STRIP

The Diary of a Hustler

LOLA DALVIA

Paperback ISBN 978-1-5272-9272-7

Prelude

> *Art and life are subjective. Not everybody's gonna dig what I dig, but I reserve the right to dig it.*
>
> Whoopi Goldberg

4 October 2019: this is when I started stripping in a well-known gentlemen's club in Central London, United Kingdom. The reason I started stripping… well, there is actually more than one reason. To start with, I have always fantasised about being on stage. I have always been attracted to anything glamorous, sexy, glittering, spotlights, the dark atmosphere of clubs and loud music; I was just born that way, it's not something I could control. Since I was a little girl, I was always the outcast of my family. Always dreaming away and being in my own fantasy world.

I remember when I was five years old, I was already telling my mum that I wanted to be like those dancers I saw on TV. Once a year, every 31 December, the national television in France would always show dancers from either the Crazy Horse or the Moulin Rouge. All those hand-made shimmery costumes, gigantic feathers, high heels that made the dancers' legs even longer and thinner, the extravagant make-up, their beautiful white smiles, hairstyles to die for, the public staring at them, everything about it made me dream away. I knew I wanted to be one of those women: confident, badass and sexy.

"Maman, I want to be like them! I want to wear costumes with big feathers!"

I knew that I was meant to be living a different life from the provincial life I was born into. I knew deep inside from a young age that something more was out there: somewhere where my life would be only glamorous, full of excitement, adventures and entertainment. I knew that I was meant to live something great, something out of the ordinary and entertain a public, just like those dancers I so admired. But I was too scared to admit what I wanted of my life, too scared to go after my dreams, just like most of us. So for a very long time I listened to my parents and society, lived through them and for them, just to be accepted but not for myself, like so many of us on this planet.

I can already hear some people thinking that professional and highly trained dancers cannot be compared to exotic dancers. Professional dancers are real artists who worked really hard to live their passion; while strippers are just "sluts", "whores", "unrespectable" women who "only show their assets for money and nothing else".

Well, at some point in my life, I thought the same. Like most people, I would judge a world I didn't know anything about. But once I stepped into the world of stripping, my whole view of strippers and everything around it changed.

And it also changed many other perspectives of my life: relationships between men and women, marriage, money, friendships, self-confidence, the power we have as women and many more aspects. This job simply changed my life forever, and by sharing my story I hope it will somehow change yours, even a little; make you start chasing your dreams, living for yourself, and make you realise that the power to change and take action is within you.

Please, have an open mind; read my story, in the hope that you will understand that strippers are not always what you think: sexual objects being forced to do this job, and here only to seduce men. We are women first, with goals and dreams; we are students, trying to finance ourselves; we are mothers, who want to offer a good life to our kids; we are also a good attentive ear for those who need to be listened to; we are a little moment of happiness for those who feel lonely; but we are also artists, just like those beautiful dancers from your favourite show. Art is very subjective, and I would like to try to explain the complexity of it.

> “ *Art is the uniting of the subjective with the objective, of nature with reason, of the unconscious with conscious and therefore art is the highest means of knowledge.*
>
> Leo Tolstoy

ONE

Where It All Started, My Childhood

> *And now we understand why Peter Pan doesn't want to grow up.*
>
> Anonymous

My name is Lola. I was born in the south of France, where the weather is always lovely, nice and warm. I never realised how lucky I was to grow up in such a beautiful part of the world. The food was exquisite, the views were more breath-taking than any others, the smell and the sound of the sea couldn't be compared to anything else. Every time I think back to my childhood memories, I feel very blessed to picture so much beauty.

Like many people around the world, I grew up with the norms and beliefs of my parents and society. As a child, you don't realise that being conditioned by them can affect the shape of your life and your decisions. Most of us end up fearing what we don't know, and never take any risk to do anything different from what society would call "normal". My parents are from a middle-class background, both of them always having worked.

My mum started as a cashier in a supermarket when she was younger; many years later, she became a sales director for a wine company. She was truly a good example of an independent woman and a hard-working person. I admire her for that. I will always be thankful for the example she showed us; we were not spoon-fed at all. From a young age we had to take care of ourselves, me and my sister, and it helped me to become the strong, independent woman that I am now. My mum was extremely pretty, with black curly hair, almond-shaped green eyes, olive skin, really small pointy nose, cheeky smile, hourglass-shaped body. She was a natural beauty, never wore too much make-up, but was always presentable and looking smart. I was a mummy's girl until I was 10 years old, until my parents decided to separate. As a child, my mum was my everything. I wouldn't leave her side for one minute, she was my whole world. Funny how things turned around after my parents separated.

My dad was a plumber at first, then became a sales agent for a building company, and then went back to being a plumber. My dad is a very intelligent man, with a huge amount of knowledge; I could ask him any question and he would have the answer. But unlike my mum, my dad never had drive; he would always do the minimum, he isn't a go getter. He is just happy living a simple, minimal life and not working hard. My dad is very tall, with broad shoulders, hairy, a typical dad. We are Italian on my dad's side, so he always talks very loud; he has a big nose, dark eyes, curly hair and dark skin. I love my dad; I always looked up to him like a hero; he always made me feel protected when I was younger, but as I got older our relationship also changed, and not for the best.

Overall I had a comfortable childhood and teenage years; we always went on holidays, never missed out on food, toys or clothes. We were not rich, but we lived comfortably. I am the youngest of my family. My older sister is two years older than me and very different from me. She is much more like the rest of the family, very down to earth, pragmatic, not very much of a dreamer like me, and clearly never thinking about another life than the one we knew. I have to say I was always jealous of her; I always felt that my parents were so proud of her. She always had good results at school without even trying. I also had good results, but I had to work hard and study for it. I really didn't like school: stuck on a chair for hours listening to adults who were looking down on me, not very supportive and always sarcastic; it just gave me nightmares. I remember being so anxious every Sunday night, because I knew that Monday was coming and I didn't want to go back to school.

My sister has always been overweight, so my parents were constantly trying to find a solution for her to lose weight; I therefore felt that she always had my parents' attention more than I did. I was always the skinny one, the one who could eat whatever she wanted and stay very slim. This was probably because I was dancing half the time; if I wasn't dancing at my dancing school, I would be dancing in my room, pretending to be Britney Spears. I grew up listening to her; I was fascinated by her dancing performance and how sexy she was. I was so skinny, without any shapes and curves. I remember that all I wanted was to have the same strong body as her, the same sex appeal, and to dance with confidence and attitude.

I always knew that dancing or performing in any form

would make me happy. When I heard music, it would transport me to another planet and I could feel joy and happiness running through my entire body and mind. The world of cinema would also take me to some other galaxy, as if I wasn't living the life I was in. I would actually believe I was the character I was watching; for the duration of the movie, I wasn't myself; I would forget what was around me and live this other fictional life. My favourite movies as a kid were *The Fifth Element* and *Titanic*. I would watch them on a loop. I knew the dialogue and the actors' movements by heart. I was so drawn to whatever love stories were happening, the costumes, the music, the special effects. I also wanted to be able to live as someone else, experiencing emotions and dramas that were not mine, wear outfits that I would never be able to wear in normal life, and even go to places that didn't exist.

When I was ten years old, we rented out the movie of *Moulin Rouge*. It tells the story of Christian, an English writer who travels to Paris to join the Bohemian revolution. He visits the city's biggest night club, a bordel, the Moulin Rouge, and falls in love with its star performer and courtesan, Satine. This movie simply brought me back to my first dream of being a cabaret dancer. The story, the set, the music, the dancing, the decors, the costumes, how everything could be so beautiful in one movie. I remember already craving and wanting the same type of love that Satine and Christian were living. I was craving for love, even though I was only a child. I had no idea back then that my life would turn into a modern version of Satine's life, more or less.

A few years later, in my teen years, when I was about fifteen years old, I tried to express to my parents that I wanted to be a performer, to be on stage, to sing and dance. But to them I had first to do something more generic, that would fit into society and help me find a regular job that would pay the bills before I even thought about doing anything artistic. Regular job? Paying the bills? Those terms to me screamed "boring". I even tried to convince my mum to attend a beauty school, as I was also very attracted to beauty products, treatments and make-up. It was at least kind of creative, but It would still lead me to a "regular"job like they wanted for me. But my mum didn't want to hear anything about it; she wanted me to do something more generic, such as business or sales.

She would always say, "Are you going to wax women's vaginas your whole life? Is that what you want to do? Lola, you're pretty, you present well, why don't you do something in sales? I'm sure you'd be good at it!" The last thing I wanted to do was sales. I was way too creative and artistic to try to sell anything to anyone – how boring and unfulfilling. But what could I do? I was only 15 years old when I had to decide which A levels I wanted to pursue. Was I really going to go against my mum? Things were already very hard at home with her since she separated from my dad.

My parents separated when I was 10 years old. They were never married, so they decided themselves on the custody quite amicably. My sister and I would live with my mum full-time and see our dad every Tuesday, Thursday and every other weekend. I don't really remember them telling us about splitting. I just have flashbacks of seeing my dad sleeping in a separate room, looking for houses when we'd only just moved to a new home, and obviously we would hear the constant arguments between them. I remember one day, we were sitting at the dinner table and my mum just started to shout at my dad; suddenly she stood up and just left the house, asking me to come with her. We went off on a bike ride around our neighborhood. I guess she needed some fresh air, to calm down. It is never pleasant as a child to see your parents arguing and drifting apart. She was trying to speak to me about how I would feel if she and our dad separated, but I don't really remember the rest of the conversation. I didn't want them to separate. I liked them together, I felt secure and loved. Why did they want to change that? I will never forget the day I really knew something was up and that they were not together any more; I wish I had never witnessed this moment…

One night my mum had to go to work to supervise the installation of a new wine range in a supermarket. My dad was looking after us, and one of my mum's friends came along with her daughter too, so we could all watch a movie together. When I think about it now, what on earth was my mum thinking? She wasn't a jealous woman at all, but still why would you let your partner be alone with another woman? I mean, I never would have. A few hours later, after my mum had left for work, my sister, myself and the other little girl were in front of the TV watching a movie. Suddenly I had this weird gut feeling, a bizarre sensation all over my body that something wasn't right. Even though I was only 10 years old, I already had this ability to feel when something was wrong. I guess you could call that a female instinct, and it never failed me. The girls were watching the movie, and I thought to myself, "Where are dad and Nathalie?" That was my mum's friend's name. I hadn't seen them in a while, where could they be and why were they not with us? I got up from the sofa (the others didn't even realise that I'd left). I walked from the living room to the kitchen and I couldn't see them. I then went to the back kitchen where we kept all the dry groceries and cleaning products. As I approached the back kitchen, which was in the dark, I could finally see my dad. He was lying down, facing Nathalie, his arms around her waist, kissing her.

My heart stopped. For a second I found it funny. I laughed, as it felt like I'd caught two kids doing something they were not meant to. I then started to shout, "Dad and Nathalie are kissi..!!" My dad interrupted me and put his hand over my mouth to make sure no one heard me.

Then I don't really remember what happened. I know I went to bed and started thinking and crying. Was that cheating? I wasn't really sure of the term, and what it meant exactly. I'd only heard this word from a soap opera that my paternal grandmother was watching, "The Young and the Restless". Every holiday we spent with her, we had no choice but to watch it, as she always put it on after lunchtime during her nap. If you don't know this show, it is all about rich people getting married, divorcing, cheating on each other with everyone, and constant dramas. Pure soap opera. So I kind of had an idea what cheating was.

Did my dad just cheat on my mum? But why? As I was wondering and thinking about what had just happened, my dad came up to talk to me. I remember him telling me that he didn't kiss Nathalie, they were just hugging as he was sad; and sometimes adults would hug people other than their partner. Did my dad really think I was dumb, or what?! Even back then, I knew when a man was bullshitting me. My dad really thought I was too young and naive to understand. Usually when parents make mistakes, they think the kids don't understand that something is wrong because they are too young to understand. But no, a child can feel and understand as much as an adult. So there I was with my dad, lying to myself. Being a grown-up cheated on and lied to is simply horrible; but when you are lied to at ten years old by the person who is meant to be your role model, your hero, the love of your life, your own dad, you can never trust any men after that. That is when my trust in men was broken and I developed serious trust issues and a lack of confidence. After that traumatising experience, my dad moved out and my mum remained friends with Nathalie. I never understood why, but if she was strong enough to forgive her, well done to that.

Weirdly, my relationship with my dad wasn't complicated after their separation. My dad was the cool one. We would only see him from time to time, so we would always have a good time, joke around and just chill with him. Life was better when we were with him than when we were at our mum's. I was young, though, so I didn't have the maturity and life experience that I have now to understand my mum. To me, my dad was the nice one and my mum was the bad guy, simply because my dad wasn't on our back all the time compared to our mum.

When they separated, things got really complicated with her. We just disconnected. She turned into this woman who wanted to live her younger years again. Now I do understand that as a woman, especially being a single mum: you need your own time to breathe and have fun, but I still think you should remain a mum, be supportive and loving. My mum was never very affectionate. I always felt that she was in business mode. When I got older and we would argue, I remember telling her sometimes, "Were you always that way? Stuck up and frigid? Have you ever been a kid, or were you born straight up an adult?" I couldn't feel any fun in her; she was so uptight and always had a negative remark to make; whatever we did or said, she seemed never satisfied. I just always felt that we were in the way, that she was happier around her friends than her kids. I know she loves us, she did a lot for my sister and me, she was working hard, she was a single mum and she did everything for us to have a comfortable life and a good education. But she was just loving us the tough way, while I needed a warm loving mum sometimes. For example, she would spend every night on the phone to her friends non-stop with a glass of rosé or white wine and a cigarette. I found it so annoying that she was working all day, and then when she was home, she would just moan at us for not doing something or doing something wrong, and then not spend time with us. We were not having dinner all together any more: my sister and I would eat in front of the TV, and my mum would sit at the kitchen bar chatting to her friends for hours. I would sometimes ask her to help with my homework, which was rare as my sister and I were really independent and we would usually managed ourselves; we had walked to and from school since we were 10 years old, and prepared our lunches or dinner if mum was working, clean the house if she asked for it and managed our homework. But sometimes I did need her to help with projects or something like that, but she was too busy on the phone and always telling me her friends needed help and that she had a life apart from us.

"What about my life?!" She would always shout this every time she and I argued. Her fucking life, I couldn't stand that sentence! The older I got, the worse it became with her. I wasn't scared of her authority any more, so I would talk back. I would also start to dress more sexily and wear make-up, and she clearly didn't like me becoming a young woman.

When I was sixteen years old I started to date my first boyfriend. I would always go to his house, which was my way to escape my mum and the bad atmosphere. We met during a night out at the only nightclub in our town – everyone knew everyone. Even back then I hated the fact of always bumping into the same people and everyone knowing your business;

that small-town mentality wasn't my cup of tea. I was only sixteen, but I'd already been out clubbing since I was fourteen years old. In France back then, the law permitted minors to go out with a member of the family who was over eighteen. Obviously I wasn't going out with my mum or my sister, but we were from a small town so it was easy to get into a club, especially if you knew the bouncer. So this is how one night I met my first boyfriend, Gabriel. He was really not good-looking: everyone called us Beauty and the Beast, and not many people understood why I went out with him, but he made me laugh so much that I couldn't resist. Gabriel was from a working-class background, very different from mine.

His parents were still together, even though their relationship was non-existent. His dad was such a small-minded typical macho man, alcoholic and probably violent, I really didn't like him. I remember staying at theirs one night and hearing glass breaking; my boyfriend's mum was shouting at him that she was fed up with him coming back home late and being drunk all the time. He was the type of man who went out to work, went to the bar during his lunch break and after work, then came home and put his feet under the table; everything was ready for him, he didn't need to lift a finger. He would watch television while having his dinner; if a good-looking woman was on screen, he would make a nasty degrading comment about her. Once he was done, he would get up from the table and plonk himself on the sofa, not helping out with anything. I don't know how Gabriel's mum could accept being married to such a jerk. She stayed at home all day, so of course she had to take care of the house; but she was also working, looking after at least three kids at the same time, so it wasn't like she was doing fuck all. She was so kind and always willing to please everyone, I don't know how she could accept being treated that way. Men in my family were not like that all; they were always helping out and respectful. I think the women in my family are scary and you simply don't want to start a fight with them. My dad knew how to cook, clean, sew, build, do electricity, he could try anything, and even though he wasn't perfect, he was a good example of the sort of man I would look up to.

But even though I wasn't keen on how things were at Gabriel's house, I still preferred to stay there. His mum was always cooking big meals for everyone and looking after us; the house was always full of family members, it just felt "homey" and that was what I needed. The only time I wasn't at his was when we started to argue. We used to have really bad rows: we were young, really jealous, possessive, and neither of us grew up in an environment that taught us how to communicate when we had an issue. So when we were arguing, you could hear us screaming from across the street. When things ran out of control, he would drive me back to mine so that I had to stay at home. This relationship was so passionate: either we loved each other very deeply, or we wanted to kill each other. I hated him even more for bringing me back home and leaving me alone… with my mum. She got so used to being on her own at home, as I was always with Gabriel, and my sister had left home already back then, that when I came back she made me understand that I wasn't welcome. She would complain that I was just hanging around doing nothing and interrupting her gathering with friends. God forbid if I cried over my boyfriend, I got no compassion. She would tell me: "If you want to act like a woman, have a boyfriend and do grown-up stuff, then act like one and stop crying."

I have to say I wasn't easy either. I was an angry teenager. Angry at her, angry at my dad, at my boyfriend, I was just angry with the world in general. When I was upset, I couldn't control my emotions and turned into a hysterical person. I would scream, shout, punch the walls, break everything, even slap my own self sometimes. But the worst thing I did was trying to kill myself. I would take whatever medicine I could find and take it. My mum caught me once, so she took me to our doctor and told him what I'd done. I felt so embarrassed and betrayed. She didn't even try to speak to me first, she just took me to a complete stranger without even trying to understand herself first why I was doing that. The only thing the doctor told me was that if I tried again, they would put me in a mental home. Clearly they had no idea about communication and love back then. It was just easier to throw you in a home. I know it must have been hard on my mum to see her child acting that way, and she probably didn't know what to do any more, but that made me dislike her even more than I already did. I really started to hate my mum: she wasn't violent or abusive, but I was feeling so rejected and unloved that I just hated her. I was feeling so much anger and rage towards her for not being the mum that I needed. But I think it really all started two years before I dated Gabriel, when I was fourteen years old.

My mum threw a housewarming party in the summertime to celebrate our new house. My mum always loved to have guests over. That night we were probably around fifty people, all dressed in white, that was the theme of the party. Everything was going pretty well actually, the weather was hot, everyone was having fun, dancing, drinking away, taking pictures. I even had friends of mine over, and we were all having a good time. At some point one of my friends started to feel sick, as she'd had way too much home-made sangria. When I saw her getting sick, I couldn't help myself feeling sick too. So I ran inside the house and headed towards the toilets. As I ran that way, I walked past the main bathroom where one of the guests called out to me as he needed my help with something. I didn't really know him, he was the new boyfriend of one of my mum's friends. I told him to wait two minutes as I needed to calm down first in the toilet and avoid throwing up. Once I was calm and not feeling so sick, I headed to the bathroom to see what help he needed. Maybe he needed a hand towel or soap.

I went inside the bathroom where he was standing. Once I was inside, he said in a very calm, natural tone: "Let me just close the door, I wouldn't want people imagining things." Then he closed and locked the door. My body froze, my heart started to beat really fast, I was breathing loudly, I knew something was odd here. Why would a man who was at least twenty years older than me want to be alone in a locked bathroom with me? He then looked at me and told me to look down at his white trousers, between his legs, right where his penis was. His trousers were covered with red marks. He said that one of the guests had dropped sangria all over him and he needed help to clean it. He also mentioned that he saw how nice my hands were, and he was sure they could do a wonderful job. For a second, the world stopped around me. Was this situation normal? I was feeling scared, but was I exaggerating things? Was I paranoid? Should I tell someone? Would that ruin the party? All those questions ran through my head. I just didn't know what was the right thing to do.

Then I came back to my senses. I told him he could clean himself up alone. I unlocked the door, ran outside and started to cry. I tried to hide, but my sister caught me and asked me what was wrong. I explained everything, but I didn't know if I was overdramatizing the situation, or if I was making things up in my head. She told me that I was not paranoid, and that he also acted up with her, openly flirting and making suggestive comments towards her. My sister was 16 years old back then, and this guy was in his 40s. He tried to tell my sister that if he wasn't already in a relationship, he would be happy to try to take her to bed. Which normal guy says those things to a 14-year-old and a 16-year-old? We wanted to tell my mum and her friend, to warn them that first of all he was not a serious guy, and second probably a sexual predator. But as a good manipulator, he tried to blame me and my sister, saying it was just a big misunderstanding and that we should all hug like a big family. I wanted to throw up: what a fucking, lying, twisted bastard! A lot of guests believed my sister and me, as he'd also made them feel uncomfortable. But my mum's friend, obviously a woman blinded by love, couldn't believe that her new, perfect-looking Ken, who was actually a policeman, could be that sort of guy. You never doubt a man who looks nice and presentable, but the devil does not always look scary.

My mum had already had a lot to drink and was enjoying her successful party until then. When we explained what had happened, she turned around, looked at me and said: "What? Do you really want me to do that? Stop the party and ask everyone to go home?" I couldn't believe that she didn't think it was an issue. I didn't want everyone to go home, I only wanted this fucker to be out of my face and kicked out of the house. As a mum, I would have expected her to believe me and do whatever to make me feel safe and comfortable. I had to stay there and watch this guy partying at my house, and still see him the day after, as a lot of people were staying over the weekend.

A year or two later, my mum's friend broke up with that guy. All I knew is that they found out weird stuff about him. No one ever told me exactly what they found out, but one day my mum's friend came to ours and apologised to me for what he did and for not believing me, which I appreciated. My mum never did the same, and I don't think I ever forgave her for that.

At least things were better with my dad: we were getting along, we didn't argue, but then he wasn't very present either. He was too preoccupied with his bipolar girlfriend. My dad dated the same woman on and off for seven years. At first everything seemed perfect, but then things turned bad. We would be home with them, or doing shopping or whatever, she would be happy and then suddenly out of nowhere she would scream, cry, worse: she tried once to kill herself. I remember my dad calling the firemen as he didn't know what to do to calm someone about to jump off the balcony. She also slammed doors the whole time, which marked me for life. I still cannot stand people shouting or slamming doors. It gives me really bad anxiety.

One day, my dad decided to leave the south of France to move really far from where we were living, to go and live with his girlfriend and start a new life. I was sixteen years old, I wasn't a kid any more, but I felt that he'd abandoned me. I needed him; I was already so miserable and sad in my life that I couldn't stand the idea of my dad being far away. When I was going out with my friends and Gabriel, I would turn into a drunken mess. I was getting really emotional about the fact that I could see my dad only a few times per year. I would cry and scream, shout how much I wanted my dad to stay and that I didn't want to be alone. Even though he knew that I wasn't in the best state mentally, he still moved to his new town with her, six hours' drive away from me. So I now saw my dad for only one week during the school holidays. I felt abandoned, and since then I always have a fear of being left behind by the people that I love and care about.

All those bad feelings towards my parents didn't help me to feel confident and beautiful. I became very introverted and shy. Every time someone talked to me, I would blush bright red and feel very uncomfortable for no reason. I hated myself. I thought I was ugly and unworthy. I was extremely skinny, no curves, no breasts, I had acne, which did not help me to feel good in my own skin. It was overall chaos for me. I was so self-conscious, shy and demotivated that I stopped dancing, which was the only thing that made me happy. I still had some hopes and dreams inside me, so when it was time for me to decide which sort of A level I wanted to study to pursue a degree, I tried to tell my parents that I wanted to attend a performing arts school, so that I could learn to sing and dance on stage in the hope of becoming a singer. The response was no. As previously mentioned, things were already so bad that I didn't have the strength to argue about my future. So I carried on with the regular college process, got my A level option in Business and Economy at eighteen years old, to then pursue a BA degree in Business. I moved from my small town to live in a really big city: Marseille. I also broke up with Gabriel: things were so bad That I was fed up with him getting wasted drunk every time we went out, and him flirting with other girls in front of me and simply treating me like shit. So I dumped him, moved to Marseille with a friend of mine and started at Business school. I was so happy to be finally away from my mum and my small town. Finally I could live my life the way I wanted, without having my mum in the background always saying something negative or hurtful, without seeing the same people everyday, and now having more than one club and bar to go to.

My hopes of succeeding at school didn't last very long. After one month of Business school, I quit. I couldn't imagine myself glued to a chair for three years, listening to teachers and being with people who had no connection with me. I felt suffocated, I couldnt breathe. So one day after class I told myself that I'd had enough and I never went back. I wrote my résumé and distributed it everywhere I could, to shops and restaurants. I just wanted to be financially independent and have a real adult life. One big high street brand was recruiting extra people for the Christmas period, so they called me for a group interview the next day. I went to the interview, petrified to talk in front of other strangers, but somehow I managed and got the job.

I remember being scared stiff on my first day. It was the first time I felt I'd had a proper job, apart from the summer job I had at the bakery shop over in my small town. Working as a sales assistant for this brand was really hard work. It was constantly busy, customers were rude and demanding, we had to carry heavy piles of clothes, run up and down to different stockrooms, but I was loving the feeling of earning money and living an adult life.

It didn't last very long, though. I worked in the store for three months, until one day I met a photographer via Facebook, an English guy who'd been living in France for many years. We started chatting and a few days later he offered to photograph me. He thought I had a really good look and would be happy to offer me a photoshoot. I had never done one before, and always dreamed of having some sexy pictures of myself. Back then, I thought the pictures were tasteful; when I see them now, I seriously want to hide myself. The day we met and shot, everything went perfectly fine. He was nice and professional. One thing that I loved about him was his ability to speak both French and English fluently. I always found it so amazing how people could speak more than one language, and I always wanted to speak English. I remember I would always translate every Britney Spears song – that is how I started to catch words other than the typical ones they taught us at school. I have always been attracted to this language, and anything to do with American/ British culture.

Ever since I was probably eleven years old, I had a passion for *Sex and the City*. This series was my Bible. I would watch Carry, Samantha, Charlotte and Miranda going to fancy places in New York City for brunches or drinks, wearing high fashion clothes, always on the go to the next big event, meeting different sorts of people, living so many different love stories and being so confident and independent. I wanted the same life, to live in a big city like New York. I couldn't imagine myself living my dream life in France, no way; I wanted to live the American dream. I remember, I would dress up, stand in front of my mirror, pretend to speak English and be like one of them. I had no choice but to learn English if I wanted to live my dream.

Good news for me: the photographer's sister was looking to move back to England, and she was looking for an au pair to help her out with her two boys as she was a single mother. He offered to put me in contact with her if I was interested in moving to England with them, becoming a nanny and learning English. I didn't hesitate for a moment, and took her number. After a few text exchanges between her and me, we arranged a date for me to move over with her and her two boys, aged six and eight years old. Within a week, I had organised my plane tickets, given my notice to my landlord in Marseille and informed my parents about my decision, which they were fine with. In less than a month I would head off to the United Kingdom, more precisely Preston, though I had no idea where that was. My plan was to stay six months to a year maximum, just to learn English, and then come back. I had no idea how things would turn out…

TWO

Welcome to England - The Reality of Being An Au Pair

> *England is the paradise of individuality, eccentricity, heresy, anomalies, hobbies and humours.*
>
> George Santayana

February 2010: I was eighteen years old, on my way to the United Kingdom without speaking a word of English. I didn't know the country at all. I obviously knew where England is, but I didn't know much about it. All I knew was what I'd heard from other people, so in my mind England was always cold, rainy and everyone was pale and ginger. I didn't know anyone over there, either friends or family, but I was young, fearless and eager to meet the unknown. I am glad that I made the move at that age, because when you are that young, you don't really realise what can go wrong; you just go with the flow and embrace the adventure. The older you get, the more cautious and worried you become. But then, I was so excited to leave my country, my family, my exes and all the bad memories behind me. It was the perfect opportunity for a fresh start and something completely new. Thinking that way made me feel that I could finally breathe again. Being away from my past was a relief and a big weight off my shoulders. Of course I was a bit scared, I can't lie about that, but still I wasn't petrified or dramatising everything that could happen.

I landed in Manchester, UK, where my new boss picked me up with her two boys to drive on to Preston. It was such a weird feeling to be picked up by strangers and going to their home without knowing anything about them. When I saw those two little boys, I thought, "What the hell am I doing?" I wasn't into kids that much back then; I found them really annoying. The mum was nice, very extravagant and loud, but she made me feel welcomed. The drive from Manchester to Preston took us about an hour. It was my first time in England. I remember looking outside the window and thinking how different everything was compared to France. The only references I had for England were Harry Potter and Bridget Jones. The houses were all so small and one next to the other, the walls red brick, and the doors all different colours. I found it very cute and funny at the same time.

We finally arrived at their home around 9 p.m. We walked inside and the first thing I noticed was how the floor was covered with fitted carpets. In France you either have wooden or floor tiles; the only place you have carpet would be the kids' room. I dropped my luggage in my room and we all met in the living room to eat dinner. I remember we sat on the floor and ate cheese on toast. At first I thought It was a joke. In my culture, most of the family eat together at the dining table. French meals are often long, as you usually eat a starter, a main and a dessert, so having cheese on toast wasn't a meal for me, but more of a snack. I was starving, so I ate it, but it wasn't enough. I obviously didn't say anything; I didn't want to seem rude, so I ate like everyone else and watched TV. The music channel was on, and even the music was not familiar. This extremely pretty girl on TV was wearing a sexy Queen's Guard uniform and singing "Fight for this love". I asked who she was, as she clearly wasn't famous in France, and they said it was the nation's sweetheart: Cheryl Cole.

At the end of dinner, I helped clean. As I was washing the dishes, my new boss stood next to me and we started chatting. At some point she showed me explicit pictures that she was sending to her multiple boyfriends. I did find it cool that she wasn't stuck up or shy, but I had met her only a few hours before, so I just thought it was a bit strange. After dinner we all went to bed. As I lay down and put the cover over me, the reality started to kick in: I was feeling a little homesick, I'd left everything behind me, friends, family, country, habits, language, everything seemed blurred, but I had to stick with my plan. I was there for only a few months, I would learn English then go back home and figure out a way to move to the United States, once I was fluent in English.

One week passed. Every day was the same: rain pouring down so I had to stay indoors with the boys, with barely any food. My boss was trying to find herself a job, so she was constantly on the go to attend interviews. She was never buying any groceries, so I had to shop and pay with my own money, as for now she apparently didn't have any money to pay me. It is unbelievable how some people can take advantage of a situation. I was young, naive and I had no one, so even if she wasn't paying me, she knew that I had no choice but to stay. As I obviously didn't have much money, I would buy just bread most of the time, and chocolate. She always promised to pay me back once she found a job, but I could see this would never happen and it would always be a constant battle to get some kind of money and stability in my job. She wasn't stable herself in her own life, so how could she offer me stability?

I should have checked all those details before my departure, as my mum asked me to, but every time my mum said something to me, I would get annoyed and tell her she was too much on my back. Well, I should have listened for once, because she was damn right, and that is how I learned my lesson. I could see I was stuck in an unpleasant situation, and I wasn't sure how to get out of it. I didn't have a contract with any details about my role, or an agency that I could call if I needed help. My boss was just a stranger at the end of the day, whom I'd met through another stranger.

I decided to call my mum, as I didn't know what to do. I told her I wanted to come back home. I explained that this woman wasn't paying me, I wasn't eating the way I wanted, I wasn't speaking a word of English, and I just wanted to leave. My mum simply told me that this was out of the question; that I'd done everything to leave France, my home and my life there, so now I had to stick to what I'd started! Thanks, mum, very supportive and comforting! I guess she didn't want me to be a quitter, and that sometimes in life you have to fight a little bit to get what you want. Once again she was showing the tough way, which I am so grateful for right now, because without my mum I would not have been able to handle all the hustles that came my way during those past ten years. I would have crumbled many times, but no, I always managed to fight, and that is because my mum wasn't treating us like spoon-fed spoiled kids. Even though she didn't want me to come home, she still helped me out. She had a friend who'd been living in London for many years; she contacted her, told her about my situation and asked if she could help me out.

Luckily my mum's friend agreed straight away and told my mum that I was welcome to come to her house in London until I found a new family to stay with as an au pair.

I was kind of relieved, but I had no idea where this would take me. I was on another new adventure within a week. I had to travel across a country that I didn't know anything about, with a language that I wasn't familiar with, and go to someone else's house whom I barely knew. But it was my only and best choice right now. I didn't know London; to be honest, I only knew that it was the capital, so I was hoping it would be more fun than Preston.

I was too scared to tell the truth to my boss, so I made up a lie that I had to go back to France for family reasons, but that I would need to go to London first. When I think about it now, it totally doesn't make sense: it was the worst lie ever, but she believed me. She was a bit upset that I was leaving, as having free help is always hard to say goodbye to, but she couldn't keep me a prisoner. I asked her to kindly drop me at the train station the next day, so I could head to London.

As I finally left her and the boys, I felt relieved, but still scared. I remember asking the man selling tickets for a train ticket to London. Bear in mind that I was only eighteen years old, I couldn't speak a word of English, and I was from a small town, so a lot of things didn't make sense to me. I asked him for a train ticket to London, but that didn't turn out as easy as I hoped it would be. "Sure, Miss, which station? Euston? King Cross? Victoria?" I could barely understand what he was saying, but why did he want me to go somewhere called Euston or Victoria when I just wanted to go to London. I was such a small-town girl that I didn't realise that one city could have more than one train station with different names. This is how young and innocent I was. I kept telling him that I just wanted to go to London. After two minutes of me repeating to the gentleman, "NO! ME... GO... LONDON, NO... EUSTON" (this was my level of English), I think he got fed up and just gave me a train ticket to London, Euston. I looked at my ticket, hoping that I would end up in London and not another city.

My train journey was about two hours and a half. The train was crowded, with no allocated seats, so I stood up the entire journey with all my suitcases. If someone tried to speak to me I would just blush and sweat out of anxiety. I couldn't undertsand what people were saying, and I couldn't respond properly. I was feeling so stupid and vulnerable, I just wanted to be left alone.

By evening time, I arrived in London, Euston. I was glad to know that I hadn't ended up somewhere where I wasn't meant to be. It was probably around 6 p.m., rush hour. I had never seen so many people in my life: a human wave. My brain was trying to process all this new information, it was overwhelming. I had my mum's friend's number; I texted her and told her I was at Euston station. She texted me back saying she'd just finished work and she was on her way. I just needed to find a coffee place, sit and wait for her. After five minutes looking around, I found some sort of bar/restaurant. I was freezing, so I ordered a hot chocolate. I struggled to make the order, and the same thing happened as with the ticket man: the waitress got frustrated with me for not understanding what she was saying. After struggling a little, we finally understood each other and I could finally drink my hot chocolate. I felt that everyone was looking at me. I looked down at my cup, trying not to cry. I felt so lonely and lost. What was I doing? Why did I not just stay in my own country, where I could speak the language perfectly, be with people that I knew and have a normal life like everyone else? Why was I always looking for something else, rather than being content with what I had?

After thirty minutes waiting, my mum's friend finally arrived. Her name was Manuela. I had probably met her a few times in my life, during special occasions such as weddings or birthdays. She kissed me on both cheeks, like we do in France, helped me carry my luggage and we headed to the Underground. It was the first time in my life I had gone down into such a big Underground with so many different lines. The only one I knew was the metro in Marseille, which had only two lines.

We took the Northern line to Tottenham Court Road, then changed to the Central line and headed to our final destination of Ealing Broadway where she lived. Once we arrived at the station, we had to take a bus for about ten minutes and then walk. That journey was so long and it was so cold outside that I was so exhausted. How could people working in the City do this every single day? Maybe that was why everyone looked so tired and stressed over here.

Once we were home, I chatted a bit with Manuela. I was reassured that she also had come to London when she was really young, but now she was all settled, had a good life and seemed very happy to be living here. She gave me a few tips for my job research and a London tube map to start to get familiar with the different areas. Remember that in 2010 we did not have most apps we have now, such as city mapper, uber and more. After our chat, I just went to bed without eating. I was so tired that all I wanted to do was sleep and be ready the next day to start looking for a new family to work for.

A feeling of confusion and fear of the unknown hit me again, just as when I spent my first night in England a few weeks before. Did I really want to do this? Was it worth it? What was I going to do?

~

Weeks passed, and after much research on Gumtree, a well-known advertisement website, I found a new family to work for. They were very different from my previous boss. They were extremely rich, Indian, and living in High Barnet, North London. I was thinking that working for rich people would be much better than someone with no job, but once again I was wrong. I was living in a mansion: I remember the first time I visited their house, I'd never seen anything like it. The entrance had a gigantic gate, and the car park was full of luxurious cars: Range Rovers, a Porsche and a Lamborghini. The entrance hall was huge with a massive staircase that was split in two. The house had a big dining reception area for special occasions on one side, and on the other side an open-plan marble kitchen with a living room. The main kitchen where I was cooking for the family also had a back kitchen, where I was allowed to cook my meal and eat. Upstairs, on the first floor, was the master bedroom with an ensuite, the twins' nursery and the little boy's room with his own en suite too. This floor also had a cinema room. The second and top floor were right under the roof, which is where my room was. I couldn't complain: my room was pretty big and comfy, and I also had my own bathroom. This floor also had a really tiny room where I had to iron and fold the entire family's laundry.

I was working six days a week from 8 a.m. until 9 p.m. and earning £120 a week. I had to take care of an eight-year-old boy and six-months-old twins. I had to wake them up, make their breakfast, feed them, make their beds, tidy up their room, cook every meal, wash all the baby bottles, change nappies, take care of the family laundry, groceries and walking the little boy to school. On top of looking after the kids, I had to clean, even though they had a housekeeper coming twice a week. And I had to serve them if guests were coming over. When I think about it now, it was clearly modern slavery. Getting paid less than £500 a month to work 14 hours per day, six days a week, was abusive. But what could I say? I didn't know my rights, this country wasn't mine, I could barely speak English, so I just had to get on with it. I was simply grateful to work, and have a comfortable place to stay and eat.

My usual day would start at 7 a.m. and finish at 9 p.m. I was exhausted and bored at the same time. I would spend most of my time alone inside the house, running my household chores. The only time I was outside was to shop for groceries or when I was taking the kids to the park. I tried to speak to the mum, but she clearly wasn't interested in having a conversation with me. Why couldn't I find some normal, regular and kind people? My previous boss was overly open and disorganised, whereas this one was as warm and welcoming as a prison door, and a never satisfied control freak bitch.

I felt extremely lonely. I was working six days a week, living far from Central London, and the only people I was hanging out with were the rich mums who took their kids to the park or came to the mansion to visit my boss. They clearly weren't interested in who I was and what I was doing. I was just part of the staff, so nothing interesting for them. I don't think they were interested in each other either, it was really weird to witness. They would sit in a circle, barely talking and having tea. None of them had a spark, they all looked very sad, I must say. When my parents had friends over, they would talk loudly, laugh for hours, listen to music, it was really lively. These women were nothing like that. Was it because they were British, or rich? They had everything going for them: money, power, help, designer clothes, so why did they look so miserable? Was it true then that money doesn't make you happy?

I realised that there was no hope of making any sort of connection with them, or anyone in my area, so I decided to go online and look for friends. I found this website for French people living in London, and you could find all sorts of advertisements, including people feeling lonely and wanting to make friends. I felt pathetic at first for doing this. Me? Lola? Going online to find friends, like some freaks? But I had to put my ego aside and go with it. One ad caught my attention: "*Hello, my name is Inaya, I am twenty-one years old, I just moved to London, I am an au pair, I feel a bit lonely so I am looking for girlfriends to hang out with, discover London and have fun. Contact me if you are also new in London and looking for friends.*" That sounded promising: she'd also just moved to the country, was an au pair and was looking to do the same thing as me. I just had a very good vibe from reading her words, so I contacted her. Not even ten minutes later, she responded to my message and we exchanged numbers so we could organise our first meeting. I couldn't wait for my next day off to arrive so I could finally have some sort of social life and get out of this gilded cage. Yes, they were rich, but I never met people that were so miserable. This house had no sparks, no warmth, everyone was hanging out in a different room, no one was talking to each other, the dad was always on a business trip, and as soon as he returned home he would hide in his office not even paying attention to his kids or wife. The mum was such a cold-hearted bitch, she was never happy with anything that I was doing, all I heard was complaints. She wasn't even working, all she was doing was watching television and having her parents or friends over for tea.

Once I met Inaya, we clicked straight away; it felt like we'd known each other for years. Inaya was the same age as me; she was from Paris, but originally from the Ivory Coast. Her skin was beautifully deep dark and she had the biggest smile that always brightened my mood. We used to go to Central London, walk around, visit, sit down to have a bite, and bitch about our horrible bosses. It felt good to have a friend who was living in the same situation as me. Inaya was from Paris, so she was used to living in a big city; but for me, somewhere like London was brand new. But every time I went to the centre, I fell in love more and more with the city. London was such a revelation to me: those historical buildings, the red double-decker buses, the phone boxes, the big screens on Piccadilly Circus, China Town, London Bridge, Hyde Park. For a small-town girl like me, I felt I was living in a movie scene.

I was also feeling that my personality on various levels began to match more with London than where I'd been living in France. What I loved about London was the freedom that I felt. I didn't feel I was being judged on anything, people were allowed to have dreams, dress up the way they wanted; they were much more positive and friendly than French people, just more open in general. I also felt much more secure as a woman. France was very bad for safety: most men over there treated women like objects, they had no respect or education. I was called "slut" many times when I was walking down the street of Marseille; for no reason, except that I wasn't responding to their attempt to flirt with me. I didn't miss this kind of treatment at all. After only a few weeks of living in London, I knew I'd be staying not just for a few months or even a year, I knew I would stay much longer. I was getting used to living in a big city, embracing so many different cultures and people coming from different backgrounds. I could see the potential of living in such a big city, and couldn't see myself going back to France.

I stayed just two months with the Indian family. I got fed up with being treated badly, hearing my boss complaining constantly, and not seeing my English improving as I was not talking to anyone in the house. The only way I was learning English, apart from when I was out shopping for groceries, was when I was watching music videos at night. I made sure the sublittles were on, and looked for the French translation in my dictionary if I couldn't understand a particular word.

I was also so depressed living with them that I developed an eating habit that I'd never had before. I was over-eating. I would eat constantly and way too much. I was so bored and sad that I would hoover up anything I could find, which made me put on two stone within two months. I had never been overweight in my life; I was always skinny and fit, even though I was never on a diet and always ate whatever I wanted. But the fact that I was staying at home all day, over-eating, being sad with no physical activity, turned me into a chubby character that I didn't recognise. I had to put a stop to this.

One day, I decided that I'd had enough of being treated like Cinderella, and I knew that no Prince Charming would pop out of nowhere and save me. I had to save myself. I decided to leave this family and find a new one. I researched online, and within a day I found my new bosses. Finally I could be with a simple, middle-class, regular family. I knew I wouldn't be living anywhere luxurious, but they seemed much nicer than the people I was staying with before. My new family was mixed: the mum was Polish and the dad French, originally from the Ivory Coast, so the kids could speak

French, Polish and English and it was great to be with a multicultural family. They lived in Woolwich Arsenal, South-East London, and I would get paid £60 a week. That wasn't a lot, but I would have less work and I knew they wanted their au pair to be part of the family, which I wanted too. My happiness had no price at this time.

The day I announced to my current boss that I was leaving didn't go down very well. She got so furious that I was leaving them at such short notice, that she had no choice now but to take care of the kids herself. She then asked me to give her the money back from the week before, pretending I hadn't give her any notice at all, so I owed her money. When I heard those words, I lost it. Was she serious? We didn't have any contract, they'd abused me the whole time, and on top of that she wanted money back that she clearly didn't need. The sum of £120 was nothing to her, but for me it was a lot of money back then, so I simply refused. She then threatened to call the police and tell them that I was stealing from her if I didn't give her back the cash. Had I had my current level of English and know-how, I would have told her that she was more than welcome to call them. She was the one in the wrong here: hiring someone illegally, paying me cash with no contracts or records and abusing me, but obviously back then I wasn't the person that I am now. I was scared and I didn't know my rights. I just let her talk, and then walked out on her to go to town to cancel my brand new gym membership.

Once I got back, I found myself locked outside the house. The bitch had locked the door, leaving the keys on the other side so I couldn't get in. All my personal belongings were inside the house. I couldn't believe it. I felt that I was in a bad movie or something. This woman was so frustrated and unhappy that she was taking out all her frustration on me. How could she be so mean, to lock an eighteen-year-old outside without her personal stuff? Every time I pressed the buzzer, she would pick up the telecom but not say a word. She was completely crazy. I probably stayed outside the door for thirty minutes, before deciding to text her saying I would give her back her money and leave. Like magic she opened the door. I couldn't believe that she was so cold and cruel to lock someone out just to get back £120 that didn't mean anything to her. I ran upstairs, packed my stuff, threw the cash at her and left with absolutely nothing in my pocket.

I was on the pavement outside, sitting with my luggage for a few minutes, exhausted from the drama. I was so fed up with people abusing their power, but I couldn't let it stop me. I would be with my new family in an hour or two, and everything would be better from now on. I managed to travel to London Bridge, where they would pick me up. I knew in my heart that the nightmare was over and I could finally live my London experience to the full.

THREE

The Lies and Abuse

> *You destroyed every little bit of me, and I let you… I let you.*
>
> Anonymous

I stayed about six months with my new family in Woolwich Arsenal. Overall, I had a great time with them, but hard times also. I was taking care of two kids, a two-year-old little girl and a four-year-old boy, which could be challenging at eighteen years old. But this experience made me grow up so much, and I wouldn't have changed it for the world. In October 2010, after six months being a nanny, I decided it was about time to find a real job so I could finally have a real social life. For the past months, the only social time I'd had was with other mums at the local park, and with my friend Inaya.

I set about it in the same way I'd done when in France

looking for my first job. I printed out my CV and traipsed around Central London hoping that someone would give me a chance. As I walked down Regents Street, I walked past a famous semi-luxurious high street store and thought that this could be a good place to start work. I went inside, asked for the manager and left my CV with them. One hour later, the manager called me back. I had a really hard time understanding her accent; even though my English was much better, I was still struggling. All I understood was that I had an interview the following day. I was so proud and excited. Finally I was getting somewhere.

The next day I went back to Regent Street and headed to the store for my first ever interview in English. I made sure I looked smart and professional. The interview was very casual and quick. After twenty minutes of talking, the manager informed me that I'd got the job. Congratulations, Lola! Now all I had to do was find a place to live, as for now I was back on living at Manuela's, my mum's friend. I went on Gumtree and looked for a room. In London, most people live in shared houses. The rental is so high that even people with a decent job have to share. I didn't even have the money for a deposit, but I kept on looking. At some point one ad caught my eye: a double bedroom for £400, bills included, no deposit; Old Street station was one minute's walk away, and it was sharing with one person only. I looked up on a tube map to check where Old Street was. The location was perfect, zone 1 in the City. I called the number to see if the flat was still available, and if I could come and visit it. A man with a Portuguese accent picked up; he informed me that he was the owner of the place and the flat was to be shared with him. Once we'd agreed a date and time for me to visit it, I asked Inaya to come with me for the viewing. The ad could be fake, so I wanted to be cautious and safe. After six months in London, and many bad adventures, I knew it was better to be safe than sorry.

The day after the call, around 6 p.m., we reached the address he'd given us. The flat was situated in a block of flats right next to the station. We entered the small estate and walked towards the door and buzzed it. The door opened and we went up to the 3rd floor. We arrived in front of the door, knocked and waited for someone to open. After not even one minute waiting, a young, tall, black man opened the door. He seemed nice, a bit sleepy maybe, but overall I didn't have a bad vibe from him. He showed us around: the flat wasn't luxurious at all, it was very dark, and cold, a bit sad. It had no warmth about it, but the room that was available was quite big, and to be honest for a flat situated in Central London, right next to the tube station, it wasn't bad at all. As many Londoners would know, finding the perfect place in London is very rare and complicated, unless you earn a very good salary; but for the person I was back then, this was perfect. After our tour we spoke for a bit: he asked me how long I was planning to stay, what job I was doing, etc. After that, I told him I was really interested in the room and ready to move in. He informed me that other people were coming to visit the flat and he would call me back later on during the evening to give me an answer. We left, and I went back down the Underground, to Ealing Broadway. I was so anxious about his answer; I really wanted that room. As soon as I reached Ealing Broadway, I received a call from the guy, whose name was Miguel.

"Lola, can you hear me? This is Miguel. I just wanted to say that you can have the room, and you can move in as soon as you can. If you could please bring me the first month's rent in cash, that would be great."

I was over the moon. Within a few days I'd found a new

job on one of the busiest streets in London, and a room in an apartment in a trendy area. Finally my London life could start.

~

After a few months working at the store, I'd made new friends. We were a group of French girls, and I was finally going out clubbing, going out for drinks after work, going shopping with the girls, and it felt amazing. On top of that, I met someone at work called Matthew. He was tall, very muscular, really nice dark caramel skin, hair in cornrows. We caught each other's eye straight away. Matthew was working in the stockroom, and I was working on the floor. I remember I would find any excuse to go to the stockroom so I could just talk with him for two minutes. The only issue was that so many girls were trying with him, even though he was really shy, because he was the only good-looking guy in the store. Every time I saw another girl speaking to him, I would rage inside and it would turn into an argument, as I blamed him for not pushing them away. That was only the beginning of many arguments, for about two years. I knew I should have stopped the relationship right after the first date, and I don't know why I kept going.

The first time Matthew invited me out was to the cinema, and I will never forget it: we were queuing to get our tickets, and when it was finally our turn, I walked up to the cashier and asked for two tickets for the movie, expecting Matthew would then pay up. But I soon realised that Matthew wasn't behind me, he was still queuing. That fucker wanted to pay for his own ticket! I was shocked: for a first date I would always expect a guy to pay, especially if he's the one asking me out. Matthew wasn't very generous or romantic, and this was only the beginning of a long list of him acting like this. If only if I'd known that dating him would turn into a nightmare…

In the meantime I was still living with Miguel in Old Street. Then one day, in December 2010, he asked me to move out. I was shocked, I mean not that shocked actually. He and I were like cats and dogs. He was nice, but I couldn't stand him. He was spending his time buying me chocolate, hoping I would agree to be his girlfriend. He also kept asking me to stop working so I could take care of his son, and in exchange I wouldn't have to pay the rent. What the fuck? I was expecting more from life at nineteen years old than being the stepmother of someone's child, staying home and being with a guy who spent his benefits money on booze and cigarettes. Miguel couldn't understand why I was refusing his offer, and kept buying me small gifts in the hope that maybe I would accept.

One day he'd had enough of me rejecting him and told me to leave. I was so hurt by the unfairness of the situation, and also stressed, as I had no notice to find somewhere else. I didn't know what to do. I had no money for a deposit, no computer to look for a room, and no smartphone. Life was once again challenging me. One of my friends told me that when she came to London she'd stayed in a hostel for the first week, and it wasn't that bad. So maybe I should check it out and think about that option. I wasn't keen, but I had no choice but to look into something easy and fast, so hostels seemed the best solution at the time. I went down the road to Kings Cross and found a hostel; the prices were reasonable, but it meant staying in one of sixteen dorms. I really didn't want to share the place where I would sleep every night with strangers, mainly tourists coming only to visit and party while I would be working, but I had no choice.

A few days later I left my apartment and moved to the hostel for about a month. I even spent Christmas there alone while my family were celebrating all together in France. I couldn't take any holidays due to Christmas sales and Boxing Day, the busiest time of the year for stores. My London dream wasn't such a dream any more. I was feeling very lonely, even though I had a boyfriend, friends and a job that was keeping me busy for more than forty hours a week. But London can do that to you: you can fall in love with such a beautiful city, full of excitement, but it can feel empty at the same time. Like Alicia Keys sang in her song *Doesn't mean anything,* "All the people in the world and you can still feel lonely".

I stayed one month in the hostel before finally moving to another house, one of many during the next two years. That was also the duration of the relationship with Matthew – probably the worst relationship I'd ever had. With time, I found out that he was a compulsive liar: he would lie about anything, where he was going, who he was seeing, but the worst thing he did was lie to me about where he was working. After six months working at the store, I got fired as management was fed up with Matthew and me arguing all the time at work. He'd been in his position way longer than I had, and he had a better attitude than me, so they decided to keep him and just got rid of me. After that I worked in many places, even in a famous fast food chicken chain in the UK. Let me tell you, I didn't like that job at all. What the fuck was I doing? From dreaming of being swept up by a millionaire, living the dream and being a celebrity, I'd descended to working in a chicken restaurant, smelling frying oil at the end of the day and stuck in a relationship with a cheap, compulsive liar. I had no control over my life and I was just letting things be, thinking it could be worse. I was not allowing myself to think things could be much better.

For the last year of our relationship, Matthew and I decided to live together. A few weeks after we moved in, he made me believe he'd lost his job so he couldn't help me pay the rent. For one year I paid everything: the rent, the groceries and bills if we were going out somewhere. All I was doing was working, finishing really late and sleeping. My life had no excitement whatsoever. I was simply exhausted, and every time I came home he would be there doing nothing. I would argue with him constantly, as in two years we'd barely been to any restaurants, never been on holiday, I'd never had flowers or any sort of attention. And don't let me not start on sex: he wouldn't even touch me. He would blame me for all the arguments, saying I was ruining the relationship with all my complaints about money; that it wasn't his fault if he didn't have a job. I would then feel guilty for putting pressure on him and acting like a spoiled brat. I should support my boyfriend and stop moaning, but deep down I knew something was odd.

On top of being cheap and pretending to be jobless, he was violent. He would lose his temper when we were arguing. He would throw stuff at me: shoes and books, or lift me up by my collar and throw me on the bed. Our flatmates had enough of hearing us arguing all the time, so we would end up arguing with them too. I thought that sort of argument was normal, so I didn't understand why they didn't just mind their own business. One day they even called the police. I couldn't believe that I was one of those women, the ones facing the police and lying, telling them everything was fine. I was obviously lying, but I couldn't see back then that this was domestic violence. This relationship was completely useless. I'd simply had enough of it. But I wasn't strong enough to leave him and be all alone. I felt that my life was pointless, I wasn't happy at all, I didn't even know what happiness would look like. I forgot about my dreams, my hopes, I had no self-esteem or confidence, I simply lost myself. I thought that what we had was love, and I would just think of the good times, however rare they were, but they kept me going and I stayed with him.

People say, "There's no such thing as coincidence, everything happens for a reason." I couldn't agree more: my entire life was filled with weird events that I couldn't explain, but that would always show me the right path or unfold a truth. I always felt that I was surrounded by guardian angels, or a powerful energy that would help me out, and one day out of nowhere I found help again.

It was August 2013; the weather was boiling hot and the city felt like a giant oven. But I still wanted to enjoy the British summer, so I decided to meet a friend for a drink in Central London. I got off at Oxford Circus and walked down Regents Street to head for Piccadilly Circus. As I walked down, I passed the store where I used to work, where Matthew and I had met, when I bumped into one of my former colleagues. We said Hi, hugged and he then said, "Are you here to see Matthew? He's not here today, it's his day off."

What did he just say? Did I hear him properly? I felt a strong pain in my entire body, as if I'd just been hit by a bus. I started to feel sick, I wanted to throw up, I think I got pale, because my friend started to worry and asked me if I was OK. I asked him how long Matthew had been back at work. He looked at me confused, and said he'd never left. I felt even more sick; the whole world stopped around me. My friend was trying to speak to me, but I couldn't hear a thing. Everything was spinning around me; I was shaking, and I could not breathe. I think I was not taking in what he'd just told me. After a few minutes of shock, I got back to my senses and realised what was going on. Then I started to feel extremely angry. My friend realised that Matthew had lied to me, but he did not want any trouble, so he made me promise not to say anything about it. Of course I was going to tell him. I wasn't going to say who'd told me, but no way was I going to pretend that I didn't know anything. I was so hurt at being lied to for so long. How could he use me like that, and worse, play with my head and make me think that I was the one in the wrong and make me feel guilty? What a fucking psychopath, what a motherfucker. I was in such a rage that I could not contain it any more. I had to confront him. So I cancelled on my friend and headed back home. Only I knew what would happen…

When I came back home, he was there on the bed on his phone, doing nothing. I wanted to punch him so badly, but I contained myself. I just wanted him out of my life and my room, so I didn't even give him an explanation. I simply told him to get the fuck out. He looked at me very confused and scared. I told him that I knew everything. I knew he'd been working this whole time, that he was a cheap ass, a liar and that I wanted him out. The rental contract was under my name, and I'd been paying everything for a year, so he had no right to stay in this place anyway. He tried to explain, but I didn't want to hear any more of his lies. He kept trying to talk, but I couldn't hear his voice.

I became hysterical and screamed, "I want you out right now!" It's not as if he had nowhere to stay: he had his family house with his own bedroom, so It wasn't like I was kicking him out on the street, he had a place to go. But he wouldn't make a move, he wanted to stay. How the hell could I force him to leave when I was half his size? I threatened to call the police if he didn't move. That made him laugh, to see how desperate and powerless I was. He kept calling me crazy, and carried on looking at his phone. How could he be so arrogant after I'd discovered that he was a liar and manipulator? I felt so hurt to be facing such a bad person, a person I'd loved and tried to trust, a person I'd spent time with for two years. What a waste of my life. I started to cry, begging him to leave, but all he did was laugh at me.

I couldn't handle his attitude and his mocking me, so I called the police. He then realised that I was serious and not playing around. He got scared and took my phone away from me and told me he was going to throw it away if I didn't hang up. After a few attempts to get my phone back from him, and being pushed on the floor every time I tried, I managed to get my phone and called the police again. That put him in a rage like I'd never seen before. He started to destroy everything in my room. He punched the walls, broke the mirror and the worst thing he did was smash my computer. When he punched it, I screamed and cried at the same time. It felt that it was me he was punching. He'd already broken me as a person, and now the only valuable thing that I owned was also ruined. I hated him so much. This guy had broken me mentally into pieces, more than anyone had. When I was in front of the door, he grabbed me and threw me violently on the bed. Finally he left before the police came.

When the police arrived, they could guess what had happened. The room was a mess, my laptop was broken into pieces, and I was here on my bed petrified, crying. One of the officers sat down next to me, asked me questions about what had happened, and suggested I press charges against him. But I didn't have the courage to do so. I just wanted him out of my life. I didn't want to have anything to do with him any more. I wanted this nightmare to be over. And even though I was in a lot of pain mentally, I was relieved because I knew this was the end of the nightmare.

After that day I never saw him or heard from him ever again. It left me with a lot of scars mentally, but I decided this was the last time I would let a man treat me that way. I would never date a man who wasn't generous and respectful. For years I had been transparent, see through, worthless, but that had to come to an end. From now on I would make the rules, and I wouldn't let anyone treat me in any way less than what I deserved. This is when I promised myself to always make sure that men would treat me like a princess *and nothing less.*

FOUR

Hostess with the Mostest

> *Sometimes the smallest step in the right direction ends up being the biggest step of your life.*

A month or two after the incident, I changed my job and house… again. I became a visual merchandiser and moved in with one of my former flatmates. She knew all about Matthew, as she, like the other flatmate, had heard us arguing many times. She and I became close once Matthew was out of the picture. We would go out and party at the 02 Centre, which was only two stops away from the house. After a while we decided to move in together, just the two of us. The flat was ridiculously small but cosy. It was situated in Greenwich town centre: an area that is quite posh and touristy, but the place we were living in wasn't very fancy. The flat was situated on a council estate, but I was fine with that. The rent was quite cheap, but after two months we realised we were never using the living room and we both needed extra money, so why not rent it out to make the rent even cheaper?

Luckily I met a charming, nice guy at work. For weeks before, we had the idea of renting out the living room. His name was Julien, he was French and two years younger than me. We clicked straight away, but not in the way you might think. Julien was gay, and at the time too scared to admit he was, even though you could easily guess. We felt that we'd known each other for years already. We were very different, but very similar at the same time. I would be a crazy party animal, living my life the way I wanted, flirting away and having many guys; and he would stay at home playing the piano all day, reading books and not having anyone in his life at all. When we met, Julien hadn't had sex for a year. I don't know how he managed it. I loved sex, and I couldn't live without it. But I loved how he never judged me on my love for sex. He always found my free spirit fascinating. I'd changed a lot since my separation from Matthew. I was single for the first time in a long time, and clearly I was enjoying myself.

It was obvious to me that Julien would be the best person to live with, so I asked him if he was interested. He had just moved to London, and for now he was renting a room the size of a closet for the price of £600 in Edgware Road. So when I offered him a much bigger room for half the price, he accepted straight away.

I was so happy to live with Julien. Life was so much better with him. I felt that I'd met one of my soulmates. For the first time I'd met someone who wasn't judging me, who truly understood me, maybe because we were both from similar backgrounds, and both of us were very artistic in our different ways, and our parents didn't really understand us. We were always laughing like two teenagers, and we always had something to talk about. He was also very supportive of my choices. He knew that the life I was in wasn't meant to be for me; he knew that I wanted something better than that. But for the first years I was in London, I'd had to learn the language, establish myself and get more confident before moving forward. My only worries during those past three years was work, getting money and paying my rent. That's what my life was about. I was loving London, but I was surviving, not living. I was only dreaming that maybe one day I could be part of those people who went to fancy restaurants and clubs, drove nice cars or took black cabs, wearing designer clothes and going on luxury vacations.

But for now my life was extremely far from that. I was getting up at 5 a.m. every day, getting ready to take public transport at 6 a.m. and getting to work by 7 a.m. This visual merchandiser job was so tiring. All day long I would open boxes, hang thousands of clothes on rails, and try to coordinate them on the floor according to the collection sent by the head office. I hated that job and the company I was working for. The majority of my colleagues and management were Spanish, as that was where the company is from, so probably 70% of the staff were from Spain. The managers would talk to us as if we were dog shit; they wouldn't even speak English, they would have full-on conversations in Spanish, which really made me feel uncomfortable to know that someone was probably saying something mean about me but I couldn't understand it. No one from management was nice, kind or helpful, which most of the time would make the employees stressed, depressed and not very productive.

The last store I was located in was within an incredibly

old shopping centre in Queensway. When I had to remove clothes from the shopfloor that we did not need, I had to take them back to the stockroom, which was outside our store. It was situated at the inside back of the shopping centre, where the bin area was. The way to the stockroom was very dark. It was really scary but also smelly, as I had to walk past the bins. I couldn't believe that I was doing this job, dragging heavy rails and boxes all day long and going through this back alley. I would come home at night exhausted. All I could do was work, travel, eat, sleep, repeat. My life was a bit better than when I was with Matthew, but still nothing was exciting at all. Most of the time I was miserable unless I was with Julien.

I didn't want to be one of those people who complain all the time and don't do anything about it, so one day, in June 2014, while I was at work, dragging my heavy rail towards the stockroom, I stopped and said to myself it was time to break out of this vicious circle and finally take control of my life and work for something better. I knew that I deserved more than this. I left work that day and never went back. I wasn't worried about money, as my rent was really cheap and my cost of living back then was way lower than the one I have now. I knew I had to find an alternative at some point, but I wasn't in a rush. For once I wanted to take time for me and figure out a way to have a better life, a life that was more suitable to me, my personality and vision.

As soon as I quit this job, I felt so relieved that I wasn't still carrying this heavy weight on my back which had been dragging me down and making me feel miserable. Changing one thing in my life always changed other things naturally, without me trying to change them. When I quit my job, my boyfriend at the time, Zach, dumped me. We'd been together for only three months, but I was still hurt by being let down.

I'd met Zach at one of the stores I was working for as a visual merchandiser. I remember the first time I met him: I was taking the lift to go to the changing room and he ran to catch the same lift as me and tried to speak to me, but I wasn't interested at all. But that didn't stop him from chasing me. I don't think anyone had chased me that much in my life. He would offer to drive me home after work; every time I needed to go somewhere, he would pick me up and drive me; if I was short of money, he would help me out as money wasn't an issue for him. Yes, Zach was loaded, obviously not from our job at the store; that was only his cover job. Zach was a drug dealer – I know, not the best type of guy to date, but let me tell you, although he was a bad boy for sure, he was a true gentleman at heart. He was the first guy who'd opened doors for me and pulled out my chair when we were eating out. If I was out late, he would make sure to pick me up or send a cab, as he wanted to make sure I was safe at all times. He would always pay for food, and offer his jacket if I was cold. It felt good to have someone so nice to me for once, so at some point I gave in and we officially dated for three months. I felt like a princess for the entire time we were together: I always had flowers, everything paid for, shopping, always eating out, he was really the first guy to show me how I was meant to be treated. And after my past relationship, it felt amazing.

Obviously, it wasn't all cute and rainbows all the time. We would argue, mainly because of me. Zach was a party animal: he was always out, on drugs, drinking and surrounded by girls. I was so jealous and paranoid, clearly I didn't trust him at all, so I gave him a hard time, called him a hundred times to check up on him and make sure what he was doing. Back then I thought that having a man on a leash would help me not to get cheated on. But obviously that doesn't work, and it probably does the completely opposite, but I was so damaged from Matthew that I was clearly acting crazy sometimes. Like any young guy, he wasn't going to get stuck with a girl with so many mental issues, and clearly not in the road of recovery. After a trip to Ibiza with his mates, where I knew he'd cheated on me, he called me and dumped me. I was heartbroken. Back then, I didn't know how to control my emotions, so I would sit at home, cry for days, thinking over and over why he had dumped me, trying everything to win him back. But obviously I was failing. I could not believe that I was being let down, abandoned and failed by another relationship.

So there I was, without a job and a boyfriend. I had all the time in the world to try to figure out what was my next step. I just didn't know what to do. I was still dreaming and hoping in the back of my mind that one day a rich millionaire would kidnap me and take care of me and make me a superstar. I don't think I was dreaming of such a thing just because I was materialistic; I think that after many years of struggle and bad relationships, I simply wanted someone to sweep me off my feet and make me dream a little. I wanted to be able to count on someone and not worry any more. Moving to the United Kingdom at eighteen had made me grow up really fast. I became an independent adult in no time, but deep down I was still a little girl dreaming of Prince Charming. But like anything in life, even dating a modern Prince Charming takes time, effort and work. Yet back then I had no idea. Most people would think that you just need to be pretty; and yes, it can help, but let's face it, there are endless numbers of pretty girls in London, from so many different countries. Men have a huge choice open to them, so you need to have this "*Je ne sais quoi*" about you to stand out from the rest. To meet those men, you need to hang out in the right places with the right people and have the right mindset. But back then I didn't know all that, and I didn't have the same mindset as I do now. I wanted this life, but I wasn't working for it, I was just fantasising about it, moaning about my current situation and just hoping that one day it would happen. Hope doesn't get you anywhere; only actions and a positive attitude can set you up for greatness, no matter what you want to do or be. I simply didn't know about it. Like most people, I was wary of my dreams and always thinking, "It only happens to other people".

One day, Julien and I went for a walk in Greenwich Park. We were always going for a walk after lunch or dinner, and while we were walking we would talk about anything and everything. We were acting like an old married couple. Seriously, we were two old farts together, but I loved it. There was something very comforting in Julien's company: I felt safe and understood. As we were walking, we could see a wedding from far off, being held at Greenwich University. We walked past it, and noticed a line of girls standing there greeting the guests. Julien looked at me and said, "*Chat* (affectionate French nickname meaning Cat), why don't you become a hostess? It's an easy job: you're just paid to literally stand there and look pretty. After all those years of hard, physical work, I'm sure you could do with an easy job like that."

As soon as he said those words, it hit me. That could be my way into a new world, the world of events, fancy nightclubs and obviously wealthy and powerful people. I didn't waste any time. I came back home and researched all the prestigious hostess agencies in London and sent out my CV to all of them. I knew I was going to get contacted, it was just a matter of time.

Within two days, I went from being jobless to being on the books of three hostess agencies. I was on top of the world. I was so excited to try something new, meeting new people and being able to work whenever I wanted. As I was available to several agencies, I was considered as self-employed, so I could choose which event I wanted to attend. All I had to do was wait for the client in charge of the event to accept my application.

From July 2014 until mid-September 2014, I was a little butterfly working in a different place every day, meeting new people and working at different types of events. Sometimes the job was fun, if we got fed by the caterer who was serving the guests. The locations were most of the time amazing, and the job was not hard. I probably worked in every luxurious hotel in London at least once. Every time I went to work, I looked at the guests, especially the women, wearing their designer clothes or evening gowns. I thought, "One day this could be me."

Sometimes the jobs were not that glamorous or cool. The two types of jobs I hated the most were promotional work and shot girl. The agencies I was working for were quite different: one of them was prestigious and had only proper hostess jobs in formal corporate VIP events; and the other was underline jobs: promo, shot girl, podium dancing and stadium jobs. The woman that created this agency was the most driven woman I have ever met. She started as a shot girl and took her job to the next level to create her own agency. She wasn't mucking about, everyone was scared of her, no one liked her. She was an extremely unpleasant businesswoman. If you were late by just one minute, or if she didn't like your make-up, she would deduct money from your pay, sometimes for no reason. Payments took so long to come, you always had to chase her. She asked for a lot but gave nothing in return. She was also mean: she had no shame in telling you if she found you ugly or overweight. But for now I had no choice but to go with the flow. I knew it wasn't a job for a lifetime, so I would keep my mouth shut and do whatever job was on offer.

Promotion was one of the hardest. Luckily I was working during the summer, so it wasn't cold while I stood outside for hours distributing flyers. But sometimes I had to get up at 6 a.m. to be ready to hand out flyers outside the tube station by 7 a.m., and that wasn't fun at all. People in London are so stressed in the morning that trying to give them flyers at that time wasn't easy. They were either rude or looked at me funny. Sometimes I would look at myself and think, "Lola, really? Don't you think you can do better than that?" The most annoying thing I'd often hear was that I was too pretty to do this sort of job; I should be a model or on television. It was very frustrating to hear it, and also frustrating for me not to be able to do anything about it. But for now I had no choice but to make money to pay my bills and eat. Those jobs were paying well, but it wasn't regular work so I was on a budget for the first time in my life.

I remember Julien and me eating only pasta for two months. On good days we would buy tomato sauce, and on even better days grated cheese. On days when we wanted some protein, we would buy cans of sardines. We never felt sad or sorry for ourselves, no, we were laughing about it. Julien always used to say that one day Madame Lola would become a superstar and we would remember this time of us eating pasta and think "We finally made it". I didn't mind being broke; I was feeling happier now than when I had a better salary but no life and felt miserable. For the first time also I was having fun. It was my fourth year in London, and I'd never really enjoyed my summers there, so it felt good just to be young, wild and free. I was feeling so adventurous that every time I was booked for a job, I mean most of the time, I would end up with a guy that I was working with, and usually it was the client, not my colleagues.

During those two months, I went on a date with an airplane pilot; we met during a birthday party where I was the shot girl dressed up as a playmate. I then kissed the manager of one of the clubs I was working for as a hostess, crammed up in a closet inside the club, very charming. I slept with a client who needed a French hostess for a few days, to look after his guests during their trip in London; then with a guy who was presenting the weather on national television; and one guy from British reality TV. I mean, I was having fun. For the first time in a few years, I felt young and careless. All the past years was about me struggling, hating my life and going out with bad guys. Now for once I was listening to me and my needs and it felt amazing. I still wasn't on the level that I wanted to be at, life wasn't glamorous and full of abundance, but it was a start of freedom and excitement.

In September 2014, I decided it was about time to have a full-time job again. I'd had fun during the summer, but it was very stressful to be always on a budget and counting every penny you earn. I wasn't working regularly, so money wasn't always flowing. Even though I was feeling better mentally, not having so much pressure on my shoulders, it was still stressful to wonder if I was going to be able to pay the rent and buy my food.

My next plan was to work as a hostess either in a luxury club in Mayfair or in a prestigious hotel. I sent out my CV everywhere, but I remember one job ad catching my eye. A new hotel was opening on the South Bank. This hotel was the new sensation in town. It was very modern, luxurious, promising to have famous guests and the crème de la crème. I could picture myself working there and having the time of my life, meeting even more important and wealthy people than I was already meeting now. My main and only goal for now was to get a job in this hotel. One of my agencies was advertising work at this new hotel and inviting staff to send in their CV, which I obviously did, but no one ever got back to me. Funnily enough, a few days later the sexfriend that I was seeing at the time, Tom, a British photographer who was thirteen years older than me, knew one of the managers working there. He promised to pass on my CV, but it never happened. I couldn't count on anyone, could I? As usual I had to take care of things myself.

I let it go for a few days and applied for other jobs. I even managed to get a trial run in a hostess job at a gentlemen's club. Naive me, I didn't even know what a gentlemen's club was back then, and that the term "hostess" was a cover for escort work. When I arrived at the club for my trial shift, I got a bad feeling. The doors were old and damaged, I would even say creepy, and the men who entered the club didn't inspire trust and safety. This is when I understood what the word "hostess" meant in certain cases. I just left and didn't even bother with my trial shift. I wanted promotion and money, but not at any cost.

In the meantime I also got contacted for a hostess job via the rotten boss, the one who had her own agency. She wasn't really clear on the job description, all she asked was who was available to party and get paid £700. When I saw the amount, I got really excited and of course I was going to accept. She then said that she would put our pictures through to the client and he would call the girls he was interested in. I had never heard of such a process, how weird; maybe he wanted to check our level of English and if we were well spoken? A few minutes later I received a call from that client. I put on my best professional voice, ready to respond to every question he asked. I had no idea what the questions would be.

But he asked me what my boss had told us he'd pay, so I mentioned what I knew we'd get paid to party in a club in Mayfair. He said yes, but not exactly, and asked me to keep what he was about to say between him and me. The conversation was getting a bit weird. He then asked me if I wanted to do the "after party" with him in his hotel room. I was a bit naive back then, but not that naive. I was twenty-three years old, and I exactly knew what he meant by "after party". He was looking for sex. I played dumb and asked how many people would come to the party and if he needed the girls to host. He then made it clear that it was only him and me, so I apologised and said that I wasn't offering this kind of service. Things started to get out of control when he offered me more money, a lot of money; and when you have nothing in your bank account, the figure he was offering me was extremely tempting. He was also very charming over the phone; he knew exactly what he was doing, he recognised my accent and started to speak French to me. We stayed on the phone for about thirty minutes while he tried to convince me. He offered me £20,000 and a shopping trip to Selfridges. I couldn't believe what I heard: fucking £20,000! That would sort me out for a few months. I have to say I was tempted, I thought of doing it, but I couldn't. I didn't even know who he was, so I hung up. For a few days and even weeks he tried to contact me; sometimes I would pick up and speak to him, and sometimes I would hang up. At some point I thought it was time to end this game. I didn't even know who I was talking to. Every time I asked for a picture or to go on Face Time, he would refuse. When I told him that he needed to stop calling me, he didn't take it well. He kept calling me, shouting, screaming the word "slut", so I blocked him. From time to time I would receive pictures of girls in sexual positions or giving a blowjob to a man from an unknown number, but I knew it was him. I was a bit scared, but I knew that if I wasn't responding to the calls and the texts, he would stop eventually, which he did. I am glad that my intuition and gut instinct helped me out one more time. I could have ended up in a very tricky situation. Money can lead you to do unexpected things, but no money in the world should compromise your safety.

While all this weird situation was going on, I came across the website of this new hotel that just opened a few weeks ago, promising to be the next place to BE at the time. That sounded promising, so I checked their job section, and lucky me they had an open day scheduled. Perfect! Two days later, I arrived at the hotel. Wow, It was beautiful, all brand new, modern, everyone wearing stylish uniforms, everything so trendy and cool. I entered via the main entrance to a lobby which was very spacious, in a brown metallic colour with small spotlights in the floor. As I was looking around, someone asked me if I was coming to the open day. I nodded yes and was guided up to the rooftop bar. I arrived on the top floor to discover a very bright, luminous, big room with a gigantic glass window that gave onto a beautiful view of London. The room was decorated with dark purple and burgundy velvet sofas and chairs. In the ceiling you could see a massive modern chandelier that looked like a firework, and at the back an extravagant golden bar. I was so impressed, I could really see myself working there. I was sure that many parties with important people would be organised in this bar. I had to get a job there, and I was going to. All the interviews were held in small groups with different managers. I was sitting with the Food and Beverage director: she wasn't very warm and welcoming, but I didn't let it depress me. I put on my best smile, pretended to be very confident and gave my best. Everything went so well that she introduced me to the manager of the rooftop bar. We had a brief chat together, and after five minutes he offered me a job as a hostess.

Yes! Well done, Lola! I was over the moon. I'd put my 100% into this and I'd got what I wanted. Finally, I would have some sort of stability, but still have fun. I would work evenings, in a party environment that exactly matched with my personality and what I was looking for at the time.

FIVE

Love Hurts

There is no heart for me like yours.

Maya Angelou

When I started to work at the rooftop bar, I never thought it would change my life. At first I was a bit lost: I'd never worked in a luxurious bar before, so I didn't know anything about spirits, cocktails, service and how to be an actual hostess. Here it meant not a simple standing around hostess, but an actual host who welcomes you, makes you feel as if you are a unique customer, manages to turn around the tables fast. You are literally the person that manages the entire place; the whole vibe and arrangement of the room depends on you. It took me some time to master, as I wasn't a people person back then, but week after week I was getting better and better. I was recognising regulars, I would always try to accommodate everyone, I knew how to be firm but remain polite and pleasant. I learned about spirits and cocktails; the world of luxury bars and restaurants was my new life. I'd always thought that going to a hotel bar or a fancy restaurant was accessible only to privileged people or members. I was always scared of not being accepted as a client, but not a bit of it.

I spent my new free time with my new colleagues, either having a drink in one of the best cocktail bars in London, brunching in a cool cafe, spending hours eating very Instagram-able afternoon tea, or having dinner in a fancy restaurant. I was finally having the same life as my favourite characters from *Sex and the City*, and it felt so good. I felt my mind expand, and I could see the opportunities that London had to offer. Until now I hadn't enjoyed the City to its fullest, I'd only been working there, but now I was actually living. I couldn't have done any of it without the help of my work colleagues: most of them were actors, models or dancers, so I was finally surrounded by dreamers and creatives. They made me understand that it was possible to follow your dreams while still working. I just needed to work for it, obviously, and believe in myself.

I was really close with one of my colleagues, Larah, who was the main host. Larah was a West End actress who played in many musicals. I found it extraordinary that she could sing, act and dance at the same time. I was really drawn to her acting, it was fascinating. I also loved the way she lived her life: she was always on the go, looking fabulous, heading to a casting or even just to grab a coffee. She looked good, no matter what; that was her motto. She was so productive and creative, it was very inspiring. When I started to work at the hotel, I was still behaving the same as before: I would work and go home and that was it. But seeing how Larah lived her life truly changed my own view on life. She showed me it was possible to do all these many things. She actually kicked my butt when we first met, asked me how I could hope to change my life and fill it with abundance if all I was doing was watching TV series and dreaming about my aspirations without taking any actions. That doesn't work. No one was going to come to my council flat, scoop me off my sofa and say, "Hey, you look beautiful, let me sign you!"

Her words made a lot of sense. I knew all this already, but I was too scared to admit that I wanted to be an artist. I was always scared of people judging and laughing at me for wanting those things. I was still bogged down in beliefs that people with money who lived an abundant, luxurious life were bad. In France, people are very judgemental of successful people, and I never understood why, but slowly I was challenging those beliefs. Another fear I had to overcome was failure. In certain countries like America, failure is a good thing: it is a way to learn lessons and keep pushing yourself forward. Where I come from, if you fail once, that means you are not a winner. You tried, you failed and that is it. Which is why not many people try, as they are too scared of being judged for failing. But Larah made me understand that failing, or not always being successful, was totally normal and part of the learning process. She really changed something in me; she managed to unlock all the fears and insecurities inside me. I really looked up to her so I decided to make some changes, real changes, not just going out and looking fancy.

The first thing I did was hire a personal trainer. If I wanted to be an artist, perform on stage, I needed to be in the best shape possible and I needed help. I didn't know anything about exercising or healthy food, and that was the best decision I made. Working out really helped me to feel more confident in my body, for sure; but I was also began to feel amazing mentally – more calm and positive. Once my body was on form, I started to organise a photoshoot with a photographer to build up my portfolio and professional page. One advice I would give to everyone trying to collaborate with photographers or videographers is always to check them out to be 100% safe.

One day, I was meant to shoot with a man pretending to be a photographer whom I'd met on a famous website that helps models and photographers to meet and collaborate. After a few emails were exchanged, we agreed on a date and time. He suggested we meet at a hotel that was near his house, and we would then walk together to his. Even before I met him, I could feel a weird feeling in my stomach, my gut instinct again: something didn't feel right, but I still went for it. I was the first one to arrive at the hotel, so I sat down at the hotel bar and waited. After five minutes a very tall skinny man walked towards me and said Hi: it was him. As soon as I saw him, chills ran through my entire body. He didn't inspire any trust; I could see from his eyes that his intentions were not good, but what could I do? I mean of course I could have said straight away I'm sorry but I have to go. But I was paralyzed. I followed him outside the hotel to walk towards his. We started walking together, and as we were walking I started to ask questions about him as a photographer. His answers were very vague, not clear or didn't make sense. I felt this person beside me had no confidence in his supposed profession.

Once we arrived at his house, I noticed something really weird about it. His front door had a window glass covered with big chunks of wood, as if he wanted to hide what was inside the house. I thought it was really creepy and realised "Fuck, I'm in trouble here!" How the hell was I going to get out of this? If he was an actual weirdo, and telling him that I suddenly wanted to leave, he would probably try to hold me back and force me to go into the house. I couldn't show that I was scared. My heart was beating really fast and my blood was freezing up, but I had to remain calm and pretend everything was fine. We both went inside, me letting him walk in front of me. The house was so messy and ugly, with stuff everywhere. To me this was confirmation that if he were a genuine photographer, the place would be spacious and clean to shoot in, but this wasn't the case. He then headed to the kitchen and I stayed by the door, which luckily was unlocked. He offered me a tea, which I accepted. As he was making the tea, I pretended a phone call was coming through and that I had to take it.

As soon as I stepped outside, I started running as fast as I could, I didn't dare look behind me once. I was petrified. Why had I not checked up about him before our meeting? In less than three minutes, I reached the train station. I was out of breath, but so relieved to have escaped this freak! I didn't have long to wait: my train was arriving in two minutes, and this nightmare would finally be over. Maybe I was wrong, maybe he was a genuinely nice guy and I was paranoid, but I didn't want to risk it. My instinct had always proved me right, so I had to follow it. I just wanted the train to arrive now and leave as soon as possible!

When the train did finally arrive, and as it was still moving, almost ready to stop, I heard a male voice behind me: "Why did you leave? Where are you going?" It was him: he'd followed me all the way to the train station, what a freak. Thank God, many people were on the platform so nothing could happen to me. I barely responded, I just said I had to go. He looked me up and down with his pervy eyes and said it was a real shame. Finally the train stopped in front of me, opened its doors and I could escape inside.

Just the thought of it still scares the hell out of me. Since that incident, I always make sure I triple check anyone before being alone with them. Thank God not all the photographers are like that, and I managed to get some great shots that I could use. My hard work paid off, as I managed to work with a few model agencies – mainly commercial. I was earning a bit of money that I was intending to invest in dancing and singing classes, but something was still holding me back… fear.

February 2015: I received a call from one of the agencies asking me If I was interested to cast for a reality TV show, *Love Island*. They needed hot, outgoing single girls available for the summer to go abroad to live in a luxury villa for some time and find their match. I fulfilled all the criteria, so my agency wanted to put me forward. I couldn't believe it: my first ever real casting. I thought it was mad how when I put work and effort into something, how quickly and easily it would come my way. I obviously accepted, as it was a lifetime opportunity. I had never heard of the show before, as I don't watch British television, but it sounded promising. I could become famous and have so many new doors open for me and finally become an artist. A few days later I turned up at the ITV studio, which was near my work on the South Bank, to pass the first casting test. I was impressed by the building: just the thought of knowing I was in the offices of a national channel was amazing to me. I didn't know what to expect, as I'd never been to a casting before, so I was really anxious. A lovely lady met me on the ground floor and asked me to follow her up in the lift .I took a seat in a room full of girls, all looking very impressive and intimidating. It's awful to see your direct competition right in front of you. We were all looking at each other and probably thinking the same: "Is she prettier than me?" " My boobs are so much smaller than hers." "She's had too much surgery." "She's had no surgery at all and looks really plain." While we were waiting, we had to fill out a form with our personal information and details about our love life. I still couldn't believe I was there at ITV, ready to go into this casting. Less than ten minutes later, the same lady picked me out to follow her to the next stage.

This is it, it's my turn, for fuck's sake, I feel sick and hot. I was sweating so much and started to feel my cheeks getting really red. At the time I was still struggling to hide my emotions and calm myself down. But it didn't stop me from doing what I wanted, any more than it used to do when I was a teenager. What is the worst thing that could happen? They weren't going to eat me alive, were they? I entered the room and someone fixed a microphone to my top. They asked me to sit down on at the back of the room. I pulled out the chair, and there I was facing four people and two cameras. I smiled at them and said Hello. I was petrified. I think my voice was shaking rather a lot. They all welcomed me and explained what was going to happen. They would ask me a list of questions, and while I answered, I should look right at the camera. They were all very nice and reassuring. I confess I had a hard time at first, having had to catch my breath, but the more I answered their questions, the more confident I got. I still can't believe how I managed to stay calm and speak English in front of a camera and a group of casting directors, but I did it! Even though I was sweating like crazy and had a massive red rash all over my chest as I was so anxious, I felt really proud of myself for not crumbling to pieces. Once the interview was done, they all thanked me and said that only successful candidates would be contacted. I thanked them back and left. Once I was outside the studios, I called Julien straight away to tell him everything! I was so excited, full of hopes and dreams. All I had to do now was wait for a response.

Another main event that changed my life while I was working at the rooftop bar was meeting the man I thought was the love of my life, the man that made me the happiest person alive, but also the one who broke my heart like no one else. He was Filip.

Filip was Swedish, tall, blond and very funny. I remember that we were working together, but I didn't even know who he was at first. He would always try to speak to me, but all I thought was why was this young boy trying to chat to me. I won't say I was looking down on him, but I have to admit that I was a bit. He looked much younger than me; he didn't seem very mature, and he was working as a barback. I was now used to dating older, established men with a good situation, and I was enjoying single life to the limit. I even slept with a reality TV celebrity from Essex after a crazy night out in a famous club in Mayfair. I knew nothing about reality TV celebrities in the UK, but my friend I was with that night was over the moon when we started partying with them, and I think she was really happy with how the night ended. I even dated a weather TV presenter, probably the worst date I have been on, but still I was having so much fun that the last person I wanted to be bothered with was a barback guy. As you know, after Matthew, I always promised myself to date someone who was more or less established.

But it felt different with Filip: in time we became friends, and then lovers. The whole team would always go out after work for a few drinks, and when you work in a bar, your after-work drinks usually run from 4 a.m until 9 a.m. Those nights were fun: I was drinking much more at this time of my life; I never liked it, to be honest, I always felt really sick even after one drink or really tired. But I was young, so I thought what the hell. You know, feeling sick is part of the drinking process. We would either go to Polo's bar on Liverpool Street, which was open 24/7 and also served food, or we would head to the Empire Casino on Leicester Square; but that was further out, so we mainly went to Polo's. I felt really happy at that time. I finally had a fun job, the people I was working with were much more interesting than the ones I'd been working with in the past, I was concentrating on myself, and I was enjoying London much more. All those bad years of working physically and mentally hard were behind me. I didn't have an abusive or lying boyfriend, and I was surrounded by good people. I was just taking care of myself, and I liked this feeling.

I always knew that Filip had a crush on me, but I never paid attention until one night when we both got so drunk that we ended up kissing. I think that was the best day of his life. I remember him smiling from ear to ear the next day at work. It was so cute, but still I wasn't planning on falling for him. After that first kiss, we started to text a bit as friends; but seeing him everyday at work, him making me laugh and always having cute attention for me, made me want to go further. I loved the way he looked at me and the way he made me feel. It just felt amazing. For the first time I didn't feel that this guy was just interested in sleeping with me before leaving, or that I was the best prize to chase. It felt much deeper than that. We were not together yet, but I felt that he cared and that was a new feeling for me. I'd never felt that a guy cared about me, apart from Julien of course.

A few months after we'd started flirting, we all went out one night for a drink after work. Everyone was mingling, but Filip and I were not interested in the rest of the group. We were in our own world, just the two of us. We couldn't stop hugging, talking, laughing, we were drawn into each other. We all drank so much that night that I was completely wasted, so wasted that I wasn't even walking straight. Filip offered to take me home to make sure I was safe. I remember us taking the DLR, at around 7 a.m., with the sun rising, and the view of London waking up simply beautiful. Filip was really drunk too, and we both passed out in our seats. At around 7.30 a.m. we managed to get back to my place, and even though we were exhausted and wasted, we were still very much attracted to each other and started to make out.

Filip was such a good kisser, and it felt so good to be close to him and intimate. It was the first time I'd felt something so strong when I was kissing someone. I'd never felt that before. It felt like our bodies were merging into one body, and my heart was about to explode with happiness. Filip started to touch me: he was so good at it, so good that I squirted for the first time in my life, and I remember being so embarrassed as I didn't know what had just happened. But it felt wonderful, it was a sexual sensation at another level. We then tried to have sex, but I don't know if it was the alcohol, or if he was nervous, but he couldn't manage to get it up. I was just a little annoyed, as this wasn't the first time it had happened to me. Every time I was close to a guy emotionally and we ended up sleeping together for the first time, the guy would always end up with a soft on. At first I thought that maybe these guys weren't attracted to me, but like my grandmother explained to me: "If a guy really likes you, he will get nervous, so obviously he'll have trouble making it work the first time." It took Filip a few times to make it work and for us to have sex. We still kissed the whole night and cuddled until we fell asleep.

I was so embarrassed when we woke up a few hours later. I had the worst hangover, I could barely move. I was feeling so rough and I looked like hell, but I don't think he cared. He looked at me, pulled me towards him and hugged me. I was feeling so good between his arms. I will always remember one of the first things he said that day. He looked at me as if I was the most beautiful thing in the world and said: "What is your story, Lola? Who are you? I want to know everything." That touched me so deeply, someone wanting to know me, the real me, my past, who I am, my hopes, my dreams. No one had ever asked me such a question before, and that made me like him even more.

After that first night, I didn't see him for three weeks as he was away on holiday in Sweden. I missed him so much, but we couldn't be together so I played it cool and didn't bother him. In March 2015, Filip came back from holidays and he finally asked me out on a real date, just the two of us in a proper cocktail bar. I remember him taking me to this very small bar on Hoxton Square, "Happiness Forgets". We were both so nervous at first, but with the help of a lot of delicious cocktails we started to loosen up and we had an amazing time. Even though Filip wasn't rich, he treated me like a princess. He always paid attention for me and made sure I was fine. After our first date we both decided to be official boyfriend and girlfriend. We stayed together for just over six months, and it was probably one of the best times of my life. I felt so loved, and in return I'd never loved anyone as much. He was the first guy who'd loved me for me, and not for my looks. I felt that I was important and that I mattered.

After many bad relationships with cheaters, liars and abusive boyfriends, I finally felt safe and loved. If we ever argued, he would sit me down and talk to me, try to calm me down. No one had ever taught me this before, not even my parents. I didn't know what communication was. Filip loved me deeply, so he had a lot of patience with me, even though he had a hard time sometimes understanding why I was so angry and negative out of nowhere. I had changed in the last few years, but I still had my demons from the past, I was still very insecure and petrified of being cheated on and abandoned. We would argue quite often, mainly my fault because I was so jealous and insecure that I confess I must have made his life hell. I was constantly making movies in my head about him cheating on me or lying. If everything was going well, I would find ways to argue. I was pushing his limits, pushing him away to see if he would still stay with me. I was constantly testing him, and he was successful each time, he remained by my side, always trying to reassure me. When everything was fine, we would spend hours talking, laughing, making love, It felt like we were one person. He was my best friend and lover. We had so much passion for one another. He was good at listening to me, looking after me like no one else before and simply staring at me, as if I was the best thing in the world. I was so in love that it hurt me sometimes. I didn't know what to do with so much love, it actually ached. I could have died for him.

June 2015: I was now twenty-four years old. After three months in the relationship with Filip, he asked me to follow him to Sydney, Australia after the summer, in around September. His sister, who I wasn't a big fan of, was moving there and he wanted to follow her and try something new. As I hadn't received an answer from *Love Island*, I thought why not? I'm young, I don't have a career, and starting a new life with the person I love most could be something great. So I accepted his offer, and a few months later I crossed the globe for him. If only I'd known…

Filip went to Sydney two weeks ahead of me, as I wanted to have a trip to New York City with one of my best friends before moving to the other side of the world. He promised to take care of everything once he was in Sydney: job, apartment etc. But before he left for Australia, we had a massive row: I was in such panic mode about not seeing him for a while that I kept pushing him away. I even told him it was over, so he got fed up with me and started packing before it was his time to leave. No! Why did I do that? Why was I ruining everything? Why couldn't I just enjoy loving him and letting him love me? Why did I constantly need to argue? I loved him a lot, so why?

I managed to calm things down, apologise for my bad attitude and make it up, but things were still a bit tense. He then left a few hours later to catch his flight, and I could feel him being very cold and distant with me. During those two weeks apart, we constantly argued. He wasn't making as much effort with me any more, and I felt that I was fighting alone. I knew deep inside that Filip had reached his limits with me, but still I was hoping for things to get better once we were together in Sydney. After two long weeks apart and many arguments, we started to get finally back on track and things were feeling better. I was annoyed at him as he wasn't organising anything in terms of work and where to live, but still I was happy that he wasn't so cold with me any more.

I set off for Sydney and I couldn't wait to see him again. Once I landed in Sydney and met Filip, things were rather awkward and cold. I could feel that even though we were trying hard, something had changed. He wasn't as sweet and nice any more. I was seeing a side of Filip I didn't like at all. He was acting like a dick for real. I knew I wasn't always perfect, but I never acted as if he didn't matter. I didn't know what to do to get his attention any more, so I did what I do best, I pushed him away even further, thinking that he would have a wake-up call and be scared to lose me. But this time I was going to regret for a long time playing that game.

On the fourth day of me being in Sydney, we went for

breakfast. The atmosphere was still tense and awkward. I'd had enough of it, and him being distant with me, so while we were eating I suggested we break up as there was no point in us staying together if we were the way we were. Inside my head and heart, I didn't mean it. I didn't want us to break up. All I wanted was a reaction, but instead he agreed with me. I was shocked. I tried to explain that I didn't know what I was saying and that we were making a mistake. But he didn't want to hear anything. He paid the bill and walked out. I tried to talk to him, to make him listen, but it was too late, he had made his decision and I was devastated.

So here I was in Sydney, by the beach, on the other side of the world. I'd left all my friends, my entire life in London behind me for him, and ended up all alone. I couldn't believe it. Things were easier for him, he had family and people to help him out over there, but I had no one! No contacts, no job, no place to stay any more. The feeling I had was exactly like losing someone in a car accident. You don't expect it to happen. I had such a big pain inside me, it was unbearable. I never thought he could hurt me that much, or do something like that to me. I had so much esteem for him, he was above everyone that I knew, he was my priority, my everything. He was the best person I'd ever met, and I never thought he would leave me in such a state, as if I was a one-night stand. I needed to wake up from this horrible nightmare. I had to find a job and a place in no time. I didn't have the energy for it, but when life gives you no choice, you just have to find strength within you.

I cried for days, I couldn't eat. I was only a body, I didn't feel that I had a soul any more. But one month later, somehow I managed to get my life back on track: I found a job, a place to stay and new friends. I wasn't all alone any more. I really don't know how I did it all. I was obviously still in pain, very sad, and constantly thinking about him. We still saw each other from time to time, but at some point I'd had enough of us seeing each other as "friends". We would still go out for dinner or go to the beach, and actually we still slept together. We couldn't lose our strong attraction towards each other, even though it didn't make sense any more. He'd dumped me, so it wasn't right for him still to enjoy the good side of me. So I told him we had to stop seeing each other completely. I knew he was having a hard time in Sydney: he didn't like the place, and the time he spent with me was the only time that felt like home. It was all so unfair on me though. Even if I loved him more than anything, being near him and spending time with him, I wasn't just going to let him use me whenever was convenient.

A week later, after us not being in contact at all, he called me. He said he was missing me and he just wanted us to get back together. I had waited for that moment for over a month, but weirdly when it happened I didn't feel so happy about it. I was very sceptical, but our love bond was so special that I couldn't just throw it away like that. So I did give it another go, but going back to something that was already broken felt weird. Yet still I had a lot of love for him, so I tried. Two weeks later, we were arguing again. He was out partying with people who were having a really bad influence on him. After hours of fighting via text, I asked him to come over to mine so we could talk and sort things out face to face. He arrived at my place at 4 a.m. and the nightmare started again. We kept arguing and disagreeing for hours, and then he dumped me for the second time and left my apartment. I followed him outside, begging him to stay, but he wouldn't listen. I remember crying so much that I was hysterical. When I think of that scene again, I don't know if it was pathetic of me, or really sad. I had so much love for Filip, I couldn't believe he was abandoning me again. It was like being hit by a bus. My heart was crushed and broken in a thousand pieces, I couldn't breathe. I remember watching him walking away from me, and me crying loudly sitting on the floor. Just the thought of it still makes me horribly sad. I just want to hug my younger self and tell her it will all be fine, but at the time I thought my life was over.

I went to bed around 7 a.m. I had no more energy. I had nothing left in me, no tears, no voice, no thought. I felt like a zombie, I was empty. My soulmate was gone, a part of me had died that day. I felt that I had no choice but to travel back to London. If he and I were in the same city, it would happen again. We were like magnets that couldn't stay apart for long, but I was always the one paying the price and suffering. I wasn't strong enough to keep on fighting for this love. Ever since I remember, I always fight to make something out of my life, I fight to get out of a bad relationship, I fight to find a decent job, I fight to make sure I don't end up broke and homeless. It feels that I am always trying and trying. When would it ever stop? When would I be at peace and have a life where everything came easily towards me without stress and worries? My life always looked like an ocean during a bad storm, never a peaceful river, and I'd had enough of it. My family and friends asked if I was sure that coming back to London was a good idea, that maybe I should push a bit more, but I was tired of pushing, for once I didn't want to be a warrior, I just wanted to let myself go and be somewhere homey and comforting.

By the end of October 2015, I was on a plane from Sydney back to London. I spent all the money I had left to buy the cheapest ticket I could find. The company I was flying with was blacklisted in Europe. The plane was uncomfortable and the journey so bumpy that I thought that on top of being dumped, I was probably going to die in a shit plane. But we finally made it to London. I remember Julien picking me up at the airport. Just seeing his face made me feel so much better. The first thing he noticed was how skinny I was, and he asked me if I was eating properly. It is not that I'd intentionally stopped eating, but I wasn't hungry. The pain I was feeling in my heart was so strong that it created a big node in my stomach. The node was so big that I couldn't eat.

We went back to our old apartment. My room was meanwhile rented by someone else, so I stayed with Julien in his room. I was back to square one: no place to stay, no job and no boyfriend. Fortunately I had Julien. He was my true soulmate, my guardian angel. I will always be grateful for his friendship; without him I think I would have crumbled away many times during my London journey, but his love and support helped me survive the tough times, and that is what real friendships are all about.

Of course Filip reached out to me a few days after I got back to London, and from time to time we would spend hours on the phone talking. Even though we were living in different countries, miles away from each other, our connection remained strong. We would even get turned on just by talking. It took us years to cut our contact completely and forget about each other. I stayed single for three years after that. Every time I met someone, it just felt tasteless. There was no other man like him. Once I'd experienced true love, it was really hard to connect with other people at a shallower level. I would find other guys so boring, selfish and simply uninteresting. All I could think about was Filip, and hope for a reunion one day. Unfortunately or fortunately, whichever is the better term to use, it ultimately didn't happen and we are not even friends any more. When such intense feelings have been involved, it is almost impossible to stay friends. We met once or twice when he got back to London, and every time we met just for a drink, we would revert to our old habits and act as a couple. But we both knew that it wasn't right, so we cut our contact. I still think about him from time to time, but only as a good memory. I wonder who he is now, and what he is about, but it is probably best for us to remain strangers.

SIX

Mayfair

> *It was here in Mayfair that adjectives such as gracious, elegant, sophisticated and sublime trip off the tongue like coins into a parking meter."*
>
> Tyne O'Connell

When I returned from Australia without any money in my pocket, I went back to all the small jobs I'd been doing before being a hostess at the rooftop bar: from shot girl to podium dancer, handing out flyers outside the tube station, hostessing at corporate events, I did it all over again. I had no money and I had to make some money fast. Those jobs were paid either weekly or the same day, which was very convenient for me at the time. I had no choice but to take any sort of job if I wanted to have enough money to get my own place. It was nice to be with Julien of course, but living out of a suitcase and sharing a bed at twenty-four years old wasn't the ideal picture to me.

After a few weeks of working here and there, one of the regular clients from the rooftop bar with whom I'd become a friend called me to have a drink and a catch-up together. A drink was always a good idea at that time. That was the only thing I was doing, apart from working anyway. I was going out all the time, partying and drinking. That was helping me to forget the pain I was constantly feeling. If I drank too much and heard a song that reminded me of Filip, I would end up in a pretty bad state.

I remember one night lying on the bathroom floor of some disgusting dodgy bar, crying. I was in such a bad state, but Larah, who I thought was my friend, put me in an Uber so I could get back home while she carried on partying. I was past moving or talking. How could she just leave me in a taxi? if the driver had bad intentions, he could have done whatever he wanted to me. I remember throwing up everywhere. The taxi driver wasn't happy at all, but the worst was that my friend didn't give the right address and we arrived at the back of the estate. I couldn't even walk, so I begged the driver to help me walk home as I was scared something could happen to me. I was blessed and lucky that the driver was not a rapist or psychopath. He walked me all the way up to Julien's appartement. I banged on the door, Julien opened and I started to cry hysterically. I think I was so embarrassed at myself and ashamed to act like this. I then started to shout about how I was missing my dad, how much of a slut I'd become, and that I wasn't worth it. Julien took me in his arms to comfort me, undressed me and put me to bed next to him. I was beyond grateful and blessed to have such an angel by my side. I always thought I had guardian angels anyway, angels that were above me, that I couldn't see. They were probably my grandparents and great grandparents, but also I had angels that were physically here with me, like Julien. In every bad, dangerous or tricky situation, I always managed to stay safe or find a solution.

Even though I kept ending up in a pretty bad state, I still agreed to go for drinks with my former regular. I had to take my mind off my misery, so dressing up, going to a fancy bar with everything paid for, seemed like a good idea. I could once again show the world of social media how exciting my life was and that a break-up wasn't stopping me from having fun. Apart from Julien, no one knew how sad I was. I was mastering the art of faking my life and emotions. I would make sure that I was always very active, always on the go, going to nice places, parties, seeing "friends" to make it look as if my life was perfect, even though deep inside I was crying for help.

My former regular asked me to meet him at a famous bar in a hotel in the heart of Mayfair. It had just got refurbished, and he swore it was the new place to be in Mayfair. He also knew all the managers, so he offered to introduce me to them as I was looking for a job. I remember walking into that bar for the first time. It was really dark, the only lights being the candles lit on every table. It was November, so the bar was packed, full of Christmas parties and businessmen. We sat in one of the booths, caught up with news, had a drink and then finally he introduced me to one of the managers who then offered me an interview and a trial shift.

A few days later I came back to the bar, worked for probably thirty minutes and then was told that I'd got the job. Easy. Finally I could see a little light at the end of the tunnel. I would work in a very fancy place and area, I would make new friends, hope to find a new lover who would help me forget about Filip, and most importantly I would make money, a real salary. I wouldn't have to stand outside in the cold at 7 a.m. any more, handing out flyers to earn peanuts. I would work in a luxurious place, full of rich men and important people. That would maybe lead me somewhere?

I worked at the bar for probably six months. I had fun, but I didn't bond with my colleagues as I'd done at the rooftop bar. My new work place was staffed by Italians; their English was very poor and they didn't have the same artistic mentality as my former colleagues. They were there only to work, earn their money and go. The clientele was also very different. In Mayfair people didn't really care about what they were drinking, they just wanted to get smashed at the end of their stressful day and that was it. "Work hard, play hard." Whereas here, during the day we served mostly businessmen in meetings, ordering coffee and water; then at night the bar turned into a lounge where the same men got into heavy drinking and flirting with any woman around.

There weren't many women, I must say, especially during the week. During the weekend, yes, many girls would come in the hope of finding their next rich boyfriend. But I would say that 60% of the women coming to the bar were escorts. Yes, Mayfair was the playground for escorts. You could recognise them straight away. They were always dressed up extremely sexily, and most of the time not looking cheap. They were wearing the most famous designers, their hair were always perfect and make-up flawless. They would always refuse to get a table and would always go and sit by the bar, waiting for a big fish to come around, that is how they would operate. As an employee, I was annoyed by them because they were using space for nothing; they were not spending at all. They would get a Coke and wait. But as a woman, I'm not going to say that I wanted to be like them. I couldnt imagine myself having sex with strangers for money, especially since most of the time they were not attractive. But I did envy their lifestyle. They had the money, the clothes, the freedom, the confidence, they were living the high life. Even though the way they earned their money was not politically correct, I never understood why people judged them so harshly. Why were they the ones people called "hoes", "whores", "sluts"? Why are we always shaming the women and never the men who pay for those women? If the demand wasn't there, the offer would not exist. No one ever gave me an answer for why it was wrong to do what they were doing. The women were answering the needs of frustrated men, they weren't harming anyone. And on top of that, they were making tons of money. Is that worse than those bankers ruining our economy? But because they were wearing suits, this made them socially correct, even though they were fucking with everyone else's money. I always thought that as long as nothing was forced or harming anyone, there was nothing wrong with being an escort, stripper or even a porn star. If it made you happy and you were doing it in a healthy, genuine way, why should anyone be so judgemental about it?

I won't lie: I thought about joining them many times. I had so many offers from clients I was serving at the bar, but I always refused. I simply couldn't do it. I think it was more to do with security. I was petrified of being raped or killed. The only time I accepted an offer was from a regular who came to the bar once or twice a month. He would always come around 11 a.m. with his friend; he always called me "sweetie" and gave me £100 tips, just because I was smiling at him, calling him by his name and sitting them down somewhere quiet. He would always order Laurent Perrier Rosé and get smashed by about 2 p.m. One day, he came in with his friend and I looked after them as usual. I stayed a bit with them to chat, you know, make them feel special. We then started to talk about the horse racing at Ascot. (Ascot was one of the main events of the year in British culture. All the men and women would dress up fancy, watch the races, bet on horses and drink Champagne. I remember seeing on social media those women wearing big hats, fancy dresses and shoes. It was so British and kitsch, I really wanted to attend one day, but this event was really expensive and selective.)

Luckily, my regular was going this year and he invited me to join him and his friends and bring a few friends of mine. I was a bit hesitant; I was 24 years old and he was probably 65 years old, how would that look? Yes, I would look like an escort. He saw that I was a bit hesitant, so he looked at me and said, "Don't worry, sweetie, I'll look after you. Are you still working at 4 p.m.? I'll be back with a little something." I wondered what he meant by a "little something". Anyway, I carried on with my day and waited to see if he would come back. He came back like he said around 4 p.m. with an envelope which he gave me very discreetly. He just explained that it was a little help for me to buy myself a dress and cover all my travel expenses to get to Ascot. We exchanged numbers so we could arrange a time and where to meet in Ascot and he then left. I couldn't wait to get home to see how much was in the envelope. I opened it and couldn't believe the wad of notes. I laid it out on the bed and counted… £3,000 right there in front of me.

Was he serious, £3k for a dress? I'd never seen so much cash in my entire life, and I have to say that it was exciting. Adrenaline shot through my body. I jumped all over my room, laughing out loud. I had to think, was I going to buy a designer dress that I would wear only once just for the occasion? It was tempting, I'd never bought anything luxurious in my life and I would have loved to see myself in a designer dress. But I had to be a bit cleverer than that. At the time I was really tight with money, as I was looking to get a flat with one of my friends; I know, I'm constantly looking for a place to live, crazy that I can't settle anywhere for more than 6 months or a year. When I came back from Australia I'd moved in with a friend of mine who'd then moved to Spain, so once again I had to look for a new place to stay. In six years in the United Kingdom I lived in twelve different houses, when I think of it, which sounds mad.

I had to use this money wisely, so I decided to put it on one side and use it for my deposit and first month's rent when we found a new place to live. Regarding the dress, I just needed to go to Topshop or any high street brand and find something decent. Anyway, people were always telling me that anything looked expensive on me, so I didn't need to go over the top. I had no choice about accepting his offer if I was taking his money. I felt a bit bad, I mean weird, to take money from a man. I'd never done that before, but what was the difference from your parents giving you money for your birthday? That's what I told myself: he was generous and only wanted to be nice. It wasn't as if he'd asked me to sleep with him, it was just money for a dress, money that he'd given me, I hadn't asked for anything. So I texted him and said that I was up for joining him and his friends at Ascot.

A few weeks later, we all headed to Ascot. I was wearing a tulipe baby pink skirt, a floral crop top, suede beige stilettos and a flowery headband. This isn't my usual style, but I loved it. I felt like a lady, a rich lady. The whole day we bet on horses, drank Champagne, ate afternoon tea, laughed, danced, I had some serious fun. Those guys were much older than us, but they knew how to have a good time, much more than guys my own age. I wanted my life to be like that all the time. I wanted to be part of this world, a world full of abundance where you don't worry about money, where everything is beautiful, fun and glamorous. None of the guys were acting inappropriately with me or my friends, everyone was very kind and respectful. I think they were just happy to be in the company of young, fun and beautiful girls. That was the only time I accepted money from a client, and I didn't regret it at all. I will never forget that day. I even saw the Queen and Prince Charles! The day could not have been more British. God, I love England!

In April 2016, after working at the bar for six months, I decided it was time for me to leave my hostess job. I was tired of hearing myself repeating the same words everyday and doing the same repeated actions. I wanted to be more productive and use my brain. I thought about what I could do, and after thinking for a while I thought that being a receptionist would lead me to the next step in my life. Even though it wasn't artistic at all, I'd kind of given up on my dreams from back then. I was twenty-four years old, I thought my dreams and goals of being someone important were over and it was time to fit into society. I had been conditioned for so long by my parents and society that I was dependent on other people's thoughts and beliefs. I'd tried to be someone, but nothing great had come out of it, so why keep pushing? Maybe stability and normality would be good for me? Maybe that is what I really needed? A stable job, Monday to Friday, 9 to 5, find a regular guy, settle and have a family, that's what people do, isn't it? By the way, I'm not shaming anyone who has a 9 to 5 job and a family. If it makes them happy, then that's amazing. But I know that a lot of people can recognise themselves in my story, and realise deep inside that it is not what they truly wanted out of life.

They only did it because they were following what they had been told.

In my case I always knew it wasn't for me and it wouldn't make me happy. But back then it sounded a little appealing, so I followed my ideas and looked for receptionist jobs across London. I thought I could start as a receptionist and climb the ladder that way. I already had a few interviews lined up, so I was halfway ready to leave my job as a hostess in Mayfair, but the universe decided otherwise.

The hotel's food and beverage director, Amani, turned up for lunch at the bar the day before I was meant to have my interview as a receptionist at another company. He sat down and asked my manager to send me over to his table to have a chat with him. I was surprised, as I'd never spoken to him before. I was petrified of this man. Every time he walked into a room, everyone stopped whatever they were doing and freaked out. I think he loved the effect he had on people. He wasn't tall at all, or impressive, but he just had an attitude and aura that said, "I am the boss, don't fuck with me." He didn't need to shout to make you understand you'd done something wrong, he just had this natural authority in him. Every time he came to the bar, I always sent someone else to look after him. I was too scared of him. But there he was, wanting to speak to me. So I went over and joined him at his table. I sat down, feeling a bit overwhelmed and shy. He asked me if I wanted anything to drink or eat. I nodded "no" and listened to what he had to say.

"So, Lola, I heard you want to leave. May I know why?"

How did he know? Jesus, nothing could be kept private in this building. What was I going to say? That I was bored of sitting people down and that this job was crap? Of course not, so I said:

"I really enjoy working for the company. I'm very grateful

for the opportunity, but I feel that it's time for me to take the next step in my career and have more responsibilities."

He looked at me, asked me what other jobs I'd done before. He listened to the impressive number and variety of jobs I'd done. He then stopped, thought and said:

"What would you think of being my Executive Assistant?"

I didn't even know what an Executive Assistant was. I think he could see the confusion on my face, so he explained the role: looking after his diary, organising the meeting room, helping out with coordinating events, sorting out his expenses etc.

"So you want me to be your personal assistant, something like that?"

Did he realise I had no experience at all in an office job, and no degrees or qualifications whatsoever? He didn't care at all, and told me I would learn. I was beyond shocked. How from being a hostess and aspiring to be a receptionist was I going to become an Executive Assistant within a day? My life was so crazy and full of surprises. I was proud of myself though. Once again, I had visualised something and it had happened like magic. I felt that finally after six years in London I was going to have some stability, a 9 to 5 job, working from Monday to Friday, and I had my own place with my friend. The thought of having a stable, normal, regular life like everyone comforted me and made me happy at the time. Many people were happy that way, so why not me?

This is how in May 2016 I became an Executive Assistant. It was the first time that I'd felt that my parents could be proud of me, and I guess I was happy to feel that I was making them proud. I had a title, a salary coming in every month, I had the possibility to grow within the company, all those elements that made my parents feel that I was getting somewhere, that finally I was done with my ideas of becoming a model or any sort of performer.

The first year was amazing: not one day was the same, everything was new, so I was excited about it. During my three years as being an assistant, I learned how to manage someone's diary, thinking of what my boss wanted before he even asked. I also learned how to coordinate events, VIP weddings, open restaurants, organise photo shoots, video shoots, create new uniforms for the staff. My role was very diverse and it kept me busy.

But after a year or so it wasn't as thrilling any more. My real personality was taking over again. Once I was settled and knew everything about the job, I got bored. We were working a lot, we were doing so many extra hours that were not paid, we would work at weekends sometimes. During the opening of a restaurant, we would live at the hotel so we were available at all times. It was getting way too much for me mentally, especially for the salary I was getting. My colleagues loved calling me "lazy" and a "part timer", just because I would go home on time and I didn't want to spend my life working. It was weird experiencing this unhealthy competition on who was going to work the most hours? They were so proud of putting up with this job that was so demanding but not giving you any financial bonus to reward you. Did they not have a life to enjoy, instead of being miserable at work? I personally did, and I was tired of not having any time for myself. If I compared the hours and the salary from when I was a hostess to being an EA, my salary was much more interesting as a hostess and with much less responsibility. When I realised that I'd started to become really frustrated with work, my boss and my colleagues, I could not stand to work like a bitch for peanuts. It didn't make sense to me any more. I had no time to enjoy my life any more, all the dreams I'd had once were over. I didn't even have time to see my friends, so forget about going to a dance or singing class. All I was doing was work. Was that how life was meant to be? People selling you the dream of being a puppet for someone else? And I was meant to feel good about it because it wasn't a hard physical job?

I thought deeply about what would really make me happy. I'd had a physically hard shitty job, and I was miserable. I'd had the nightlife job, hosting people, but also got bored. And now I was finally one of a normal crowd with a comfortable life, but still I felt unfulfilled. On top of that, I never felt that I was growing as a person. I was still feeling very insecure, scared and anxious about the future. This normal life never helped me with my confidence. I'd had good times, for sure. It wasn't a nightmare, either. My job was never the same any day, and my team was simply unique. I was surrounded by guys, ten to be precise, and we were only two girls. We were like a little fucked up family. I liked my colleagues, but I never felt completely understood by them.

Every day they would have something to say about what I was wearing, or the way I did my make-up or what I was up to during the weekend, as they could see what I was doing on social media. They were always making fun of me as I was out clubbing. I am not sure what was funny in that. I could sense some jealousy, as they were stuck at home with their wife and kids; the fun, the free days were over for them, so they simply made me feel bad about it. They thought that I was just a pretty girl partying, not very clever, with no hope of having a husband and a family one day. I always felt that I was judged. I know they didn't mean any harm, but hearing all those comments every single day was very annoying, and I felt a lot of social pressure.

Sometimes I would go to my office and cry, as I was fed

up with always feeling misunderstood and judged. I really felt that because I was a woman past 25 years old, I was a failure for not being able to keep a man and still being out having fun. My team wasn't the worst at making me feel bad about myself though; they were just silly guys who were not releasing the power of their words. Women, however, we know when we hurt someone and it is always intentional. The other departments at work were much more women-led and they hated me. If you could see them, they were real hyenas. They were always looking up and down me, talking behind my back, not making me feel welcome, sending nasty emails complaining about me to my manager, in the hope that I would get into trouble. It was probably only because I always made sure that I looked fashionable and sexy. I wore make-up every single day, I had trendy clothes, which I have to admit did not match with the rest of the company. My director was against uniforms and corporate suits, thank God for that, so our department would dress up "smart casual", unlike the others who had to wear the company uniforms. So I presume a lot of people didn't like us, and especially me as a woman.

You know how women can act competitive between them, which I find ridiculous. Instead of embracing and helping each other, we would take each other down. I am not saying we should all be friends and have the same way of thinking, but if you simply don't like someone, why don't you just ignore it instead of making that person life's hell? I always felt that I had to apologise to be who I am and not wanting to be like the rest. Some of my work colleagues would used to say that I was over the top. What does that even mean? That maybe I should wear less make-up, be more conservative, less sexy, so I would fit in more and probably attract a good man? As if being sexy, I would only attract bad guys. I was so angry at them for trying to change me, and saying that because my appearance was glamorous and sexy I was only attracting the wrong kind of men. So it was my fault once again. We all know that quote, "You shouldn't judge a book by its cover." And that's exactly what my life had become, always being judged on my appearance instead of trying to get to know what was inside me. I know that I'm not perfect, of course no one is, but I know how much of a good person I am and I wish more people could see how much I have to offer. If I was with the right person, they'd see how serious, faithful and dedicated I was to them, as much any other girl who looked more ordinary. I felt like a caterpillar with no confidence or self-esteem who couldn't wait to turn into a beautiful butterfly.

With time I realised and understood that being surrounded by people who are mediocre, hate their jobs, dislike their partners or are unhappy with their life in general can really affect your overall energy and self-development. How can you improve as a person and become the better version of yourself, if you are surrounded by negative energies or people who don't follow the same principles of life as you? Believe it or not, your environment is key to your success and happiness. Understanding this principle changed my life. When I realised it, it felt that something was shaking inside me that I couldn't contain, a change was happening, I was growing and I felt that I was unchaining myself.

I knew deep inside that I was meant to live a different life, where people would understand my creativity, my weirdness, my sex appeal and not judge me for it. All I wanted was a glamorous life, full of excitement and adventures, without people stopping me with their negativity. Even though I started slowly understanding that I had to do something about my life to be happier, I was still stuck with all the beliefs that my parents had taught me and my fear of failing. All those negative emotions and thoughts were controlling me. I could still hear them: "You should be worrying about having a stable job that pays the bills." Those thoughts in my head were stopping me moving forward. I was the only person able to stop myself. I was the only person responsible for my choices and actions, but an unfortunate event changed my life forever…

SEVEN

You Must Die a Little in Order to Be Reborn

> *Often it's the deepest pain which empowers you to grow into your highest self.*
>
> Karen Salmansohn

February 2018: I was now twenty-seven years old, and I'd been in my position as Executive Assistant for about a year and a half. Life was still the same, boring and tiring, until one day I woke up feeling extremely tired, unusually tired. I was hit by an intense fatigue. Maybe because I'd slept on Inaya's sofas the night before, when I'd visited her? I also had weird dreams that night: I kept seeing myself touching my stomach and feeling that it was alive, as if something was growing inside. Like every other day, I took the Underground to head to work. But even though I'd had a coffee, I was still feeling exhausted and a bit sick. I hoped it was not a cold or the flu. I couldn't afford to be sick, as I had so much work to do, I needed to feel 100%. I really needed to sit down, but every time a seat became available, a pregnant lady would jump into the carriage. I'd never seen so many pregnant women in such a short amount of time: how weird, did they all decide to get pregnant at the same time?

I arrived at work and headed straight to the canteen to grab another coffee. I felt a bit better, still very tired, but I had no choice but to stick it out. We had an important day and I didn't think I'd be able to get a break, so I put up with it and got through the day. We finished work late, and I could no longer move. I felt so drained that I was just dragging my body, no chance I could manage public transport, I just wanted to go to bed, so I ordered a taxi. On my way home I kept wondering what was wrong with me? Was I being sick? Should I go to the doctor? Was it something bad? But I could hear a voice inside my head telling me that I knew exactly what it was. I kept thinking about my weird dream, of me touching my stomach, all those pregnant women in the tube this morning, and worse, I was late for my period by a day. Could I be?

At the time, I was single and not really having sex. I'd literally just started to see this guy, Arber. He was a London club promoter. We knew each other via social media: he was always messaging me to join his guest list, but I never went for it, I'm not sure why. Then one day I went out and bumped into him. We recognised each other straight away and started flirting. One day we eventually slept together. I slept with him only once: it couldn't be possible, could it? He didn't even finish inside, so no chance. How naive and immature I was.

Once I reached my estate, I went to the corner shop and checked if they had any pregnancy tests. Lucky me they had two left, so I bought them just in case. As soon as I opened the door, I went to the toilet, sat down and peed on the stick.

For fuck's sake, what if I was? What the hell was I going to do? In a way, I wouldn't mind seeing if I was, just to reassure myself I was able to have kids. All those years having sex and I wasn't being very careful. When I was taking the pill, nothing ever happened. Having a baby and a family was never at the top of my dream list. I never felt that maternal gene inside me, and if I didn't manage to have a family one day, I was fine with that, but surprisingly that also changed.

Three minutes passed. My heart was pounding, I was really anxious about the result. I looked at the test and there it was. Nothing! The test wasn't positive or negative, no cross or one straight line. I could see a half bar, which didn't make sense at all, for fuck's sake! Why wasn't the result straightforward and simple? Anyway, let's see the positive side. If it was positive, the results would have shown up straight away. I was only late by one day so it wasn't that worrying, and I was obviously exhausted because of all the stress at work. I was a bit paranoid and dramatic sometimes, I just needed an early night, relax and everything would be fine tomorrow.

Two days passed and still no sign of my period. I was having a really hard time getting up in the morning. I was lying in my bed wondering how I could get to work. I was too tired, I just wanted to sleep the whole day. I snoozed my alarm for ten more minutes, and as I was turning my duvet to wrap myself inside, I saw the other pregnancy test on my bedside table. I looked at it for two good minutes and then got out of bed, ready to do the test again. I sat on the toilet, put my panties down and peed on that stick for the second time. Within a minute the test started showing. A clear blue cross appeared on the results screen indicating that yes, I was pregnant. I checked the box probably ten times to make sure that it meant the test was positive. Then when I realised that I was pregnant, I burst into tears.

I was devastated. Why did I get pregnant now? With a man that I don't even love, with a man who was not even my boyfriend? I could only blame myself though, I should have been more careful. How stupid could I be? Acting like a grown-up in all the areas in my life but fucking up my own health, as if I was an unconscious teenager. I think what got me really sad was that I knew I wasn't going to keep it, I just couldn't at that time, I didn't have anything to offer to a child, and it broke my heart to know that I had to go through an abortion. I'd never expected to get attached so quickly to something that barely existed, but I guess human nature makes us that way. The feeling of knowing something that I'd created was growing inside me, and eventually knowing that I could be a mum, made me feel completed in a sense. I felt a lot of love, a love that I'd never experienced before, but even though I was already loving this baby, I had to make a smart choice for its sake and also for mine. I was living in a council flat, still sharing, the genitor wasn't my boyfriend, I didn't have any family members in the UK with me. If I was going to bring a new human being onto this planet, I would want a better situation for it.

I called my boss and told him the truth and that I needed a day to rest and organise whatever was necessary for the abortion. Even though my workplace was tough and very demanding, my director was always listening and very understanding. He told me to take as much time off as I needed, and to not worry about a thing. I also called Arber to inform him about the situation, and he obviously wasn't happy, but he promised me to be by my side. I thought it was actually really nice and mature of him.

Planning an abortion is never a quick process, especially in London. Waiting lists are long, but I managed to book mine two weeks after I found out I was pregnant. Until then I carried on working, feeling exhausted and getting more and more attached to this human being growing inside me. I would catch myself talking to it sometimes, rubbing my belly, I was full of love for it even if I didn't like the constant tiredness and the acne appearing on my face just as when I was fifteen. I was still seeing Arber: he always came to see me each time I had to sleep at the hotel due to a work commitment. How good it was for him: free food, free hotel room, nice bath. I mean, I didn't care about taking advantage as long as he was with me until everything was over. That's what mattered to me; but once again I would be disappointed in a man.

The day before the abortion, I received a text from Arber telling me he couldn't come with me to the appointment as he had to help his brother to move out. What the actual fuck?! Was he being serious?! I was fuming. I called him and we got into a massive row. I was so upset that he'd kept seeing me, having a good time, but when it was time to be a man and take responsibility, he'd let me down. Another disappointment, again! The only thing he had to say was that we were not an item, so he didn't have to come with me. I wasn't his girlfriend, so he didn't owe me anything. That felt like a knife in the heart. What a fucking dick! I was so angry at him, but especially more at myself for giving my body to someone I knew wasn't worth it from the start. How could I be so mature and independent most of the time, and sometimes so naive and unwise? I could blame him all I wanted for being a coward and heartless for not supporting me, but if I'd been more careful when he and I were having sex, this would have never happened. This was down to myself, no one else.

Even though I wasn't lucky with men, I was blessed with my friends. When Julien found out that I was all by myself for my appointment, he offered to be there and come with me. I was so lucky and grateful to have this angel by my side once again. Julien was always there during good times and bad. I wish I could marry him sometimes, my life would be much easier. So Julien and I again, the two of us were together during a difficult time. As usual he managed to make me laugh, even though I was crying loudly inside. I was smiling and laughing, but my heart was bleeding. One more time, I really wondered when disappointment would stop and when men would stop letting me down.

During my recovery I started thinking, thinking a lot. I was tired of always being treated like shit by men. I was tired of all this negativity around me, either at work or from people you think are your friends. My environment wasn't bad, don't get me wrong, but it didn't feel great either and I wanted greatness. I didn't feel that I was improving or moving forward as a person. I wanted to feel truly happy, confident and stop worrying about what others were thinking and finally have my dream life, be married to a kind, educated, funny man, live somewhere beautiful, have money and finally become someone: either a model, singer, performer, whatever!

After a little research on the Internet and asking around for recommendations on how to be more confident, someone suggested that I simply read *The Secret* to start with. I am sure many of you have heard of this book. If not, I truly suggest you have a look at it. Basically it is based on the law of attraction: "You attract what you are," and that simple idea changed my life and the way I live. Reading this book made me understand that everything that had happened in my life was the result of my actions and thoughts. At first I was a bit sceptical, but the more I kept reading *The Secret* and thought about it, the more it all made sense. Everything was linked and everything happened for a reason, it was no coincidence. Everything that I truly wanted at some point, I got because I visualised it and felt that it would be right for me. I really wanted to work at the rooftop bar, so the universe put multiple signs in my way to help me to work there. Once I was really happy there, I attracted something that I never truly experienced: true love with Filip. I wanted to work in a luxurious part of London, to meet important people, and what happened? One of my regulars introduced me to the perfect place and people. I was in need of money badly to pay my deposit and rent, and there I was with one client giving me £3,000 out of nowhere. Or every time I wanted to find a new place to live, a good opportunity came my way.

But it was also the same for the bad things that happened to me. Yes, I was attracting a lot of good things, but back then for many years I wasn't a very positive person. I didn't even know what being positive meant. I was constantly moaning about something, complaining about whatever. I swear I would spend 60% of my time having bad thoughts. If only I'd known then that those bad thoughts could lead me to negative outcomes. For example, I was always worrying about being cheated on and lied to, and that was always happening. I would get scared of doing something bad at work, and as a result I wasn't performing. I was worried that I couldn't get pregnant, and would think deep inside myself that I would love to get pregnant just to see if I could. And what happened? I got pregnant. Until now my mind was all over the place and I never really had a positive vibe about me. Everything was always confused in my head, so this is why my life was the way it was. Not bad, but not great either. It was just a big rough draft, and now it was time to create the masterpiece. This book brought so much sense into my life. I could now see that everything that had happened, everyone

I'd met during my journey, was one element of the lesson and a key to my success.

I started to follow the process of *The Secret*. I would turn anything negative into a positive, even my abortion. I was treating this mistake, this hard time, as a blessing, as a life lesson. I felt that I was living my own birth for the second time and growing up. I was practising the secret exercises, such as writing down my dreams and goals. I would create a vision board. I would try to stay positive, even in a difficult situation, and try to change my mindset. It was hard at first to change a mind that has been set for so long, but once I understood the principles, I could see a change and it felt amazing. I wasn't so fearful, negative and anxious any more. I became much more positive, which helped me heal mentally from all my past relationships with friends, lovers, work and of course to be at peace with my abortion. I could see such an improvement in every aspect of my life. Nothing changed drastically, but life was more pleasant now that I was positive and feeling grateful. Please don't believe that my life or yours will change overnight, but slowly I felt that the energy around me was changing and opportunities were coming my way.

Another thing you need to know about the law of attraction: you obviously have to be positive, feeling good, have a good vibe and energy about you, but without actions it doesn't work. You cannot think yes, I want to be a performer, dance and sing on stage, but stay in your room and hope that a genie will appear magically out of nowhere and make you a star, no. You need to work for it, and that was what I was doing. I was more determined than ever to be finally out there and let the world know who I am.

EIGHT

Reality TV

Sometimes life doesn't give you something you want, not because you don't deserve it, but because you deserve more.

After reading *The Secret*, I decided that it was time for me to stop pretending that I would be fine having a regular job and life until I die. I knew that it would never fulfil me, that no matter how hard I tried to fit in, it would never make me happy and I would always go back to the same cycle of being satisfied for a little while and then getting bored again. It was time to take my life in my hands and do what I always wanted to do: be a performer, be on television, be someone important and earn a lot of money. Back then I thought the only way to reach my goal was to be part of a reality TV programme. I was called two years in a row for *Love Island*, but nothing more, and I always thought that being French might be the issue. Maybe if I tried to join a French programme, that would probably work for me and lead to a lot of opportunities.

For the new generation, the reality TV stars are the new versions of Michael Jackson or Britney Spears. These characters are inspiring and influencing millions of people worldwide; social media founders and brands understood the potential and lucrative businesses that could be made around it. They managed to use reality TV fame to create businesses and sell products to the public through the influence of those TV characters, and hence a new category of job has been created that didn't exist a few years ago: the influencers. The biggest ones are usually from reality TV, especially in France. I thought that if I played my cards properly, I could become famous, become an influencer and once I was taken seriously by the showbusiness world, some big music producer or agent would reach out and see how talented I was and then I could finally become a performer, have my own business and finally live my dream life.

Once I had this goal, this vision in my head, I did everything in my power to succeed. I applied for every show possible and contacted all the TV producers in France. After a few days, the best producer at the time, the one that was producing the most lucrative show, responded to me and put me in contact with his casting director. I contacted her straight away, we exchanged a few messages, talked about when the next casting would be open, about the process, where I was from etc. She then said she would keep my number and contact me when the next casting was officially open. I was really proud of myself, at least it was something, all I had to do was wait and keep working on myself in the meantime.

I was still being much more positive, visualising my goals, but I could feel that I wasn't quite there yet. I was still working more and more hours, the girls that I was hanging out with, who I thought were my friends, didn't bring any positivity into my life. I could feel pressure and jealousy from them. They were always judging me, what I was doing, who I was seeing, what I was wearing. Those friendships didn't feel genuine and didn't seem to bring more positivity into my life. Once you choose to be positive and experience a spiritual growth, you realise that most of the people you are "friends" with don't have anything in common with you and don't share the same view on life. Everything still felt very cloudy at the time. I could see the beginning of the light at the end of the tunnel, but I knew it was a long work in process. My life couldn't change drastically from one day to another anyway. I had to learn to be patient and take things slowly. I knew deep inside that I was on my way to something great, so it helped me to stay positive and I felt much happier than a few months ago.

Around June 2018, the French casting director finally contacted me and put me through the official casting process for a famous show. The concept of this show is the same as "Geordie Shore": a group of friends go abroad with the possibility to party and have fun, but in return they must work in different types of jobs if they want to stay and live in an amazing villa. The public love it: parties, summer, dramas, love stories, everything to make the public watch this show for a decade. I always wanted to participate in this show; it seemed such fun and the people who participated usually got a good outcome. The casting director sent me all the different forms to fill out, with every personal detail, such as name, surname, date of birth, where I was born, dress size, what would I bring to the programme, how far would I be ready to go to be part of the show, what was the most embarrassing things I'd done, the sexiest thing, I mean many quirky and unusual questions. I was also asked to send alongside the documents some photographs of me, including in a bikini. Once I'd sent all the required information, she told me that if I was successful, a Skype call would be arranged.

A few days later, she messaged me again to arrange the interview. Great, at least I'd made it to the next stage of the casting. We arranged a date and time for us to call each other, even though it was so hard for me to schedule anything as I was living between London and Manchester back then, due to work commitments. We were working on our biggest project so far, the opening of a new restaurant. I was so tired of travelling every week between the two cities and always sleeping in hotels. I know it sounds ridiculous to complain about sleeping in hotels, I loved it, but sometimes I just needed the comfort of my own place and space. I was constantly with my colleagues and I needed a break sometimes, but knowing at the back of my mind that I was in the process of changing my life kept me going.

The day of the Skype call finally arrived. I was so stressed, because I'd never done that before, but once again I would make sure to give my best. She called me, I picked up the video call but her screen was black; I couldn't see her but my camera was on so she could see me. It was really weird talking to someone I couldn't see but knowing they could see me. She started to ask me to introduce myself, and then she asked me the same questions that I'd already answered via email. At the end of casting, she asked me to wear a bikini so I could dance in front of the camera. What the fuck! Really? I didn't expect that. I know how to dance, I have no issues with that, but in front of a stranger via Skype, that was a bit weird and intimidating! But I had no choice, so I executed it somehow. Lord, did I look ridiculous! I felt like a right idiot. I couldn't move, I was paralyzed by my emotions. After three long minutes she asked me to stop, thanked me for my time and informed me that we would be in contact soon. At the end of the call I was literally covered in sweat, due to the level of stress and anxiety of this casting process.

Months passed, June, July, August, September, still nothing. I didn't think at this point I would hear anything more. I knew that the filming crew was about to leave France to start filming the show. For the third time, I had not succeeded through the casting.

Then out of nowhere, in October, the casting director called me and asked if I was still willing to join the show. Could I be ready to leave the United Kingdom to travel to Asia? Was she serious? I mean I had a job, I couldn't just leave like that, I had to organise myself with my director, he would probably hate me for the rest of his life for leaving so suddenly without warning during an opening. Also, I didn't feel ready physically, mentally or materially. I had no summer clothes, my pedicure wasn't done, I hadn't been to the hairdresser in a long time, I was really pale, so many questions went through my head. What was I meant to do? She then said that I still had to redo my Skype interview so she could pass it on to the channel director before any decision was taken. Another casting? Again? I was fed up with doing the same performance, answering the same questions, doing the same act but it was maybe my last chance, so I did it all over again, including dancing like a weirdo in front of my camera.

Weeks passed and still nothing. I found it really rude that they could call me out of nowhere, ask me to pack my bags, give me hopes that I was maybe leaving for Asia, stress me out and then not even take two minutes to inform me if I was successful or not. Never mind, I guess it wasn't meant to be. Once again, I was doubting myself and thought that maybe I was meant to have a normal life. If I was failing, I could always tell myself that maybe it wasn't worth it, I hadn't fought for it the way I was meant to. Maybe I didn't really believe in being a reality TV star, so that was why it wasn't working out for me the way I'd hoped. I'd thought that I wanted to be a reality star, but deep inside, was it really what my heart and soul aspired to? Was it my life's purpose?

In the meantime, around mid-October 2018, I started to date the hottest guy at work, so my mind was a bit off career and more relationship-focused. His name was Lukas. I don't think I'd seen someone so beautiful in my life. Lukas was from Latvia, extremely tall, blue almond-shaped eyes, full big lips, blond hair. We started to get close during the staff training, before the opening of the restaurant. He was the head waiter, so technically I was his boss. I felt really lonely back then, so it felt good to have some male's attention. We started texting, mainly because of work, and then I found out that he had a crush on me. I got close with the head waitress, and she told me how Lukas was jealous every time a guy tried to flirt with me. I found it really cute and flattering. I was craving for attention, and that sort of news flattered my ego; so once I knew that he liked me, I started to flirt with him.

Our texts had nothing to do with work any more. We would talk until 4 a.m. about anything and everything. I was so happy to have someone to talk to. One night after work we decided to actually talk face to face. As we didn't have the same shift, and he was finishing much later than me, I invited him to come to my room once he was done with work. It was very practical living in the hotel where we both worked. I was so scared while I was waiting for him. I hadn't had a sort of boyfriend experience for a very long time. I knew he wasn't the type to have fun or a one-night stand, he was a relationship sort of guy. For the past three years, since my break-up with Filip, I'd probably gone on two dates, three maximum. I obviously slept around and flirted, but nothing serious, so I was really nervous to be all alone with a guy who could potentially become my boyfriend. I also had the usual thousand questions going through my mind: "What if he also breaks my heart?" "Will I give my trust again?" "What if he doesn't treat me like a princess?" "Will he cheat?" "Is he talking to other girls?" "He seems too nice to be true."

Every time I started something new with a guy, I had those questions running through my head, which always made me ruin everything. I would talk to myself on loop, creating fake scenarios in my head, telling myself that it was too good to be true, and whoever I was with was automatically lying and hiding something. Even though I was much more positive now, I was still having a hard time with my relationships with men. I was still extremely jealous, possessive and wary of being abandoned, which is why I always came across as extremely guarded and distant when I started a new relationship, because I always felt that once I showed my true self, my soft side, opened myself and gave my all, men would start to run away.

But it felt it could be different this time with Lukas. He seemed really sweet and kind. He came up to my room around 11 p.m. It was the first time we'd been alone, face to face, talking. It felt really awkward at first. I was on the bed, he was sitting on a chair, really far away from me. We started talking and we didn't stop until 2 a.m. I started to get really tired, so I lay down on the bed. I clearly wanted him to cuddle me, I needed affection so badly, but he wasn't making a single move. I guess he was trying to act like a gentleman, something I'd never really experienced before. Whenever I'd been alone with a man, usually something would always happen.

As he was still not making a move, I ended up asking him

to join me and give me a cuddle. He obviously didn't refuse. He finally stood up, switched off the light, came over, lay in the bed next to me, pulled me close to his chest and cuddled me. That felt amazing, being in a man's arms, feeling protected, exactly what I needed, a bit of warmth and comfort. Believe it or not, we didn't sleep together. He didn't even try to touch me. I actually doubted his attraction for me, but I was enjoying it for now, to not be seen as just a sexual object. I loved feeling desired and sexy, but I wished men could see more in me and see past the sexual body and discover a genuine girl who needed love, but most of them didn't want to, so it was good to feel respected. We carried on talking until 4 a.m. and then I asked him to leave. I was exhausted and I had to wake up in a few hours. I don't even think we kissed that night. I was so happy to start something so special with someone so sweet, I mean this is what I thought.

Only one day after that night, I had to come back to London and Lukas was going to Singapore for work. On top of working within our company, he was part of a catering agency that needed staff worldwide. While he was away, I already felt the anxiety of him being far off and probably surrounded by girls, so I did what I do best, I harassed him every time he didn't answer my texts. All I could think of was him surrounded by girls and playing me around. Lukas wasn't making things easier. I was really paranoid, but he would turn his phone off every time he was out or hang up when I was calling. That clearly wasn't a good start for our relationship.

While Lukas was away for work, the casting director called me once again out of the blue. What did she want this time? I picked up the call. She talked to me as if we'd been friends for years. They're very good at that in this industry, making you feel like you're really important and probably the next big star. She explained that the production was working on a new show and needed single girls looking for love. Well, technically I'd started a relationship, so I wasn't looking for love; but I was definitely looking for fame, so I didn't mention that part and asked her to tell me more about the show. She didn't want to give too much information away, but simply said we were here to seduce men, go on dates, play sexy games but also have the opportunity to attend professional casting for modelling or somesuch. I wanted to be famous and be on television, but I wasn't sure I was ready to have the role of seducing guys just to be on TV. I wanted to stay true to myself, and I didn't want to "give" myself just to have two minutes of fame.

She could hear that I was hesitant. She reassured me straight away and explained that the programme would be family-friendly and nothing sexual would be shown on television. Also we were in 2018, and the image of women has changed a lot. TV programmes had to be really careful about how they portrayed women. She explained that it was more about love, that we would be there just to just be friendly with the boys and see if a real connection developed. I have to say that reassured me a bit, but still I was at the beginning of a new relationship, so what was I meant to do? Then I thought that Lukas and I had just met, it wasn't as if we'd been together for two years, nothing was serious, and I might not be successful, so why not try one more time and see where it would lead me? So I accepted, and for the second time I went through the entire casting process and had a Skype interview for the third time, but I made sure that I was looking and feeling my best this time. I knew the whole process now, so I was more than ready. After my Skype interview, the casting director thanked me and told me she would get in touch.

Once again I had to wait for a response that might never come.

I decided to not tell anyone about this casting, not Lukas, not Julien, no one. I didn't want any energies, good or bad, to influence the casting process. I am a big believer in karma and the energies that surround us, which is how we attract certain things. I wanted everything to be neutral so I stayed quiet.

Weeks passed and I was still with Lukas. Our relationship was good overall, I felt calm when I was with him, a bit too calm I must say. At first it felt amazing to feel secure and have someone different from myself. I am very loud, always on the go, constantly talking, laughing, my mouth open, making stupid jokes. So it was good to have someone opposite to balance everything out. But after a few weeks and then months, I could feel that I was getting bored, really bored. Being different is great, but I realised that being completely the opposite in everything wasn't a good match either. We were different in our attitudes, but also we had different views on life. I am a go-getter, always on the next move, ready for the next adventure to improve myself, dreaming of living a life full of abundance and luxury. Lukas on the other hand was content having his job, doing his hours, coming back home, watching television, eating and sleeping. I obviously knew that he wasn't rich when we got together. I knew that he would probably never be able to offer me my dream life and gifts. Which is why I wanted to make sure that I would be able to provide for my expensive needs. But still, not being filthy rich is no excuse to my mind for not surprising or spoiling your girlfriend. There are always ways to make a girl happy, even with a regular salary. He could have made a small effort to surprise me, or make me feel special. But no, I never got flowers, a bubble bath ready with candles (I don't think that cost much), or simply getting my favourite food when I was coming to his, things that I would do, for example. The main thing we did was watch Netflix in bed and get a take-away. We would only go out if I suggested it, or moaned about it. If I was swearing or speaking loudly, Lukas would feel embarrassed.

The worst thing was needing to ask for sex; Lukas didn't have a very high sex drive, whereas for me it was a big issue. I'd always had partners who loved sex, and so do I. At first it was kind of refreshing to be with a guy not constantly wanting to grind on me, but after a while I started to doubt his sexuality, and even my own sex appeal. Was I not attractive? Was he gay? Was he seeing another girl? Why did we have so little sex? Bear in mind we were seeing each other only once a week, or sometimes once every two weeks. We had a long-distance relationship, so it was even weirder to me that he didn't want sex. I was feeling so frustrated not getting the amount I needed. I liked Lukas a lot, and to me sex has always been a way of showing my affection and appreciation to my partner. Then when we were having sex, it lasted, I'm not lying, probably about five minutes all included. I was so frustrated that I started my bad girl attitude again. I would flirt with my colleagues, text some exes and I was watching porn constantly, something that I never usually do! I love masturbating, I have always done it, it is the best way for me to fall asleep, but I have always used my imagination, I don't need porn.

But in this case of extreme frustration, I felt I had to go beyond my imagination. It felt that because I was deprived of something that I loved, my needs got to a level I'd never experienced before. I would watch S&M porn, although I wasn't usually into this sort of sexual act, but the fact that I couldn't have my regular dose of sex pushed my desires up to a new dimension. Maybe that's why married men have to use escorts after all? Because they have needs that their partner can't fill? I was so tempted to cheat on him, but at the end of the day, even though we were very different, it didn't mean he wasn't a good person, and he didn't deserve to be cheated on. But I really didn't like that feeling of being in a ten-year-old relationship when we'd only been dating for a few months. I knew it could not always be romantic and exciting, life was life at the end of the day, I wasn't living in a Disney movie, but still some efforts should be made on both sides to keep things exciting. I think I had butterflies probably for just a week or two, and after that it was all gone.

I knew from the start that we were very different, but I thought it would be good to be with someone much calmer than me who could bring stability. But Lukas's lack of drive for life, work, sex, surprises and life in general put me off him. He was so handsome, like a Greek god, but I couldn't feel any sparks, vibe, excitement towards him. After a while I wasn't finding him attractive any more. Every time he picked me up from Manchester's train station to take me back to his, he would open the door, put on his slippers, switch on the television and put the news on. He never surprised me with unexpected romantic dinner, flowers or simply just throwing me on the bed to have sex. He would sit there on the sofa, very content with his simple life, happy that I was there and that was it. I know it sounds wrong: I had a guy who adored me and was happy just to be in my company, but I was twenty-seven not seventy years old and looking for companionship. Even my grandmother had a better dating life than mine at the time.

When I got really frustrated with him, I would moan and tell him I was fed up with him taking me for granted and never making an effort. But it didn't seem to bother him. He would say he was trying his best but it wasn't in his DNA to be full of life. So everything remained the same. Our conversations were also so plain and boring. Lukas never experienced anything in particular really. His life was always very stable and steady, so he couldn't relate to a lot of things that happened in my life, or debate about any sort of subject. He wasn't curious at all. Of course I hadn't experienced everything in life, and I certainly have a lack of book knowledge, but I am curious and I always ask the person I am talking with: How? Why? When? And made sure I got an explanation. I remember bringing the subject of my abortion, and he had nothing to say about it. Lukas didn't have any depth, that was also a turn-off for me. Nothing about him was intriguing, exciting, appealing.

I think I was looking for a similar relationship to what I'd had with Filip, which was my mistake. I would always compare the two of them and get angry for not feeling the same. But how could it be when those two men were completely different? I was probably annoyed at myself for being in a relationship that didn't fit me at all. But I stayed because I thought that he was nice, and maybe things would get better with time. Filip and I had too much passion for each other, and we crashed pretty quickly, so maybe going a bit slower and letting my feelings grow would work. My grandmother always told me that passion didn't last, so maybe I had to learn to wait and develop my feelings for Lukas in a more stable way. Which I did. I took my time, I learned to get to know him, to be patient, and I started to feel comfortable around him. Could I accept just being comfortable, forgetting my dreams of living an exciting life and being treated like a princess?

End of December 2018: I was spending the holidays with my mum this year. For once I was glad to spend Christmas with her. I was calm and content with my life, so it felt good mentally to spend time with my mum. My grandmother from my dad's side also joined us; she didn't want to stay alone and didn't have the energy to visit my dad in Corsica, where he lives. My mum and my nan haven't seen each other since my parents split. I was a bit scared and sceptical about the two of them spending a few days together in the same house. I remember the two of them arguing when I was a kid, over the family gathering and holidays; they couldn't agree on anything. They didn't get along back then, but surprisingly, more than a decade later and with my dad out of the picture, everything went well. We all had a good time together, we chilled, spent the days watching Christmas movies on television in front of the fireplace and eating chocolate. It felt good just to relax and not do too much for once. The past months at work had been so hectic that I was happy to do nothing. I remember crying from exhaustion at work on the opening day of the new restaurant, as we'd been working non-stop. I was so tired that my brain couldn't function properly any more. I really needed to find a way to get out of that place; it wasn't human to work like that, and I knew I deserved better, even though I'd grown closer to my colleagues and boss.

Luckily the universe heard me, and while I was chilling during my well-deserved holidays, I received the call I had been desperately waiting for. One day after Christmas, the casting director called me and asked me to come to Paris to do the final interview face to face, recorded on camera. Finally, after months of casting, I was getting closer to reaching my goal. She and I arranged a date and time, she bought my tickets to Paris and a taxi to drive me to the production offices. Now I had two things to do: tell my mum that I was being cast for reality TV, and tell Lukas that I was being cast for a show where I was meant to be single. We'd been together for three months now, so I had to tell him what was going on, I couldn't hide it from him any more, it wasn't fair. So I called him on video call and explained everything: how it had started, the show, the concept, what I would be doing and when it would be. He listened, he laughed at times, I think he was nervous, but surprisingly he was fine; he understood it could be an opportunity, but at the same time he didn't want us to talk too much about it in depth, as we didn't even know if I was going to be taken on. We agreed that once we did know the final answer, if I was successful, we would have a proper conversation about all the rules of what I could and couldn't do on the show.

I was so happy about his reaction, because I didn't want to have to lie to him and do something sneaky behind his back. I always thought that honesty was the key to a healthy, successful life, even if sometimes it hurt, and that's how I was trying to live my life from now on: being honest with others, but also with myself. On the other hand, I don't think any of my exes would have accepted it, not even Filip, who was very open-minded. I think he'd loved me too much to be able to let me go on a show to"pretend" to be single. That was the sort of love that I was craving, feeling like I belonged to someone. Things were definitely not like that with Lukas, I never felt that we were a team, like Bonnie and Clyde, my ride or die. But never mind, it was actually perfect for me at the time, I could pursue whatever I wanted to do without a guy breaking my balls about it and trying to stop me.

Now I had to tell my mum and also my grandmother. I knew they weren't going to stop me, but I knew that I'd have to face all the questions about why I wanted to participate in such a show. For them, reality TV was the worst thing that the human race had created. They thought everyone participating in it was stupid, fake, uninteresting, and had a really bad influence on the younger generation. Even knowing what they were thinking, I took my courage, explained everything about the show, how it was going to be, what my goals were, the outcome I was hoping for. Last off, I asked my mum if she would drive me to the train station in two days so I could head up to Paris. As expected, they didn't really understand why I wanted to break off my stable "career" in hospitality to start doing TV. But they said that I was young and if I wanted to try something like that it was the right time to do so. Amazing, I had no bad or negative energies trying to stop me in this process. I could peacefully head off to Paris and give my best. I knew that this time I would make it…

27 December 2019, 10 a.m., I was on the TGV from Avignon to Paris, my face immaculately made up, my hair done to perfection. I had brand new clothes for the occasion, so all I had to do was change my trainers for high heels in the taxi. I could not believe I was on my way to an official casting for one of the biggest channels in France. I was so nervous that I felt sick at times. The journey was just over three hours, so I decided to sleep and rest as much as possible to feel and look my best.

At around 1 p.m., I arrived in Paris, Gare de Lyon. My taxi driver was waiting for me with my name on a board. I approached him to let him know who I was, and we then headed to the car. The car was so luxurious, leather seats, smelling good, sweets and bottled water on offer, it was very different from my usual Uber driving experience. I was already liking this sort of exclusive treatment. During the car journey, I probably checked my hair and make-up a hundred times. I wanted to make sure I was looking my best. I checked my teeth, my nose, my skin, my breath. This was my last chance, and I had to make sure that everything was impeccable. I also changed out of my trainers and put on my high-heeled boots. They went perfectly with my skin-tight checked leggings and red cropped jumper. I deliberately chose to not wear a dress; I wanted to be different from all the other girls. I wanted to show my London style. My leggings were tight enough to show all my curves, my boots complimented my long legs, and my crop top was showing my tiny waist.

Twenty minutes later, we finally arrived at our destination. The building was all glass windows and very tall, it was really impressive. I entered through a curved sliding door and followed the instructions that the casting director had messaged me earlier on. I found the lift and pressed the button for the third floor. Once I was on the right floor, I looked for the door bearing the production company's name. There I was in front of that door. I didn't know what to expect on the other side. I took a deep breath in, closed my eyes for a second, reopened them and buzzed the doorbell. This is it, I can't go back… show time.

A young woman opened the door. I put on my biggest smile, introduced myself and explained that I was here for the casting. She welcomed me in, asked me to take a seat and wait. The offices were much smaller than the ITV ones where I'd been for the casting of *Love Island.* Also, I couldn't see anyone else waiting. Was I the only single girl attending? After two minutes, the casting director finally came out of her office and walked towards me. I stood up and we both smiled at each other:

"Hi, Lola, I'm Alix, glad to finally meet you. How are you?"

I was trying my best to look confident and bubbly. I was over-smiling, looking right in her eyes. I was walking as if I was on a catwalk and trying to speak as clearly as possible. She asked me to follow her. I thought she would take me to another room with all the other girls, but no, we entered a very small room with nothing in there apart from a camera. I asked her if other people would join. She looked at me with surprise and said it was just her and me. It was way less impressive than the audition I'd had in London for *Love Island*. If I hadn't crumbled a few years ago at an audition where I'd had to speak a different language to my native language in front of a panel of strangers, I was sure I could nail this one.

Alix placed herself behind the camera and explained she would ask me pretty much the same questions we'd already done via phone and Skype. In my head I thought, seriously, again? The thought of hearing myself repeating the same thing all over again bored me already, but I had to pretend to be as excited and confident as possible. The whole process went well until she asked me to put on my bikini so I could dance in front of the camera. What did she just say? She never asked me to bring one. I had no issue being half-naked in front of a stranger, but I'd had no warning, so I was clearly not ready! It was winter time, I hadn't seen my boyfriend for two weeks, so I wasn't shaved anywhere at all! I told her that I didn't have a bikini because she hadn't asked me to bring one. She said it was fine, I could just dance in my underwear.

I think that was one of the most embarrassing times of my life. There I was being cast to be a seductive single lady, dancing in my non-matching underwear and hairy as a bear, fuck my life. Anyway, what could I do? Refuse? Of course not, I'd come all the way to Paris for one thing, to succeed at this damn casting lark, and I was going to, so I removed my clothes. I asked her to play "Paradinha" by Anitta, and I started dancing. I was doing my best to look sexy and flirt with the camera while twerking and moving, until someone opened the door without even knocking. People don't have manners or what?! I recognised exactly who it was. I'd seen him in many online articles and social media stories. It was Bob, one of the main producers. Alix stopped the music straight away and told him to leave. He looked me up and down and left. That was actually weird and a bit odd, but I'm pretty sure it was done on purpose, but never mind. She put the song back on and I started dancing again, trying my best not to show my hairy armpits and bikini line, that was clearly out of control. After two minutes of me dancing, looking at the camera, flicking my hair and smiling whenever she asked me to, the casting was finally over.

I did it! The torture is done, I can put my clothes back on and stop acting, because clearly it was all an act. She thanked me and said she would give me a definite answer the following week. She then asked me to confirm that I was available at the end of February for two weeks. I had no paid holidays at work, our agenda was full, I wasn't sure how I was going to manage two weeks off work, but I told her that of course I was free. I knew that I was taken, I could feel it in my gut, this time I'd made it, my life was about to change, and it did, but not the way I expected…

~

The following week I received a call from Alix. I was at work in my office, not doing much, to be honest. My motivation for my job went down to a fat, round zero. I think I was more on social media and taking selfies than doing real work. I was so demotivated with work since the opening of the last restaurant. I had no energy left for it, all I wanted to do was spend quality time with myself and for myself. I knew anyway that I was going to be part of the show, I just needed that phone call as confirmation. I picked up the call, even though my colleagues were next to me. Good thing that no one understood French enough to follow what I was talking about. Alix confirmed what I already knew: at the end of February I would take off to a paradisic island, all expenses covered and being paid on top of that. Let's face it, I'm not Kim Kardashian, so yes, I was being paid, but nothing extravagant; everyone would get minimum pay. People always think that you're getting a crazy amount of money when you participate in a reality TV show; but if you're not famous, you get nothing. Still, I was beyond happy and grateful for finally succeeding! The secret was working! I'd made it! Finally, after years and years of trying so many castings, I'd succeeded. I thanked Alix for her help. Before hanging up she told me that Bob the producer would call me later on for a brief chat.

I wasn't allowed to tell anyone I was going on the show, apart from parents of course, but in my case I had to tell so many people: my parents, my boyfriend; but the main person I had to tell was my boss. I immediately sent him an urgent meeting invitation for him and me to have a chat. He knew that I was on the edge of leaving, as I'd mentioned a few times before that I wasn't happy, but he always found the words to keep me motivated a bit longer and stay within the team. He really didn't want me to leave, which I found flattering. Maybe I was doing a good job after all?

We met not even an hour later in our meeting room. He looked so scared, he straight away asked me if I was leaving. Technically I was going to at some point, but he didn't need to know that. I was allowed to take two weeks of non-paid holiday, but I needed his approval first. I didn't know what to tell him at first, should I lie? But as previously mentioned, I didn't want to live a life of lies any more. I wanted to be as honest as possible. Honesty is always a winner, and a lie always comes out anyway, so I told him the truth. I said I needed two weeks of non-paid holiday to be approved because I'd got selected for a part in a reality TV show in France and I didn't want to miss this opportunity. I was so scared of his answer, very anxious, but he looked at me smilingly and congratulated me.

"Of course, Lola, you can go. You work really hard and you deserve to take time off to experience something unique. Go for it!" Wow! That was so unexpected! I was very lucky to have such an understanding boss. We were working hard, extremely hard, but my boss always made sure we were looked after and acted as if we were a family. I thanked him, probably a million times, but asked him to stay quiet, which he did. Now I had to tell my parents, Julien and obviously Lukas… I texted them all. My parents and Julien congratulated me and supported me of course. Lukas, on the other hand, was a bit shocked. I think he hadn't thought I would get the part. I reassured him that it would all be an act, that I would just be myself, be funny, of course flirty and open with the guys, but I wouldn't cross the line of kissing and having sex. He said that he had no choice about me accepting it, but he didn't want to speak about it any more until we could watch the show together. OK. I mean, I knew he wasn't going to jump for joy, that made sense, but I didn't think he would be so cold. Never mind, that wasn't going to stop me.

A few hours later, Bob finally called me. It was a really brief chat. He congratulated me and told me how much the channel loved my casting tape, that they were all amazed at how beautiful and special I am, that I had all the tools to be the next big reality TV star. I was so happy to hear this, full of hopes and dreams. I'd made a huge impression on everyone, I knew now for sure I would become rich and famous. Of course I realised later on that they say the same thing to everyone new in reality TV. Producers love to make you feel special and sugarcoat everything in order to make you trust blindly in them. The more they flatter you, the more you give yourself to them. This is how it works: an obvious sort of clever manipulation.

He then said that he could see me in the bigger and more established shows he was producing, if I played my cards right. And back then, that was all I wanted, so of course I was going to give my all for the production to be happy with me and put me in other shows. I was so naive and delusional, but back then I didn't realise all the tricks of reality TV. I am far from stupid, I always had good gut instinct and common sense, but when you've desperately wanted something for so long, you can get blinded by it. Bob also mentioned that a psychologist would call me to make sure I was able mentally to be part of this sort of experience. Production would also schedule a doctor's appointment, confirming I was able to work. French law doesn't allow you to start a new job without a doctor's note. I liked the whole idea of the production looking after our health. It made everything sound more serious and in order.

A few days later I received the phone call from the psychologist, and let's be honest, I could have faked and acted everything if I'd wanted to. I realised they probably had to make us have a conversation with a psychologist by law, but she had no way of checking if my information was true; nor did she have physical contact, to see if I was actually stable and able to handle the pressure of being on television.

The same day, production booked me an appointment with a doctor on their partnership list. I could not just go to any doctor, it had to be a private one that they allocated to me. The clinic was located in Sloane Square, which is a very posh area in London. I found the clinic and sat down in the waiting room. The place was very different from the usual GP's I go to. The entire wall was full of celebrities posing with the same person, I presumed the doctor I would be seeing shortly. After not even two minutes of waiting, the doctor asked me if I was Miss Lola and asked me to follow him into the consultation room. I stood up and joined him in the room, sat down at his desk and we had a brief chat. The doctor had the production contract in front of him. He had to follow a number of processes to examine me and validate that I was able to work. Once we were done, he asked me if I was an artist, or singer or actress. That really flattered me. It was the first time someone asked me that question. He said that I had a very particular face and should definitely be on stage or TV. He then asked what the contract was for, so I told him it was to participate in a reality TV programme. He looked at me disappointedly and said that I was better than that. It melted my heart. I knew deep inside that I was meant to act and do better than reality TV, but I was too afraid to accept that and I didn't have the confidence yet to pursue singing and dancing classes. Something was still blocked inside me. Maybe I was just lazy and wanted to take the easier route?

~

End of February 2019: there I was at King Cross station, waiting for the Eurostar to take me to Paris. Lukas came along to help me with my luggage and say goodbye. I was actually really sad to leave him. He didn't seem to be bothered. I mean, I couldn't be sure: as usual I couldn't feel or read any emotions in him, he always seemed in control of everything; it was annoying to be with someone so steady. We were not going to see each other for two weeks, and wouldn't even be able to speak at all. I'd got used to being with him, I'd started to have feelings for him, so I felt really guilty at leaving him alone in the cold of England while I would be flirting away with strangers on a paradisic Island. We hugged and kissed goodbye for at least ten minutes. I think I almost didn't want to go any more, I was feeling so confused. It broke my heart to see him walking away, back to the Underground, while I was queuing for the security check.

On the Eurostar I felt the same way I'd felt nine years ago when I was on my way to London. What was I doing? Why didn't I just stay in my comfort zone, in my simple life, with my job and my nice boyfriend? Why did I always need to look for something else? Always looking for the next step. What was wrong with me? Why couldn't I ever feel content with what I had?

I couldn't believe that I was going to get paid to be part of a TV show and a few months later see my face on screen, on national television. Even though I was scared, as it was clearly unknown to me, I was proud of myself. I'd always wanted to be part of a reality TV show, and there I was on my way to this brand new adventure. Once again, I'd wanted something and I'd got it, even though it wasn't easy. It had been a long process, but I'd still made it. This was my proof that the Law of Attraction was working. But like the book says, "Be careful what you wishing for." "Every thought becomes reality." At the time I was still not sure what that meant. But later on I would find out the power of thoughts…

I arrived in Paris, Gare Du Nord, around 11 p.m. I hated that part of Paris. It was always full of the homeless, pick-pockets and just untrustworthy people in general. I felt very unsafe. Thankfully the production company had pre-booked cabs for all the girls to take us to the hotel where we would meet with our "nanny" and some people from the production company. Our nanny was not an actual nanny, she was a woman from production in charge of all the candidates for the programme. She was the first person I met when I arrived at the hotel. She welcomed me, showed my hotel room and told me to be ready to leave the hotel by 4 a.m.

Most of the girls had already met, as they'd arrived much earlier than me, so I felt a bit disadvantaged. I was sure a few of them would have made bonds already, and as usual I would be the outcast. Living with a group of even worse French girls for two weeks was one of the main reasons I was anxious, probably more than for the actual filming. I never felt comfortable within a group. I always end up being really quiet and alone. I am way better at a one-to-one friendship. I went up to my room where I met one of the girls. I tried my best to be as social and bubbly as possible. My roommate seemed nice, nothing more, nothing less. She was way younger than me, which made me feel I was maybe a bit old to start in television. I really didn't want to look desperate to be starting TV at over twenty-five years old. Her body was so small and toned, she didn't have one bit of cellulite; which made me feel like a whale next to her, even though I am really slim. She obviously had big breasts, something I clearly didn't have, and back then I wasn't in love with the way I looked so I started to feel really insecure next to her.

Alix came to our room. I was surprised to see her here, but happy to see a familiar face. My roommate went for a smoke outside downstairs, which left Alix and me alone. Bob had asked Alix to get us to try on bikinis and send pictures to him so he could choose which one we would wear for the first day of filming. I tried all of them on, but each time she sent him a picture it got a negative comment. I knew exactly what was the problem: my breasts. I had no idea that production would be checking what we wore, and I was far too naive to imagine they would check every single day, every outfit we wore throughout the day. Can someone tell me what is real in reality TV then? At the end he wasn't happy with any of my bikinis and said we would decide once we were in the villa. What a good start for me! It wasn't a good feeling to know that someone isn't happy with the way you look in a bikini.

Before Alix left, she hugged me and said, "Give your all! I count on you! I know you're the next big star! I want to see you in bigger programmes, I know you can do it!" Those words lifted my mood immediately and gave me a huge boost of confidence. I felt that production loved me already and that I had lots of chances to pursue my career in television with their channel. How stupid of me and how clever of them; they knew exactly what they were saying to every single one of us...

I went to bed with a crazy mix of emotions: happiness, hopes, scared, anxious and confused. I had only a few hours for sleep, but I didn't think I would manage any. I called Lukas discreetly, told him that I was already missing him and that I didn't know why I was doing all this. I felt so homesick already, and confused. I think I was just scared of doing something I had never done before that would possibly change my life forever.

At 4 a.m., I was downstairs in the lobby, finally seeing all the other girls. My fear of being uncomfortable in a group showed up within five minutes of being with them all. Let's not forget that I'd been living in London for nine years. I was a Londoner now, not a typical French girl any more. Even though I was born and raised in France, my culture wasn't still French, so I had a hard time sometimes when I was surrounded by French people. I never really understood their weird sarcasms that they called humour.

I could already see a few girls I would not get along with, but I knew no one would try to act up with me. I just had this aura, this vibe that people were scared of. When people meet me for the first time and simply don't know me they can think I'm vain and cold. I can be like that if I don't like the vibe of the person in front of me, but generally I'm a very sweet and open person once you get to know me. All my friends I've known for years say the same thing after few hours talking to me for the first time: "You're actually a really nice person, I wouldn't have thought so, you just have this bitchy face that makes you look really unapproachable; but in the end you're really sweet." I've heard that sentence so many times. But *"Never judge a book by its cover."*

Two big coaches were waiting outside the hotel to take us to the airport. Everyone was smoking. But as I'm not a smoker I jumped into one of the coaches immediately, as I was freezing standing outside. By 7 a.m., we were all in the plane, ready to take off for the Caribbean, for this brand new adventure.

Once we'd landed, our nanny took our phones away. I couldn't believe I wasn't going to be able to talk to my boyfriend for a long period of time. Obviously production didn't know that I had a boyfriend, no one knew, but funnily enough after talking to a few girls, or overhearing private conversations, I realised that I wasn't the only one to have someone in my life. Practically all the girls had a boyfriend, or were seeing someone. I guess I wasn't the only one ready to put my relationship in danger to get famous.

After more than twelve hours of travelling, we finally arrived at our destination. I was so tired, I just wanted to sleep in a comfortable bed and be by myself. But we still had another hour of bus journey. For the first night we were not staying in the villa where we would be filming, but at a hotel a few kilometres away from the main villa. As soon as we arrived there, our nanny told us to get back in the coach because Bob wanted to have a meeting with us. Were they serious? We were all exhausted and feeling dirty from the long hours travelling. Why did he need to see us right now, late at night? Anyway we didn't have a choice, but I realised that it was going to be like that for the whole duration of filming: unplanned meetings at any time of day and night.

After fifteen minutes' drive, we arrived at the villa where we would stay for the entire duration of filming. It was kind of exciting to see it for the first time. Bob and a few other people from the production were waiting for us by the main door. They welcomed us and showed us the villa. I have to say I was a bit disappointed: yes, of course it was beautiful, but I was expecting something much more extravagant. I had watched all the reality TV shows and knew the sort of villa they usually rented. We headed outside to have a look at the pool and the garden. The garden was beautiful, way bigger than the house itself and open to the beach. Another house with two levels was built right next to the pool. The producers told us straight away that it was our house for the whole duration of filming, where we would get ready, sleep, have our breakfast and no cameras were allowed in there. That was another unexpected surprise: we were meant to seduce the boys, but we were not really living with them, and of course the public wouldn't know that. Production wanted to show us only when we were looking our best, no filming when we were waking up or having breakfast, only the boys would be. Again I really started to wonder what was real in this "reality" TV show. Everything started to seem so staged.

We then headed back inside the house and the producers

asked us to sit down so we could all have a brief chat. They explained again our purpose on the show: that we were there to create a connection with the boys and make them fall for us without being too sexual. The goal wasn't to forge a relationship overnight by making them sleep with us; they wanted to see real love stories growing. Bob also mentioned that we were not allowed to wear inappropriate clothes such as a g-string bikini, a very low cleavage or anything too "slutty". We also needed to perform responsibly and classily. We couldn't be wasted while filming, be seen fighting or being too sexual. Those rules sounded good to me, but weren't they killing all the ingredients for an exciting programme? It didn't sound very promising to me, but if it was what production wanted, that was what they'd get. But I was sure they'd regret it. I was happy, though, because at the back of my mind I had Lukas, and I knew I couldn't cross certain lines, so having so many strict rules was working in my favour.

Then Bob started to say something very contradictory to everything that had been explained. He started to talk about the after- show: fame, our contracts with influencer agencies, the possibility of other programmes etc. You could see all the girls being very attentive at this point. He explained that at the end of the show several agencies would approach us, and they could help us choose. He then explained that the more we were with the boys, the more we talked to them, flirted and the more we were in front of the camera, so the more we would be shown on television, which meant more followers, more money and more opportunities to do bigger programmes with the same production. Literally, if you want to succeed in reality TV in France, you needed to be in a relationship or at least to fake one. Obviously he didn't say it as clearly as I just said, but only someone really stupid would misunderstand what he was trying to say. No one from production is forcing you to do anything, of course, but they have their way of making you understand that if you act in a certain way with a certain person, the cameras would be on you, which would give you more time on screen, and of course more visibility, which meant more money.

I was listening to everything he said, but I thought it didn't sound right. There is a big controversy in France regarding reality TV. It used to be really good a few years ago, but now there are so many programmes with so many candidates that the competition is getting really hard. You can tell that the shows are not as authentic as they used to be. Everyone was in a "relationship" with anyone for about a day or two, and then became "exes". That was the best way to exist. Journalists always blamed production for staging a lot of the scenes, and asking candidates to do certain things to make the programme more interesting, but they had no clear proof of that. It would be a constant battle between journalists attacking production and them denying it. But only people in TV would know the truth. Well, I was slowly discovering the truth about reality TV. There we were, being subtly manipulated by production. For me it was fine, because I knew I was playing a role anyway so it didn't bother me that much. I felt that I was the one who was going to manipulate them, but I didn't realise I was playing with a much bigger adversary than myself…

We started filming a day before the official filming day, to get some good takes in case we were fucking it up on D day. Tensions started to appear between the girls, myself included, even though I was trying my best to get out of it. But the competition is so high in this world that some contestants could not stop themselves acting bitchily, thinking it would lead them to success. Our nanny didn't try to makes things better; no, not at all, it was as if she was enjoying all the cattiness between the girls.

After a few takes, we were finally over. Now it was time to go back to our hotel and pack to move to the villa. It was only three days I'd been away from London, and yet I felt more and more homesick. What was I doing? Living with girls when I couldn't stand half of them, a nanny who was encouraging the arguments, and production who were trying to manipulate us. And now I had to learn the most ridiculous lines ever for my introduction. At first they asked us to write it down, but it got changed completely. Once again, can someone tell me what is real?

The first official day of filming arrived; we were finally going to meet the boys. My level of anxiety was so high, I wasn't sure I could do this any more. Production were rushing us to get ready at 7 a.m. in a hotel room, one room only for ten girls. That day we didn't even get fed in the morning, as they pretended we had no time for that. We all got ready in a rush, and were then hanging around. I was so hungry that I started to get really moody. I really didn't like the whole backstage of reality TV, it was nothing like I'd imagined. I found out that you spend half the day waiting, for what I wasn't sure, but during the whole adventure I remember us constantly waiting for production. They were always rushing us to be ready by a certain time, and then making us wait. It was really getting under my skin. I wouldn't have minded doing the same for a photo shoot or a real movie, of course, not but to do reality TV while getting paid peanuts, so yes, I was having a hard time.

How was I going to do this? "Please don't fall," "Please don't stammer," "Please don't forget your words." All those thoughts went through my head. I thought about it so much that I started to shake and feel sick. I couldn't control my emotions. As I was trying to calm myself down, someone from production finally came to our room and shouted to us to hurry downstairs. Fuck this, it was my first time talking in front of a camera ever.

We all headed downstairs and hid somewhere near the pool waiting for Bob's signal. "Guys, everyone in line, please. Same order as yesterday, we are about to start!" Sounds, cameras, journalists, everyone was there, making sure everything was perfect for our walk towards the boys, who were sitting a bit further away on the sofas positioned by the hotel pool. As we were all waiting, we all started laughing nervously. My heart was beating so fast. Imagine if I actually liked one of the guys? Imagine if I fell in love? I couldn't cheat on Lukas, he didn't deserve this at all.

"1… 2… .3… .GO!" That was our signal from Bob to start walking… Show time! The two sides discovered each other. At least I had an answer to my main question: I wasn't going to fall in love. None of them were my type at all. One of them was overly muscly and looked as if he spent more time in the bathroom than me. Another one had the typical cute fuck boy face, and the other two were simply not attractive. We stood there, smiling, flicking our hair, biting our lips, looking at them with intensity as if we'd been wanting them already for five minutes. I just wanted it to be over, to say my stupid speech and be done. My heart was beating so fast, I was praying I'd remember my lines. The best way for me to hide my nerves was to put on a brave face with a huge smile. I couldn't stop smiling. At least everyone thought I was confident.

The presenter asked the boys who they wanted to hear first. One of them asked Angel, one of the girls I was getting along with, to introduce herself, and she stepped forward and approached them. She had a really hard time speaking. Her words weren't coming out properly, and I was praying for mine to be fluent. The next guy asked for me to step forward: this is it, this is my entrance, oh my Lord, "Please don't fall, please don't fall, please don't fall." There I was standing tall, smiling, looking at the boys, the adrenaline inside me giving me such a boost of confidence that I hadn't expected at all. It felt as if I was in someone else's skin, not mine. I said my lines to perfection and came back to my spot with all the girls. I was so proud of myself for doing so well. All the girls said their lines one by one, and then when we were all done, the boys had to pick the girl they preferred. One of them chose me, so I thought that was a good start for me. I would probably get a chance to flirt with one at least. After that we were done with filming the main shot for the day. All the girls left and went back to the hotel room, waiting for the production instructions. While we were waiting, a few girls started already acting bitterly and jealously for not getting picked as a favourite. One of them even cried. She was probably the hottest girl, I'm not lying, she was all plastic for sure, but still very pretty, so she couldn't believe that some girls got picked and not her. Was she for real? This is when the competition started and the dynamic changed drastically. We then all jumped in the coaches to go to the villa. The adventure had officially started.

I was surprised how comfortable I was in front of the camera, or even talking to the boys I didn't know. As soon as the cameras were on, I felt that I was another person; not that I was changing my attitude, but I had this confidence that I didn't expect to have, a confidence that I didn't have in my everyday life. The fact that I had a goal and a role to play conquered all my insecurities. It felt like acting, I mean it was acting really, but I felt that I was in someone else's skin. I was still Lola, for sure, but I was meant to be a seductive single girl, so I was acting as such. Not one of us single girls liked the guys. They were first of all not attractive, second not interesting, and third so boring and difficult to talk to. Because we were trying so hard to flirt with them, they actually believed that it was real and their egos just got bigger. It was disgusting to experience. I was still determined to accomplish what I was being paid for, so I worked hard. Even though it was very difficult as the boys were really distant and shy, I would still make the most of it.

Production loved me at first, I wasn't shy at all, I would speak to everyone, dance, speak loud, act silly, literally everything they were looking for in a good candidate for TV. I was listening to every bit of "advice" from production, on what to do or what to say. Yes, I was a really good puppet. I remember the first night someone from production told me that I should try to flirt with one of the boys, Jules. Apparently they'd overheard a conversation between the boys and him saying how hot I was. At first I believed it, but now I wonder if it was not one of their tricks to move things forward. Never mind, I really wanted to please them, and I thought that the more I was cooperative, the more I would be on camera. One night, after a few days of filming, I had a date with Jules. Someone from production took me aside and reminded me how much Jules liked me and that I was a real danger. She then "suggested to me" to say certain things to trick him. I was actually excited and proud that production were counting on me, or shall I say using me. Let's face it, reality TV production will only appreciate you if they can use you. Once you're not useful to them or not cooperating the way they want you to, you're out. I could see they liked what I was doing, always calling me the "star of the programme". It made me truly believe I would become someone once the show was over. If only if I knew… .

So I was briefed to the teeth and ready to give the best of myself. We arrived at a restaurant by the beach, all set up with a bottle of Champagne waiting for us. Yes, you always have alcohol all the time on set, I guess it helps people loosen up. I wasn't having a bad time, but not a great time either. I was just flirting as much as I could and trying to get something out of Jules. After an hour, the date was over. I got into the coach first while Jules was doing interviews outside. One of the journalists congratulated me for the best scene so far. I have to say production was having a hard time with everyone. Not everyone was comfortable in front of the camera. The boys were cold and distant, and most of the girls simply didn't know how to hold a conversation. Production was actually very worried about the outcome of the show, as nothing major was happening. The journalist then said that it was obviously easy for me to be natural and flirty with Jules, as we both had a real connection. I turned around, looked at him and said that I wasn't interested at all, that It was all an act. He couldn't believe it. He said, "But the way you were looking at him, your laugh, the conversation, it looked so real." This is when I felt the confirmation that I was meant to be on stage. I knew how to become someone else naturally, create a persona. I just needed to develop my singing and dancing skills.

Days passed and the dynamic around me changed. We couldn't see to the end of this adventure, time was so slow, the days were just long and boring. We had nothing to say to each other: every time we approached the guys or asked them personal questions, they would move away and not play the game. What was their reason to participate in a reality TV show if they refused to do or say anything? I simply couldn't be bothered with them, their ugly faces, stinky attitude and having to pretend to be interested 24/7. After a week of making a really hard effort, I stopped "working". Production wasn't happy at all as nothing was happening in there for them to put together a decent show to air on TV. I didn't feel bad about it though. I'd done everything I could, it wasn't my fault if they cast stuck up people. I was just enjoying my time left, either at the pool or the beach. That was the only thing we could do. We had no phone, no TV, the only time we could go out was to our "castings", you know the ones had Alix promised me over the phone when I was hesitant to participate to the show, but that was a complete joke. They weren't even real castings, they were fake, all created by production. Thank God I was finally getting along with a few of the girls. I have to say we had some serious fun between us, thank God for that. It made our time in the villa much livelier and more entertaining. Some other girls though were a nightmare, constantly aggressive or acting weird. Their personalities used to change from one minute to another. It seemed that if they didn't have alcohol in their system, they weren't fun and happy.

It reminded me of someone I know very well… my mum. I think I never realised that my mum had a problem with alcohol when I was living with her. As a teenager, I just thought it was normal to drink wine with the meal or while she was on the phone to her friends. I am from a country where it is in our culture to drink, it is social and there is no issue most of the time. I think I started to realise that she had a problem with alcohol when I came back to France for a quick visit. She would drink every night as usual while having dinner or while she was on the phone, but I could feel that it was annoying me more and more. I couldn't stand her being so cold and annoying when she was sober, and then being all melow and nice every time she had a drink. She would always drink rosé with ice. I couldn't stand the smell of her breath when she was speaking after drinking and trying to get some affection from us. She would always repeat the same thing multiple times, then obviously forget about it and repeat it the day after.

I wasn't close to my mum at all, but my distance in the UK and her alcoholism drew us even further apart. You would think that being an alcoholic would mean drinking vodka at 11 a.m. and being completely wasted, that is how most people would classify someone alcoholic. But my mum was only drinking wine, so to other people it didn't seem a big issue. How could you call someone alcoholic when they drink wine only with food or with their cigarette? It couldn't be any more French. A really big problem in our society is to recognise that it can be a problem to drink more than one glass every day, as it is just classified as being social. But drinking everyday, alone or more than half of a bottle, is not classed as social or being a healthy drinker any more. Yet my mum never wanted to admit it. Every time we brought up the subject, she would always say the same thing: "I am your mother, you can't say anything to me, you owe me respect and that is all you have to do." What she didn't realise is that we were not kids any more, or teenagers, we were grown-up adults and worried about her. But my mum is the sort of person who would never recognise she was wrong, and was really worried about appearances. She had a really hard time accepting that she wasn't perfect, or recognising her wrong towards us. My sister and I knew that deep down she was a good mother, she always did everything for us, we had a roof, toys, holidays, clothes, food, we never missed out on anything. But she had so many personal issues that she didn't want to deal with. She was angry, holding grudges from her past. She was simply a very unhappy person and she was putting all her frustration onto us, which made the relationship between the three of us very difficult, and especially for me.

Which is why as I was getting older I barely drank. I realised that I didn't need alcohol to have fun. I was getting more confident as a person and felt much better for not drinking. I really didn't want to become like my mum. I wanted to be healthy physically and mentally, and deal with my mental issues; to be the best version of myself. I wanted to know when to apologise to someone, recognise my wrongs, put my ego on the side when needed, deal with my anger issues, jealousy and fear of abandonment. I could see the damage for people who were not taking care of themselves, and I really didn't want to be that person. Being healthy and true to myself was one of the first steps. I never liked alcohol, so why drink? To be part of a group? To be social and not seem boring? Now I am strong enough to say no and not care if someone calls me boring.

After more than two weeks we finally finished filming and it was time for us to go back home to our normal life until the show aired on television. Even if the days had been long and we'd probably moaned 90% of the time, we were all sad to leave. It was a bittersweet feeling, but I couldn't wait to go back to London, to my life. But weirdly I wasn't missing my boyfriend so much any more..

I got my phone back. I had about 500 emails from work and around 30 emails from my boyfriend. Every day he had emailed me to tell me about his day and how much he was missing me. That was actually really sweet. I called him straight away, and as we were speaking I asked him if he had planned anything for my return, such as a night out or something a bit out of the ordinary as we hadn't seen each other for so long. He said he'd not planned anything, I wasn't surprised, but still I was really disappointed. I knew I was a demanding person, and I always wanted to feel like a princess, but he never made any effort. So after being apart for so long, I really thought he would do something special, like a trip to the spa, a gift, heart-shaped balloons round the room, flowers, unicorns, who knows what. But no, he had just planned to come to mine, and that was it. I wasn't even in London before I knew that I wasn't going to be content with the life that I'd had for too long…

~

When I got back to London, I knew I had to make some changes if I wanted to pursue my career in TV and follow my dreams. I couldn't carry on working more than 40 hours a week and have the same lifestyle. It didn't make sense. The show wasn't airing yet. I didn't know what the outcome would be, but I was fed up with my job anyway. I had no motivation any more. I would just act as present, my body was there, but not my mind. I had to leave, but as you know, London is a very expensive city and I couldn't afford to stay and not work. But if I was getting another job to pay the bills, it would have been the exact same as staying in my previous job. I had to stop working completely to figure out what I wanted to do and see the outcome of the show. I could see that my only option was to go back to France and take a break. My mum offered for me to come back home and stay with her. I was hesitant, but I thought why not? I would spend the summer in a nice comfortable house with a swimming pool, rent free and just enjoy my time for once. I knew it would be hard, as my mum and I didn't get along, but maybe that would be the occasion to re-bond?

I also broke up with Lukas when I got back to London. I couldn't stand his lack of drive for anything in life: sex, desire to succeed, desire to make me feel special. He was so attractive, but the fact that nothing in his personality had any drive really put me off him. We broke up for a few weeks when I returned from the show, but then he somehow managed to win me back. A few flowers here and there, a few nice words and dinners, and the next thing you know we were back together. How weak of me. So we decided to stay together and see each other from time to time. Either I would go and visit him in Manchester, or he would come to France.

I remember a time before I left London to go back to France, I hadn't seen him in a week as he was away in Dubai. Before he left for his trip, he asked me what I wanted from Dubai. I said nothing really, I just really wanted one of those NYC hats, so if he pick one up at the duty free that would be great. I didn't think a £15 hat was too much to ask for.

While he was away, I organised for him and me to stay in one of the hotels we were working for, so we could have one fancy last night together in a luxury hotel. I bought his favourite chocolate and a card saying "Welcome home". Every time I saw him, I would make sure to take care of him. I expect to be treated like a princess, for sure, but I am a very giving person, I am not a brat, I love to spoil and take care of the person I am with, but I do not like to be taken for granted and not do the same in return.

As soon as he landed, he called me saying he couldn't find my hat so I shouldn't expect anything. He also said that he was tired, so could just stay in if that was OK. I mean no, it wasn't OK, I hadn't seen him in two weeks and we were just going to sleep? Did he realise the number of guys who would have been happy to take me out? I couldn't believe he was doing this again.

On his birthday a few months ago, I had organised a wonderful night in a beautiful hotel room, Champagne, all his gifts, a cheeky drink in a fancy bar and the day after a surprise dinner with his sister who'd travelled all the way from Latvia. He was meant to join me when I finished work, but as he was in London he wanted to catch up with his friends first, which I obviously understood, as it was his birthday. I finished work and waited for him in the room. He texted me saying he would be an hour at the most as he was finishing his last drink. Three hours later I was still waiting for him. I was fuming. It was his birthday, fair enough, but how rude to make me wait when I had organised stuff for us. I'd finished work at 6 p.m. and he only turned up at midnight. I couldn't believe it. I ended up drinking the Champagne by myself and ordered Deliveroo, how fucking sad. And obviously we didnt have sex. I was so horny, but also so frustrated and angry, that I ended up masturbating while watching hard sex porn in the bathroom while he was sleeping. This is how sad this relationship had become.

So this was happening again, me organising something special for us and him not giving a flying fuck about it. He got to the room before me as I was still working. When I walked into the room, he was already asleep. He hadn't even texted me a thank you for organising everything. I woke him up to say hello at least. We kissed and then he asked me to give him his bag as he had something for me. I thought that maybe even if he hadn't found my hat at the airport, he'd gone to a store somewhere in London to get it for me, as he knew I really wanted it. What an idiot for even thinking that! I got his bag and passed it to him. He opened it and pulled out a plastic bag and gave it to me. I opened it and discovered a sack of hotel samples from his hotel in Dubai. I actually thought it was a joke, I had no words. I looked at him and asked him if he was playing or if he was serious? Hotel samples? For real? Can you be any more cheap and inconsiderate? I threw it back at him. How had I let myself be in a relationship with someone so uncaring and boring?

Anyway, I left London and obviously things didn't get better between him and me. It got worse. We kept arguing, and I really had a serious doubt that he was cheating on me. We were meant to meet again on my birthday to fly out somewhere I didn't know. That was meant to be the surprise for my birthday. A week before that, he called me to break up with me and said that he'd booked the wrong dates for our holidays. Did he really think I was stupid? That was the lamest excuse someone has ever given me. I was sad and angry for being dumped over the phone one week before my birthday, but I think my ego was hurt more than my actual feelings for him. For once I decided to not let my emotions take over. I cried for possibly ten minutes, then thought that I'd lived without him for twenty-seven years, so I could live without him for many more years. My 28th birthday was coming anyway, so I decided to go on a trip with a few friends to Vegas to celebrate my birthday, the way I deserved. I wasn't going to let a guy ruin my birthday.

We had so much fun in Vegas: the casino, the gigantic nightclubs, luxury hotels, the sun, it felt really good to let my hair down. The show started to air on TV while I was away in Vegas. I was so embarrassed to see how I looked on screen. I didn't like my image at all, which made me understand why so many girls from TV are going through surgery. Seeing all your imperfections on a screen can make you feel really insecure. On top of criticising yourself, you have to face all the "haters". Those people are strangers who you know nothing about, who go on your social media and attack you for your physique or what you did on the show. To be honest, I haven't had many of those, usually people were nice to me, but I have to say that I had a few and the words can be really harsh. But

I decided that the best solution was not to read those messages or comments.

Once I got back from Vegas, a famous radio presenter wanted to interview me. He was quite well known, so I was glad to be interviewed by him. He seemed very kind and genuine. During the interview he asked me how I'd ended up on TV so I decided to be open and mention my abortion. The thought behind it was to show that even after a hard time, you can always fight and do something positive with your life. I thought I was doing a good thing here, but I realised that as a "public figure" you are always criticised about anything and everything. The number of negative comments and messages I received because I'd talked about my abortion was ridiculous. Once again I was called a "slut", "whore", " bitch", only because I'd talked about a subject that wasn't socially acceptable to mention out loud. I didn't see what the issue was really, all I wanted was to help other girls out there, saying that it was OK to go through with it and you can always make something good out of something bad. After reading a few comments, I decided to not read the rest. It wasn't doing any good to me or my soul, so why make myself suffer? I didn't know those people, so their opinion shouldn't matter in the end.

But I also received negative comments from some friends of mine, I mean people that I called friends but really were not. One girl I used to go out with in London texted me saying how crazy I was to talk about such a personal subject to the entire nation. All she did was keep criticising me. I still don't understand the problem: we are constantly watching girls twerking, dancing, wearing the shortest dresses and getting wasted in clubs, including herself on social media on a daily basis, but talking about an important subject is wrong? Sometimes I have a really hard time understanding how people can be so judgemental. I felt attacked by her anger at me for talking about it. Why was she so upset? Was it really because I'd talked about it, or simply because I was doing an interview? When you start to have a little notoriety or fame, you either get people from your past that you haven't spoken to in ages suddenly wanting to hang out with you; or people that you actually hang out with who suddenly change their attitude towards you, they become mean for no reason and just criticise everything. I wasn't affected by it too much. It did hurt me a little of course, but all I could think about was the people who got famous really fast and on a bigger scale. They must have to deal with so much shit on a daily basis. I don't know how they cope with it, seriously. Receiving constant negativity and nasty comments must really damage your self-esteem and soul. People don't realise the damage they cause another human being, and I think it's a real shame. Government and laws should really look into it and do something about it. We keep hearing about people killing themselves due to social media pressure; it shouldn't happen. I always thought that we should include self-esteem and self-love in school classes; also how to be kind to one another, and explain to kids why it is wrong to say certain words to one another.

Being part of this TV show didn't really make me famous and rich, let's be honest, but it helped me to grow so much. I began to understand the importance of mental health and how important it is to not to criticise someone else who doesn't have the same life and thoughts as you. I mean, you are allowed to think differently, but what will you get out of saying nasty stuff to another person? Nothing. I was also getting really good at not listening to people criticising me: whether my family, friends or strangers. I would listen to constructive remarks and advice, but if I felt attacked or that the comments were not helping me grow as a person, I would simply not listen, and that was the best thing I could do for myself.

The episodes came out, but the show never picked up. The audience wasn't there. I mean, I wasn't blaming the public for not being interested in the show, it was simply boring. Even my mum, who is a bit uptight, thought it was very disappointing. But even though the show wasn't that popular, I was still earning money from it. I managed to get a contract with a very famous agency in France, so I had products delivered to my house and all we had to do was promote them. As I was new at the agency, I was paid €250 per post. It wasn't the amount that I was expecting, but still good for a beginning. I was disappointed with the agency, though. I didn't expect it to be so disorganised and unprofessional. I didn't feel that someone was looking after me like a real agent. I thought I would sit down with the main boss and talk about how they were going to make me famous and as lucrative as possible. The agency was known as one of the best influencer agencies, because almost everyone from TV was part of it. But in the end, the agency was prioritising quantity over quality. I never even met the main boss, this is how unstructured the agency was. We often received the wrong product, the payments were late, we always had to chase them, it was simply not what I expected.

I know that in the UK if you are part of a reality TV show you always end up with a real agent who looks after their clients properly and finds very lucrative contracts. In France we have so many reality TV programmes and candidates that you simply can't make a lot of money straight away. You have to be in the game for a long time and do many shows. Luckily for me, even though production barely showed me on screen and cut off many of my scenes, I still got noticed by another production channel who wanted to cast me for other TV shows. I really thought, back then, that those programmes would make me famous. They were established programmes watched by millions of people, so if I managed to be part of one of them, I would finally succeed.

So there I was on the road to Paris, attending all the castings I was being called for. I have to say that I had a really good summer that year: from VIP events I was invited to, to castings in Paris, trips to Cannes and St Tropez to party, I have to say I was enjoying life. I was also trying to avoid being at home alone with my mum as much as possible. My mum and I simply couldn't stand each other. At some point we almost got along, as I was trying to put the past behind us and concentrate on the present. I started to read a book called *The Magic* which is the next chapter of *The Secret*, if you like. This book transformed my life, it truly made me understand what it is to be grateful, to appreciate life the way it is. And the more grateful I was about the present, the more I would receive. I also started meditating, which helped me to stay calm, centred and positive. I was feeling really good.

So for a little time, things were slowly getting better with my mum. I was trying not to pay attention to our small disagreements, but after a while I felt hopeless with her. I was trying to be as positive as possible, but she was making it really hard to appreciate her. Everything I did or said she had to contradict. I would say black, she would say white; I would then say white, and she would say black. It was a constant mental battle with her, she was never happy with anything. She always had a remark or something negative to say. She simply didn't like me being there. If she did anything for me like cooking, she would throw it back in my face, that she'd done it for me, like I owed her something because she'd cooked. That's what I was dealing with my whole life. She would talk about the past, about how she'd driven me to dance school or to see my friends, that she'd looked after us when we were kids. But I mean, isn't that what a mum is supposed to do? I was grateful, but why was she constantly making it sound as if we owed her everything because she'd done those things for us? It felt that she'd done it because she had to, not because it was a pleasure to do so, and she constantly had to throw it back in my face. I couldn't stand this pervasive negative battle and energy around me. I felt that no matter what I said or did, it would never be enough.

I knew that I had to leave before things turned nasty. We were now in August 2019, I'd been in France for five months already, and that was more than enough time to spend there. I had what I wanted: time for myself, time to rest, time to concentrate on my casting, time to go to every event possible, but I was ready to come back to my London life. I managed to be successful in one casting: I was scheduled to leave for Miami at the end of September 2019, so everything looked as if it was going in the right direction for me. I was happy to be part of a show that had been established for years, but I wasn't thrilled about it. I was again going to have the role of a single girl coming to seduce a guy, which I'd had enough of. I wanted a bigger role, showing my true personality and not just the seductive side of me. But it was still an opportunity, so I accepted it. Production also kept repeating to me that I was going to be the next big star, that they loved my personality, the show was established, famous characters would be there, so I was guaranteed time on screen etc. Once again, I could feel that they were trying to manipulate me, but for now I felt that I had no choice.

The entire time I was in France, I didn't even flirt with anyone, no one was interesting to me, I really didn't like French guys. But around May 2019, while I was in France, I flew back to London as I was invited to another event from my former company. It was the first time I was a guest, and it felt great. Usually I would work like a maniac at those events: I would wear a black costume, an earpiece and run around making sure everything was running smoothly. This time, it was different! I would wear a fancy dress, have my hair done, I would be all tanned, slim and looking more rested and glowing than ever. For the occasion I was wearing a long, silky, orange, open-back dress that complemented my curves. I blow-dried my hair, my skin had a beautiful caramel colour, I had orange stilettos matching my dress and sophisticated make-up. I felt like Cinderella going to the ball to meet her prince. As I walked up the stairs to head to the welcoming drink area, I could feel everyone staring at me. I knew all those people and they were not used to seeing me like that. I was getting stopped every five minutes by someone telling me how stunning I looked. I felt quite shy about the compliments, but truly grateful as for the first time in a long time I felt confident and beautiful.

Throughout my life, I'd always had a hard time accepting the way I looked and feeling good about myself. I'd had a bad skin for years due to a hormonal imbalance, and unless I was on contraceptive pills, my skin would break out. I know a lot of people cannot relate to that and think it is only superficial, but having bad skin can cause as much damage as being overweight. You feel so self-conscious about the way your skin looks: all you think about is how people look at you, and probably think you're just dirty and don't wash your face properly. Having a bad skin made me wear make-up for years. All I wanted was to cover those disgraceful spots, marks and redness. It took me so long to accept that I was born that way and find a solution to treat my skin effectively but with kindness. With a good food regime, good sleep, a better mind, working out and natural products, I managed to have a much better skin, which makes me confident about myself.

My body was also amazing. I'd had so much time to work out that I finally had my dream body. I wasn't skinny, I was looking healthy and glowing. I was so much more confident. I knew a bit more about what I wanted out of life. I knew how to handle conversation and critics. I'd learned how to screen out negative comments. I just felt invincible, and I think everyone could feel it.

After a few chats here and there with my former colleagues, I headed to the main area where dinner was being held. I was sitting at a table with few people I knew, and right next to me on my left was Sebastian. Sebastian is a famous influencer who has been invited to many launch parties we organised with my company. I saw him briefly once before I quit my job, during an event in Manchester. I didn't really pay attention to him and he didn't pay much attention to me either. I was one of the staff, so I don't think he was really bothered about me; but this time I was privileged to be one of the guests, and I was sitting right next to him.

Sebastian is extremely tall, olive skin, curly hair but cut very short, beautiful green brown eyes, simply looking like a god. He has such an aura and charisma about him, and I think he knows about it, he is simply trouble. As soon as he sat next to me, he introduced himself. Oh my God, his Mancunian accent was driving me nuts. I was having a hard time understanding what he meant sometimes, but I didn't really care. I felt quite nervous next to him. We both started to talk about our backgrounds, work and life in general. After five minutes of us talking, he clearly started to flirt with me. He knew that he was extremely good-looking and all the girls would fall for him without him even trying. During the after-party he clearly tried to get me to sit next to him on one of the sofas. He took my hand, but I rejected his move. I was still thinking about my ex, and I didn't have the heart to sleep with another man, even though he was famous, rich and very attractive. My head just wasn't there. So we exchanged numbers and social media, and that was it for that night.

Then a few months later, here I was on my way back to London. I was going back earlier than planned as I was invited by my former boss to the launch party of a new restaurant. I'd be attending another party, and this time I was over my ex, prettier and happier than ever. I was really excited about it, as again I was a guest and not a member of staff. I could dress up and enjoy my time there. I was also excited about it as I knew my crush was also invited, Sebastian. All I had in my head was how could I be the only one who Sebastian would look at. It was a launch event, the place will be full of beautiful girls, influencers and celebrities, but I wanted him and this time I wasn't going to let him go.

After spending the whole summer in France, my skin was very brown and glowing, my face was radiant and my hair really long, brown and shiny. I had to wear something that would make me stand out. I always wear sexy dresses, but this time I wanted to be different. I wanted to look sexy but cute. One day as I was walking down the street in Avignon, I passed the window of a small boutique; and there it was, my perfect dress. It was baby pink, with a bustier top and Bardot sleeves, and the bottom was short and open like a tutu. I had to get it tailored as my waist was really tiny, but we finally had the best result possible. I looked like a sexy ballerina, a sweet candy ready to be eaten. I loved this look, very different from my usual femme fatale attire. I was so happy that I'd found the perfect dress, the way I'd visualised it.

So it was now August 2019 when I returned to London. I was so happy to be back. I'd missed the London buzz so much: Mayfair, the fancy restaurants, the busy streets, all the women dressing up smart and fashionable, the men in suits always running after the clock, but still having time to have a cheeky look at women, the tourists taking hundreds of photos per minute, the old and modern architecture blending together. I was truly in love with London, and it was about time I came back to my London life, especially now that I was more confident and readier than ever to have the London life I'd always wanted.

For the occasion my former director treated me like his VIP guest and offered me a room in a famous luxury hotel for the weekend. I was treated like a celebrity. I was so excited to attend this event. The weather was warm but not too hot, I was rested and simply very happy. I was ready to roll. I didn't arrive on time, you never arrive at the time when everyone else arrives, you always need to wait for the place to get busy. I took a taxi there, no chance I was going to take the Tube with my tutu dress and heels. As I arrived at the place and got out of the taxi, photographers were standing in front of the restaurant. I walked towards it and all of them were paparazzing me. I felt a bit shy and confused, as I was no one famous in England, but still felt amazing. I posed in front of the steps with all the flash photographers screaming how beautiful I was. I was loving it, I'm not going to lie. The feeling of being admired and recognised cannot be compared to anything else.

I finally entered the restaurant. It was packed, the music was loud, the place beautifully decorated. I was proud of my former team for pulling off once again such a wonderful event. As I walked in everyone was stopping me or staring at me to tell me how gorgeous I was. I felt overwhelmed by all the compliments, and for the first time in my life I was accepting them and feeling good about it. Before, I couldn't stand compliments; I always had to put myself down. I couldn't accept the fact that people could find me pretty, interesting or even nice. I thought it was wrong and pretentious to accept who you are and love yourself. I always concentrated on the negative in my appearance, skills and mental issues, and that never helped me to move forward. Now I am embracing myself. Don't get me wrong, I am not overly confident, I still struggle from time to time, but I was learning to love myself for who I am. If people were supporting me, that was amazing; but if people didn't, I learned that was also fine. Everyone has an opinion, a voice, a way of seeing life and what sort of individuals they like, and I know I couldn't be everyone's cup of tea and I made peace with that. From now on, I accepted when someone was complimenting me, I was grateful for it, always thanked the person and returned the compliment. It feels good to receive, but it feels even better to give, and that is also something I learned.

As I was talking with a few of my former colleagues, I noticed a lady standing to my right. Suddenly I saw her looking sideways, eyes wide and mouth open. She looked shocked. She then said, "Who on earth is that? I've never seen anyone so beautiful in my entire life."

I turned around and it was him, Sebastian, beautiful as a god as always. As he walked across the room, you could feel his presence, his energy. This guy had such a powerful aura, it was incredible. Our eyes caught each other's and we both smiled. I was feeling so shy deep inside, but tried my best to not show it. He looked at me for a few seconds and seemed hesitant to come over. I think he was also impressed. He still came over to say Hi. We both smiled at each other and he gave me a kiss on the cheek, saying how stunning I looked. I think my heart dropped, I was melting on the inside so much.

I could feel fireworks, butterflies, rainbows inside my stomach. It felt like I was sixteen years old again. Sebastian had such an effect on me, and that was really rare for me. I obviously acted cool and did not let my emotions take over. I still gave him a cheeky smile, as a sign for him to understand that this time I was ready for a flirt, and I'm sure he understood.

Throughout the night, every time I walked past him, he would stop listening to whoever was talking to him to stare at me and smile. We were both flirting. I loved it. Later on, when the party kicked off and Sebastian had probably had a few drinks, he finally came over to talk. I really think he also was feeling shy about talking to me. He sat next to me as I was chatting with a former colleague. He asked me how I was, and we talked briefly. I couldn't really understand what he was saying, as I think he'd started to get really drunk. All I took in was how differently I came over to him compared with the other girls. No one had ever given him the cold shoulder before, and he thought it was very attractive. I guess refusing to give myself to him at the previous event in May had an impact. I knew he had slept with another girl that night, which I didn't stop myself from pointing out to him. He obviously started to deny it and bullshit, but I stopped him straight away and said, "Sebastian, I don't care what happened with that girl, all I care about right now is the present, and I just want to make sure you are doing me tonight."

I don't think he expected me to talk like that. He started to laugh nervously out loud and hide his face with his hands. He then said, "This is why you are so different." I knew he was a sweet talker, he would say anything to get me into bed, he was that sort of guy, but I knew he had a good heart. I don't think he was the type to promise a girl the world just to get her into bed. He was just really charming, very good looking, and he knew it, so he was using it to his advantage. But I still liked to believe he had a soft spot for me.

He then left, embarrassed, and texted me five minutes later to ask me where I was staying in London for the occasion. I knew how my night was going to end... Meanwhile the party was simply amazing. I had such a good time catching up with everyone, dancing, laughing, the night was simply a success, and it was now time for me to head back to the hotel.

I didn't know where Sebastian was. The last time I'd seen him he was completely wasted, and I wasn't going to chase him. As I got back to the hotel, Sebastian called me. I could barely understand what he was saying. I knew he wanted me to come to his hotel, but I couldn't understand the name of his hotel and room number, so I told him to come and pick me up at my hotel. As I was waiting for him, I decided to go down to the bar for a drink. As I was drinking my Coke, I felt someone looking at me. I looked to my left and couldn't believe who I was seeing: one of the most famous US rappers. He was there alone, looking at me, what the actual fuck? I couldn't believe it. Then Sebastian called me to say he was outside waiting in a black cab, so I made my way out. As I was leaving, the rapper stopped me to hand me a piece of paper with his number. What was my life about now? How could I attract so many crazy happenings in less than a year? For the past eight years nothing major had happened, but as soon as I changed my attitude and way of seeing life, the universe threw me one crazy thing after another. I was flattered by the gesture, but for now all I wanted was Sebastian.

We were at his hotel in no time. As soon as we got into his hotel room he started to kiss me and dragged me towards the bed. He was exhausted and just lay on the bed, grabbed me to cuddle him. Even if he was drunk and tired, my heart was melting. I fancied Sebastian so much, and I don't know why it was but I had feelings for him. I could sense something really sad about him, just as I'd been earlier in my life. He was smiling all the time, always looking the part, pretending to be very confident, but I could feel sadness deep inside, and that made me care for him. I am that sort of person. I can't help it. If I feel that someone, especially a man, is not feeling mentally well, I cannot help wanting to rescue that person; maybe because deep inside I wish someone would do that for me. I wasn't sure about the psychology behind it, but I knew that every time someone was feeling low or sad, I was truly happy to help and be a shoulder to cry on.

After about ten minutes of him talking nonsense, about me giving him a chance, and how much he liked me, he kissed me. He was such a good kisser, I was really drawn to him. He removed my trousers and panties and started to go down on me. Let me tell you that he was really good. I am usually not a big fan of it, but the way he was doing it with so much passion and desire, I could feel it run through my body. He kept saying how beautiful my vagina looked and how it tasted so good. I didn't want it to stop. We had sex the whole night. It was amazing, but also really weird. He would stop sometimes suddenly, to put on some weird music like Disney songs, which I had no issues about as I am a big Disney fan, but I wouldn't expect that from a guy. He also stopped sometimes and just sat at the end of the bed and started talking about suicide, death and social media. I could see in his eyes how sad he was, but I wasn't sure why he was telling me all this. He then looked at me and told me to be careful with fame and make sure I always had support. I thought that was really sweet of him. I was assuming that he or someone close to him was depressed due to fame, or even dead due to the pressure of being famous, maybe? I couldn't believe that we were living in an era when people are so mean and harsh towards each other, bullying one another, that it would end up eventually in suicide. I felt so bad for him, I didn't know what to say. So I took him in my arms and hugged him. He looked at me for a minute, smiled, said he loved me and we started to have sex again. I knew he didn't love me, I didn't take it seriously. I think he just needed to say those words as he needed to be loved.

Around 6 a.m., Sebastian was finally asleep. I wasn't, so I left quietly and let him sleep. He heard me leaving, so he begged me to stay. He didn't want to be alone, that really broke my heart. I went over, gave him a hug, kissed him on the forehead and waited until he fell asleep again. Once he was asleep, I left.

I took a taxi back to my hotel room, with so many thoughts in my head. I knew that Sebastian and I would never be an item. I mean not for now, as he was at the beginning of his career, which he was really concentrating on. He had a million choices of women and I couldn't imagine him committing, but I still felt for him. The fact that he was so attractive, but still kind and broken inside, made me like him even more. I could see myself in him, a beautiful damaged soul that not many other people would perceive. Most people could probably just see the playboy that he was, and that was it. I don't think many people could see behind it, but I could. Even though I had feelings for him, I had to tell my heart that he wasn't for me, not for now. I had to control my emotions; if not, I would end up hurt. I went to bed at 7 a.m., feeling happy and grateful that I'd spent the night with Sebastian.

I woke up a few hours later, around 11 a.m., and looked at my phone. I had two missed calls from Sebastian. I texted him straight away and asked if everything was all right. Within seconds he texted back, just saying he wanted to check on me and make sure I was fine. How sweet of him. He was a player, definitely, but he wasn't an asshole. He knew he could have a different girl every night, but I do believe he remained respectful at all times. I mean with me he was, and I truly appreciated him worrying about me. We exchanged a few texts, I kindly reminded him he'd said the L word yesterday. He said that he probably was in love with me. I knew it wasn't true, but I appreciated him not being a dick about it. Sometimes guys can act up when they're embarrassed about something they did or said, but not him. He needed to stop being so imperfectly perfect, as the little girl inside me was already imagining a white dress, a beautiful diamond ring and a big family. But the grown-up woman I am knew it was only a fantasy and I had to move on.

I carried on my weekend away in London: spending time at Sketch London for a fancy afternoon tea, shopping at Selfridges, walking down New Bond Street, eating out at Bagatelle and partying at The Box Soho, my favourite club. I was having a true blast. Many people thought I was an escort. Frequently I had people asking me how could I afford this lifestyle? But when you're a girl in London, it is easy to get a lot of things for free. First of all, I knew many people in the hospitality industry, so I always had good deals on restaurants or hotel rooms; sometimes it was even complimentary. I was also on many nightclub promoters' guestlists, so I never paid either for entrance or drinks when I was going out. But mainly when you're a girl who looks after her looks, men who live in a city like London like to pay. Without me even asking, I would always have some guy offer me drinks or even dinner sometimes. Some would offer an afternoon at the spa, getting a massage, or offer me a ride home. I had many options that helped me to save money and live the high life. Many people would think that was wrong. I didn't see why. I wasn't asking, they were offering, so why refuse? This weekend definitely reminded me how much I was loving London, how much I'd missed it, and I was glad to be back and start all over again with the best intentions. I just had to be successful in the show I was going to participate in, and I would finally live my dream life…

Before I was even on my way to this new adventure, my head and heart were not excited at all about going abroad to film. During my first show, I'd definitely been scared but I was also very excited. This time I was dragging myself there. I clearly didn't want to do it, I had a bad feeling about it, some gut instinct that I couldn't shake off. I was once again playing the role of a single girl coming to find love. But just the sound of it was boring. I could feel that I was being used, even before the show started. I was finally recovering mentally, so why would I go somewhere that didn't make me feel good? Somewhere where the atmosphere would be fake and negative? I almost cancelled my flight, but I was still hoping a little inside me that this was maybe my chance to shine. Production also promised me a lot of key scenes and the chance to be part of the main cast, so I thought I should try one more time. I didn't know that this show would change my whole perception on life and what I wanted to achieve…

I met three other girls at the airport. I got along with two of them, but the third one was weird. I could sense people's nature straight away. I could feel that she was acting nice now, but once the cameras were rolling she would be a backstabber. What I'd learned from my previous TV was always to listen to my gut instinct and not trust anyone, especially people in reality TV who want everything to shine a little. As we were chatting, we all realised that production had manipulated us. They had said different things to all of us, and we realised that we would be used as little puppets who could play for one night or two to spice up the show a little, but we were never going to be part of the main cast. Another weird thing happened with this production: we signed our contract only at the airport, and we had no doctor's or psychologist's appointments. It really felt wishy washy.

After a twelve hour flight, we finally landed in Miami. The weather was so hot and humid, I wasn't sure how I was meant to stay glam while sweating like a pig. A coach was waiting for us outside the airport, and our chauffeur took us to our resort. We arrived an hour later, and I was pleasantly surprised. We could tell that the budget was high and the production was much bigger. Our resort was amazing: it was not where we were filming, but where we would stay until we started filming.

Our nanny was waiting for us at the main entrance. She seemed much nicer than the previous one: she was younger and much more innocent, let's say. She was new in the industry, and I could feel she wasn't yet manipulating us. Our nanny took us for a tour of the resort.

I'd never stayed anywhere so big and beautiful. It had five different pools, seven restaurants and bars, a spa, a beautiful private beach with white sand and a nightclub. I felt really lucky to experience such luxury for free. I wasn't keen on filming, but having a free holiday all inclusive made up for it.

The same night a few people from production came round to speak to us and explain our roles. We all sat together, and had the usual chat about how we were doing, if anyone was feeling stress or anxiety, etc. Then they explained our roles in the programme and how we were going to be introduced to the main cast. But what I heard did not appeal to me at all… .

When the producers told us we were coming to meet the boys to spend a weekend with them and seduce them, I thought I was going to throw up. We were here to tempt the guys, as a few of them were already in relationships with the girls from the villa. I felt so betrayed. Production knew that had been my role on my first show, and now they were making me come for an entire weekend just to seduce the boys, and not to mingle with the rest of the cast? Was that a joke? How would that make me look? Like a full-on desperate girl ready to play the seductive role one more time just so she could be on TV. I'd accepted the role of single girl looking for love to live with everyone in the villa, but coming to seduce boys who were already in a relationship with other girls, this is not what I'd signed up for. I wanted to be on TV, for sure, but I didn't want to humiliate myself just to get famous. I was twenty-eight years old, not eighteen years old. I was a grown-up and I had some self-esteem and dignity. They carried on saying that if we were doing our "job" properly, we had the chance to stay longer. The more we played the game, the more the camera would be on us. So I was getting paid one more time to seduce guys I had no interest in, talk to them, flirt, kiss, and more. That reminded me of a well-known famous job that has been on the market for hundreds of years. Do you follow me?

Yes, I felt like a prostitute, let's put it that way. It was obviously not prostitution, but to me it felt exactly the same. No one was forcing you, of course, but they had brilliant ways of tricking your mind and making you understand that the hotter you were, the more seductive you acted with the guys and the more actions you took with them, the more you would be on camera, which means more time on screen, more followers, so more money. To me it was clearly disguised prostitution, and on top of that not even being paid for the part.

I did a little research and found that new participants in

reality TV in the UK are barely paid, but they know that the outcome can be huge, lucrative contracts, real agents; most of them are set up for life. So I guess that acting a little seductively and stupidly for the camera is OK for the outcome you get. In France you had no guarantee, reality TV was saturated, there were so many programmes. For new people, it was hard to become someone, so the best way to get noticed was either to show you could argue with people and create dramas, or be in a relationship with someone. Everyone in French reality TV is going out with everyone. Most of the time the relationship is fake, but it doesn't matter as long as the media and the public are talking about you, that is what matters. I have nothing against people who wanted to act like that to get famous and wealthy, but it wasn't what I wanted to do myself. It was against my beliefs. I didn't want to risk my self-esteem, mental health and dignity for peanuts. Maybe if I played the part, I would end up earning much more. But I simply didn't want to risk it, it wasn't me. I was so disappointed, but I didn't let any emotions show. Production had no idea that I wasn't going to give them what they wanted…

The day arrived; we met the boys. I was petrified of meeting them. This time we were meeting guys that had been doing TV for a long time, and we were… well, no one. I was sceptical about meeting them and finding myself in an awkward position if they were acting arrogant. And I wasn't wrong. We all met by the pool of a hotel; everything was staged, obviously, with the boys already sitting on sofas. We had to wait for ten minutes in the corner until everyone was set. Before doing reality TV I actually thought everything was done in the moment, I was so naive. But most of the scenes are set. It is not like you arrive and your date is magically sitting there with Champagne. Everything is orchestrated by production, and the waiting time is always really long. Sometimes scenes are shot multiple times if they didn't catch what you said properly. For something that is called reality TV, it wasn't so real to me any more. It felt more like filming a bad soap opera.

The crucial time was finally there. As we were walking towards the boys, I was so stressed and anxious that I felt sick. But I had to be really strong and put on my biggest smile and bravest face. I didn't want them to think that I was scared. I don't know why, but I could feel someone would throw back at me that it was my second show playing the single girl coming to seduce men.

When we finally saw the boys and said Hi to them, we all sat down. Within two minutes someone asked me if I was Lola from that other show, as if it was already planned for that question to be asked. Of course it was; production had probably briefed them before meeting with us. I didn't even have time to catch my breath and calm myself: I was already in the boxing ring, ready to fight. I started to explain to all these people I didn't know and in front of the entire production crew that I wasn't just about that, and I was more than a seductress. But one of the guys, famous for being a serial cheater and an asshole, cut me while I was talking and asked me if it was my "thing" to seduce guys for fun. As soon as he said those words, I knew that I wasn't going to stay. I'd ask to go home. Why on earth would I stay with such ignorant and mean people? What a fucking idiot! Who was he to give me a lesson? He was always cheating publicly on his girlfriend, so how come he had the audacity to try and make me feel bad about myself? He was so arrogant and rude. Technically I wasn't doing anything wrong, was I? But in this world, men love to blame women. A lot of guys take on a role of seducing women, but for them it's fine. They're never judged for it, so why was I being attacked for the same thing? I couldn't even respond to this idiot; meanwhile someone else cut in to talk about something else. Production probably had what they wanted out of the confrontation, and wanted to move on to something else. The thing is, no one had anything else to say, we were all sitting in silence, it was so awkward. I thought why am I here, wasting my time with people whose brain is the size of a pea head. Everything was so fake and meaningless. I'm not saying that I'm the deepest or most intelligent person, but I knew that I had more to offer mentally than them.

Next thing you know, production is asking us to wear our bikinis to go and swim with the boys. What a surprise, to show us in our bikinis to attract them. I have no issues with nudity at all. I love my body, and I think women's curves are amazing, but it was just this whole atmosphere that I didn't like. As previously, I reckoned our role was close to prostitution, but that also applied to the boys. They also knew that if they didn't have any love stories to show, they wouldn't be on camera. In every single show you can see them trying to pair up with a girl just for the sake of lasting in the show. They then end up cheating on them and breaking up with them after five minutes. It was so pathetic. They were acting as "prostitutes" as much as the girls. To me they were "selling" themselves.

While everyone was pretending to enjoy their time in the water, I stayed by myself on one of the pool chairs, hypnotised by the chaos in front of me. I wasn't talking or moving. I was what I call an accessory. You know the sort of girl who is pretty but can't hold a conversation and just sits there and brings nothing to the table. Well, that was me. A real nonentity. At some point one of the guys came up to me and tried to chat to me, flirt with me. Then all the other boys started to shout to him to be careful, that he was playing with fire and that maybe I should come to the villa to meet his girlfriend. What the fuck? What were they trying to do? All they wanted was for me to come up to the villa and stay with them for a bit so they could tell his girlfriend that he'd flirted with me. And then she would probably get angry at me, and get an argument on camera. But I didn't want to do that. Technically I didn't do anything. He came to flirt with me, not me to him, so why would I pretend to like him and argue with his girlfriend? For fun? For the sake of the show? No way, I wasn't going to give everyone that satisfaction.

Production then cut short these uninteresting moments of us all pretending to bond and have fun, and asked us to go and get ready for the evening. We girls had one room only and one bathroom to get ready in, with only two towels and no lights. That was a complete joke. We couldn't see anything; they expected us to look the part, but didn't give us any time or space to get ready. Obviously this wasn't being filmed. On top of that, we were starving; we hadn't eaten since noon. All they'd given us was alcohol to loosen up. I'd got ready the best I could, but I knew there was no point in me doing so. Once I was ready, I went to someone from production and asked them if I could go home. They asked me why, and tried everything to make me stay. Of course they still needed me to argue with that guy's girlfriend, but I didnt want to be a puppet any more, fuck that. I had to get my dignity back and stop this whole masquerade. I'd had enough of acting the fool to the king, production's little marionette. I was better than that. Yes, I wanted to be famous. Yes, I wanted to be wealthy. Yes, I wanted to get recognised. But not at any cost; and mainly I wanted to stay true to myself, and reality TV wasn't matching with my beliefs and personality any more. I realised that I'd changed, I'd grown up, and the sort of programmes that were out there weren't for me any more. My real goal was to be a performer, to sing and dance, and if that was what I wanted to do, I had to work for it and stop trying to think I could do it the easy way by being part of the reality TV world.

They obviously couldn't keep me against my will. They just asked me to keep filming for the weekend, and then I could leave. I was still annoyed that I had to spend time with those idiots, but extremely relieved to know that I'd soon be on my way back to London, where I truly belonged. That was my last experience with reality TV. I promised myself not to try to be part of any show that did not suit my personality. I am not denigrating reality TV and putting every single show in the same bag; I am only discussing my own experience with the shows that I did. Not every production is the same, not every programme is about the same thing. Reality TV can be a very good platform for some people and very beneficial. Unfortunately for me it doesn't match with the way I see life. I am still a big fan of reality TV shows such as *Keeping up with the Kardashians*, but I simply cannot watch French reality TV any more. I think the process in France is very manipulative and malicious, the competition is too high and it can make people do weird things, hoping they will get famous and then regret it later.

As with any experience, good or bad, you always need to look on the bright side. It didn't work out for me, but reality TV brought some good things into my life and did actually change my life, not in the way that I imagined it at all, but it did change my life drastically. The experience brought me confidence and opened my eyes to what I was really meant to be on this planet: a performer. I realised that I was extremely comfortable in front of the camera and I was enjoying playing a "role". I just had to take this experience to the next level, onto the stage, not onto the set of a half-real half-fake

TV programme. I finally had the courage to admit that this is what I wanted to be, and not let my fear control me.

I could have taken singing and dancing lessons a long time ago, but I always found excuses not to. The real reason why I never did it was my fear. I was my own blockage. The only person that can stop you from doing something is YOU, no one else. For many years I'd feared being judged for wanting to be a performer. I feared failing, of course, so I did what many people do: I chose a path that wasn't mine, but a path that was easy and common so that I wouldn't risk anything. But now, because of reality TV and many life lessons, I broke my circle. I quit my job and I did what I had to do to understand my life journey. I wasn't afraid any more, and I was more determined than ever. This entire summer became a learning process. I read a lot about the Law of Attraction, about gratitude and having a better, more meaningful life. I learned, I visualised, I took time for myself. Everything was clearer and made much more sense.

You see sometimes that you think you want something, and that thing will be the key to your success. Then when it doesn't work out, you wonder why? If your heart is not fully committed to something, and you don't believe in it, then how can it work? How can you feel good about it and have a good outcome? That is what I understood: living in France and doing reality TV didn't make me feel good and happy. It wasn't a positive and productive environment for my personality, so it was obvious that I wouldn't succeed. I was still grateful for all the life lessons it had taught me, though.

I was really excited to leave Miami, stop doing reality TV, and finally determined to have the life that I'd always wanted and concentrate on what truly mattered. It then hit me. The idea didn't come out of nowhere, it had always been at the back of my mind for a very long time. But just as with taking singing lessons, the idea of doing this job petrified me. However, now I was fearless and confident, so nothing could stop me. I played back the movie of my own life in my head: my childhood, wanting to be a cabaret dancer, the stage, the spotlights, the crowd, the men desiring women, costumes, glitter, luxury, all my past boyfriends breaking my heart, all the people putting me down, those hard jobs I did, working long hours for an insignificant salary, all those years of hard work, reality TV and actually feeling like an underpaid prostitute. Clearly I had done it all, gone through everything. It was time to take action and not care about what others were thinking. I would listen to me, to my head, and do my best to get where I wanted without any fears. I would take singing classes, commercial dance classes and live a life full of abundance. And for that I needed a flexible job that would give me the time and the money to do everything that I wanted. I was ready to become a stripper..

NINE

The Club, the Girls, the Money, the Clients

> *Once you've been naked in a room full of people, nothing scares you. I am not saying everyone should become a stripper, but forcing yourself to do something terrifying can change your life. You realise you can do anything.*
>
> Jodie Marsh

Once I was back in London, I didn't waste any time. I researched the top strip clubs in the West End and found a few clubs where I could work. I wrote them down and checked when it was possible to audition. On Wednesday 2 October 2019 around 9 p.m., I made my way to the first club that was on the top of my list. I buzzed the backdoor and security let me in, checked my bag and showed me the way downstairs to the audition.

I was pleasantly surprised by the club. It was very dark with a beautiful lighting setting, naked women status, a crystal chandelier and deep red velvet chairs and sofas. Nothing was creepy like you see on TV or like you imagine. Even the girls were all looking very sexy, but classy. No one was walking around just in underwear. No, all the girls were wearing cocktail dresses, their hair and make-up were perfectly done. None of them looked unhealthy or trashy. I was understanding why the club was known as a gentlemen's club and not a strip club.

I headed downstairs, feeling a bit shy, and waited for someone to turn up and explain how the audition was being held. Two other girls were already waiting downstairs: one of them was really young, and the other seemed much older but very confident and relaxed. After waiting for ten minutes, a very nice, beautiful lady around her early forties came over and explained to us that we would go on stage one by one; we had to remove our dresses straight away, but keep our panties on and dance. I was the first one to be called on stage. I was mortified. The lady that just spoke to us was named Jackie; she sat right in front of the stage with a guy who I was sure was the manager of the club, called Leo.

The music started playing. I removed my dress straight away. I have to say, the way I removed it wasn't sexy at all! I was feeling clumsy and shaky, but once I was half naked, I made sure to look fearless and confident. I remembered all those music videos of girls dancing, and tried to reproduce the same. Luckily we didn't need to know how to pole dance, they weren't interested in that, they just wanted beautiful girls who presented well and could move on stage. After less than two minutes, Leo made a sign to me saying "done". His face was so serious, I couldn't see any emotion on his face, so I wasn't sure if he was happy or not. I really hoped I'd done well. I got off the stage to let the other girls perform.

Once all the auditions were done, Jackie called us one by

one to tell us if we were successful or not. Jackie called me first. I sat down next to her and she smiled at me to say I was successful. I screamed with happiness. I don't think I have ever been so happy to start a new job. Jackie explained how the club worked, her voice really soft and sweet. Her face was kind and charming; I felt really good around her, she seemed very maternal. After a brief chat I agreed with Jackie to start working on the next Friday, 4 October 2019.

I couldn't believe that I was officially a stripper! What was my life about? From au pair to sales assistant, to hospitality, to Executive Assistant, to reality TV, to stripping in London. My job line made no sense! It did feel good, though. I was going to experience this new adventure, feeling so happy. I looked around one more time and I already felt at home: the stage, the big curtain, all those spotlights, the loud music, I sensed this was somewhere I could belong.

Friday 4 October, my first official night working as a stripper. I felt stressed and anxious. Was I actually going to do this? What would my parents think if they found out? Or people from TV? So many questions ran through my head, filling my final two minutes. Now that I was there, I had nothing to lose and I needed the money. So I stopped worrying and walked inside the club. I met with the main house mum, Nina. She was a lovely woman, very maternal. To be honest, she carried her job title to perfection. Like so many people at the club, she'd been working there for a long time – around twenty years! She introduced herself and started to explain all the rules of the club:

- £20 house fees every time we came to work
- We had to work a minimum of three nights per week

- The club took 50% of everything we earned, even tips
- We had to wear a cocktail dress every night
- No grinding on clients
- No touching when dancing naked
- No bending over while dancing naked
- Not allowed to pretend to masturbate while dancing
- No kissing with clients
- No touching with other girls
- Not allowed to leave the club with a client
- Not allowed to exchange numbers with a client

I was surprised by so many strict rules. Was I working in a strip club or a church? But in a way that was very reassuring, I felt safe knowing that no clients could touch us. Most men in regular night clubs are much more touchy feely than in a strip club. Which is why I couldn't see any wrong in doing this job. It was so safe and clean, why feel bad about it? One thing I wasn't happy about though was the 50%! But I guess this is the price to be paid for working in a luxury gentlemen's club. After listening to all the rules, signing my contract and getting changed, I went back upstairs to the floor.

All the girls were staring at me, of course: one attractive new girl. Obviously the girls would be curious! Half the girls were East European, the other half British. I sat at a table by the bar to observe the atmosphere a bit and take everything in. As a stripper, obviously you have to dance, but what you need to be really good at is hosting! You are simply a pretty hostess in lingerie. So at first I had a bit of a hard time going to talk to complete strangers, getting to know them and getting to the point: going to a VIP room for as long as possible.

Here is the price list Jackie reminded us of when we got on the floor: one song: £25; 15 mins: £100; 30 mins: £200; 1 hour: £400.

By the way, one thing I totally forgot to mention: my name, I mean my stage name. Yes, when a stripper is giving you "her name", it is never real. I decided to be called Satine, as in my favourite movie, *Moulin Rouge*.

Back to my first night at work. After I'd been less than twenty minutes sitting by the bar, the manager Leo asked me to follow him. He mentioned that a really good regular was here having dinner and he wanted me to join his table with a few other girls. I didn't think twice and joined him and his friends at his table. Three other girls were there already. All we had to do was chat, flirt, have a laugh, nothing more than being at a regular club or on a date, to be honest. We actually had a good time with them. After about fifteen minutes, they decided it was time to have a real party. I was confused, I didn't really know what to do, what was the process? Did we have to tell them the price? Did we have to pick a guy? Did they know how it worked? I was so lost so I just followed everyone. They seemed to know where they were going. We walked down the stairs, past the stage and into a huge private VIP room, the "Glitter Room". The room was a really big VIP area with four little private booths inside the area where you could also do pole dancing.

Once we were all in the room, the cash lady came over to give us our "Angel Money". Let me explain, "Angel Money" could be compared to Monopoly money. When a client pays for your time, he obviously pays with real cash or a credit card, and in return the dancers get "Angel Money" which at the end of the night is put into an envelope with your name on it. The next time you work, you get back your envelope with real money in it.

That night I sat down for two hours with this group, which guaranteed me £400 at least! I was over the moon! The first night ever, the first hour of work, and already making money without even trying. Trust me, it felt amazing! At first I wasn't sure what to do. Should I dance straight away? Should I sit down? Should we go with a guy each? I was a bit lost, to be honest, but quickly things felt natural. I sat with one of the main client's friends, Valente.

Valente was this cute, not very tall man, half French half Norwegian, with mid-long curly blond hair, 40 years old and extremely charming and funny. I chatted with him for about ten minutes, and then decided it was time to dance. My first private dance ever, I couldn't believe it. Deep inside, I was laughing. I started to dance in front of him with my dress on, then slowly removed my dress, bra and then G-string. Within ten minutes I was totally naked. I loved it. I had no issues with being naked. But it was not just about being naked, it was also about teasing Valente. I was dancing close, but not too close; showing the front of my body, then the back; moving slowly like a snake, looking him deep in the eyes, biting my lips. It was like pretending to have sex. I could see how much Valente was enjoying my company, and it felt so empowering to see what dominance I had over him. All these new feelings and environment were very exciting. I was so happy, feeling sexy and sexual, that it turned me on too. Believe me, dancing for a total stranger who is cute, has money and is not able to do anything about it is the best foreplay ever.

I was starting to understand why men came to a stripclub. You just get that rush, that adrenaline of being turned on, but without being able to go all the way. It feels as if you are playing with fire. Also, I believe most men who come to stripclubs need to escape their everyday life. It is some sort of get away for them, a new fantasy to feel free and wild for the night without any stress and responsibilities. Most of the clients are rich, powerful and obviously married, which I guess can be stressful. A famous series on television once said, "Strippers are the angels sent from heaven on earth." I actually started to believe that for those men we were their little angels, we were the perfect fantasy to release their tensions and help them dream away for a few hours.

For two hours we chatted, laughed, danced, flirted and even ate: yes, our club provided great food and snacks for clients. Obviously they weren't cheap, so they always offer you something to eat if you're hungry. I then thanked Valente and his rich friends, hugged them and wished them a good night. For a first sit-down I was beyond happy. I wished every night could be like that! Who wouldn't like to be paid £400 an hour to party?

Right after, I was called on stage for the first time. I was actually more nervous to dance in front of so many strangers. I put on my poker face, my sexy eyes and my sass. The DJ started to play "Ride it" by Dj Regard. It was the first time I'd heard the song, but I felt possessed by it and started dancing. The music was taking me to my core. I was feeling alone in my own world, feeling the pull of the song. It made me so happy and sexy feeling that I imagined I was making love to the pole. I guess I was doing a good job, as all the clients eyes' were on me as they clapped.

Two gentlemen were sitting right in front of me. One of them didn't stop looking at me for a second. We made eye contact, and I knew straight away that as soon as I got off the stage, he would try to talk to me. When you are on stage you have to dance for three songs:

- Song 1: dress on
- Song 2: bra off
- Song 3: G-string only.

After my three songs I got off the stage, and what I expected happened: the gentleman that was sitting right in front of me approached me, introduced himself and asked me to spend some time with him in private. We started with one dance only, but ended up doing thirty minutes. For my first night I was doing really well.

I barely danced. He just wanted to talk, spend some time with a beautiful girl, have a laugh. With time I understood that what most men wanted was to spend time with the stripper they chose. Most of the clients don't really care about seeing the girl they pick naked. If the client really likes the girl and takes her for a long sit down without asking her to remove her clothes, that's when you know they are falling for that stripper. We came back on the floor after our sit down in private and joined his friend who was still sitting right in front of the stage. His eyes were hypnotised by the dancer who was performing at that moment on stage. She was the complete opposite of me: big fake boobs, blonde, fake lips, very skinny with tiny legs and no hips.

My client sat next to his friend, and so did I. I didn't want to go back straight away on the floor, so I chilled with them for a bit. My client's friend was so turned on by that girl that I could see drool coming from his mouth so I asked him:

"Are you enjoying the view?"

"Yes, I love big fake boobs."

"Thank God you didn't take me to a private booth then; you would have been bored with me and my small boobs!"

We all laughed. I thanked my client again, gave him a kiss on the cheek and left. From then on I was pulled out from everywhere to give clients single dances. Back then I wasn't negotiating anything, I was just doing what the client wanted. If they wanted a single dance, that what I was did. I wasn't trying to spend more time or anything. I was still an innocent and naive stripper. I was happy to be so popular and busy on my first night.

I was in my happy bubble when suddenly Mr "I like Big Boobs" came looking for me. Surprisingly, he wanted me to dance for him. I was a bit shocked, but oh well, I wasn't going to refuse... I took him to a private booth, sat him down and started my show. The way I dance could be described as like a snake: I moved very slowly around him as if he was my prey. I was making sure he was feeling the tension to its maximum. Looking deep into his eyes, I was close enough to him so he could smell my perfume, see the shape of my body without really seeing every detail. I was making a circle with my waist, like waves moving, as if I was grinding on him. The red lights inside the private booth made anyone look good, to be honest. It was the perfect way to hide any imperfection.

I could feel how turned on he was. He kept moving in his seat. He couldn't sit still. His hands were naturally coming towards me as if he wanted to touch, but I was putting them down on the sofa straight away, and telling him he was a naughty boy for trying. At some point I could see his boner. I wanted to laugh, but I didn't think it was appropriate. I didn't want him to think I was mocking him, but deep inside I found it funny. But I also felt powerful to know that I could have such an effect on a man without even kissing him or touching him. Once the dance was finished, he thanked me and left with the biggest smile on his face. In a way, I was making those men happy; and it actually made me happy too.

Not even ten minutes later I bumped into Mr "I like Big Boobs" again with another dancer. She was probably trying to get time with him, but he didn't seem interested. As soon as he saw me, he moved her aside and walked towards me. He then asked if we could go to the private booth again for another dance. I said, "For someone that doesn't like small boobs, I guess I'm doing something right here."

We went back to the same booth, and I started dancing again. But this time he couldn't shut up. He kept saying every second, "Oh, Satine!" as if we were having sex, then saying he was ready for me; and to keep going. I was laughing so much inside, he looked possessed and obsessed by me. Men are so weak, I swear. Throw them a pair of boobs, a pretty face, and here they are offering you the world. At the end, he asked for my number, the first of many who would ask while I was working at the club. Even if you're not allowed, I used to give my number to some of them, when I felt they were nice or when I thought I could get something out of them.

That night I left with £600 for myself. Congratulations, Satine, on your first very lucrative night.

~

After a few weeks working at the club, I still felt very happy. I was actually having a lot of fun. For the first time I was surrounded by girls who were on the same page as me in a workplace. In my previous jobs I never liked hanging out with girls, always felt the hate, the jealousy, because I was speaking my mind, being straightforward, dressing up well and sexily. It would attract a lot of arguments. Obviously not every single girl at the club was my friend: half of them would probably never speak to me and feel competitive when a client was around. But apart from that, everyone minds their own business. With most of the girls I was getting along; I didn't feel any hate or jealousy; they were similar to me, girls with dreams and goals, sassy and sexy, but very kind, deep at heart. You see what really annoys me in our society: that in 2019 we are still judging someone by their clothes or jobs. I do not drink or take drugs, I work out, I meditate, donate to charity, but still I will be classified as a "bad girl" because I speak my mind and dress up sexily; and most obviously because I'm a stripper. On the other hand, you could have a girl who doesn't wear make-up, dresses like a grandmother but drinks at the pub every night, smokes like a chimney, sleeps with the entire company, but still she won't be classified as a slut or bad girl. That doesn't make her a bad person either, but just because of a job or an outfit, people will quickly pick on who to classify as "not respectable". WHY?

It did feel good to be surrounded by the same sort of girls as me. As we were all in the same shit together, trying to hustle, make money for whatever plans or dreams we had, a few of us became really close. I especially became friends with one of the girls, Jasmine. Jasmine was the only Asian/Indian girl in the club. She had beautiful full lips, a narrow nose, Asian almond-shaped eyes and very dark straight hair. She was much younger than me and was acting as such, not very mature sometimes, so I felt that I had to take her under my wing and act like the big sister. We had such a good laugh together though; we were hustling together and being a very good team to get those men's money.

One night we were working together, and I swear that I never laughed so much. There is a moment in life when you think life is worth it. Jasmine had her period that night, and a little fact for you about strippers on their period: it's never pleasant, you feel heavy, gross and always scared that a red sea will dribble down your legs while you're on stage. You have no choice but either to wear a tampon, or some girls wear those sponges, cup things which I am not familiar with.

If you do wear a tampon, you have to cut the string really low so it doesn't pop out of your underwear while dancing. We then put the rest of the string between our vagina lips. Very glam, isn't it?

Jasmine had a tampon that night, which she had to change at some point, so she asked me to come to the bathroom with her and wait until she got changed. You know, girls always go to the bathroom together, for what reason I'm not sure, but that's what we do. She went to one of the cubicles and within two minutes I heard her screaming "Satine!! I can't grab my tampon. I cut the string too short! Im stuck!"

I offered to grab a mirror for her so she could have a look at what was happening down there, but she didn't want to! She wanted me to help! What the actual fuck did she want me to do? Remove the tampon for her? Yes, that's what she wanted! I didn't think twice, I washed my hands and went to her cubicle to see what I could do. I wasn't going to let this girl struggle for hours. Here I was, on my knees, my back facing the door, while Jasmine was standing with one of her legs up, full vagina in my face. I had to ask her to open her lips so I could see where the hell was her tampon, but we were both laughing so much that it was impossible for me to concentrate and do anything! I was laughing so much that I almost peed myself. So we swapped places, I ended up sitting on the toilet pissing, and she was standing in front of me, one leg up again. We were still laughing like two idiots, but I couldn't stay in there forever. As you know, time is money, so for a few moments I concentrated and managed to get her tampon out! If you think about it, it is really gross to remove someone's tampon. But when you're in this world, you all become more like a family; you help each other, support each other and hustle together. I will never forget that time. I wish you could all laugh as much as we did, but I don't wish you to have to remove someone else's tampon!

As a hustler you become obsessed with money, though, which is good as you are always trying your best to get more. But you realise that everything is about money, and you truly understand the expression "time is money". I didn't even want to bother to meet regular guys outside; I was not a big fan of dating, as I always found dates awkward and a waste of my time. But now that I was a stripper, why would I go out and spend my time without getting any money? As a stripper, you are constantly talking, laughing, putting on your best smile and faking being interested in the guys in front of you. Clearly strippers are actresses; I am an actress, every night I play at being Satine. She was this ultimate fantasy: charming, funny, light but not stupid, naturally beautiful and mysterious. I think that what my clients really liked about Satine was the fact that she had no filter. I just say what is going through my head, even though sometimes it is not politically correct. It always making them laugh a lot. I have a lot of conversation to hand, due to my life experiences, so I can speak about many subjects. Plus I am a good actress, so they really felt that I was genuine with them, and that was what they needed. I mean, I was kind of genuine with them, not all the time, but most of the time. But it was very draining to play Satine, believe it or not; talking to multiple strangers every night, looking your best and being the best is very tiring. And then you start thinking, overthinking about every single aspect of your life.

The first thing that hit me hard in the face is how men… well, are men. We always know as women that men are hunters, and always tempted to flirt or cheat with another woman. But somehow I always hoped that some men would be different. As a stripper, I faced the truth every night, and it felt like a big slap in the face. Poor, rich, educated, non-educated, good-looking or not good-looking, men are men and will always try to seduce and prove to themselves that their charms are still working. I guess it's an ego thing. I also realised how pervert and fucked up they can be, especially when they have power and money. The more money, the more fucked up.

One of my clients told me once that the more money you have, the more you do with your life, the more you experience, the less adrenaline you get as you get less impressed and less satisfied by what life has to offer. You get a new norm or a norm that is not on the same level as someone with a regular life. Which is why most of them are on drugs all the time: it helps them to keep going, keep that buzz. This small adrenaline that makes them happy is obviously an artificial and short-term adrenaline, but it does the job for some of them. On top of that, they have this need and desire to be surrounded by beautiful women, multiple women, escorts, strippers, models, young girls ready to do anything to also experience the high life. Those men always need new fantasies to try to reach that new satisfaction and go beyond.

I went to sit down once with a client, and all he wanted was for me to stand, legs apart, arms crossed behind my back, look up and just stand. All he was doing was staring at me looking at him, and he got so excited by it! What a fucking weirdo, all he kept saying was, "I have the power," "I know your legs hurt." If you could have seen my face at that moment: my left eyebrow was raised so high, as if I had the biggest question mark on my face. Another one that had a weird fantasy of feeling powerful and in control, another fucked up man who didn't care about seeing boobs or ass, that wasn't enough: at some point he asked me to open my mouth while standing the way he'd asked me to. I told him to fuck off, that I wasnt getting paid for that and that he could put his power in his ass. He got so shocked that I'd spoken to him that way, he felt lost and apologised to me straight away. I swear that sometimes I had to put them back in their place. No one has power over me unless I choose them to! These are just a few examples of the many weird clients and requests I had while working in the club.

And trust me, it does drain you and make you wonder if love is still a thing, and if I will ever be able to love someone again… It is quite sad, if you think about it, because we all want is money. We all want to live comfortably and get whatever we want. But when I see those men, I wonder if the money is worth it? They are not happy, they are actually sad. Why would you live a life never feeling fulfilled and satisfied? I was a bit like that, though. After living ten years in London, I experienced a lot, went to all the best restaurants in Mayfair and across town, went to many VIP parties, travelled to beautiful cities across the world, slept with guys from different countries and backgrounds, I mean it's not as if I sat on my ass for ten years, but it did become harder and harder for me to feel impressed. Even though money was driving all of us crazy, and my job was really draining and hard mentally, I just couldn't stop. I was addicted to the hustle every night to get cash. The feeling of getting an envelope full of cash every night was so satisfying. With this cash I could live my London life without worrying. I was able finally to pay for all my activities, beauty treatments, clothes and invest in my goals. As well as getting money and living the life I'd always wanted, I was meeting really interesting people, key people to my journey, who I thought would help change my life…

TEN

It's Raining Men

> *A man is not a necessity, a man is a luxury, like dessert.*
>
> Cher

As a normal healthy human being I still needed affection, real affection, even more now I am a stripper. I was spending my nights making men feel good. I needed someone to look after me. At the end of the day, even if I had a hard time, I had to admit I wanted someone to love me for who I am, and truly care for me, even though it wasn't the right time at all to be in a relationship. So here I am, night after night, feeling more and more needy and craving for sex. But even though I love sex, getting older didn't make things easy in bed for me. I know what I like, what I want, and I didn't want to waste my time with bad sex. I am the sort of person who needs some sort of connection, and with my personality it became harder and harder to find someone

I was really attracted to. So I could spend months without having sex. At least I could masturbate. I obviously had a few boys that I liked and talked to, I'm not saying that I was a nun and ready to say goodbye to men and sex and promise chastity.

The first one I'm going to tell you about is Teddy. I met Teddy at the club, and at first I didn't know who he was. I remember I just saw this really tall, blond sexy Scottish guy in a suit. I thought he was a client. "Damn, I'd dance for him for free." Later on I found out he was just part of the security team. As soon as we saw each other, we couldn't stop making eye contact; and everytime I walked past him, I could feel this crazy tension between us. One night Jackie, my house mum, came over and asked me if I had a boyfriend. She then asked me if I liked Teddy. That made me laugh. How old was he to send someone else for him? I found out he was twenty-two years old! For real, I wasn't going to waste my time with a baby boy, even though I couldn't hide and control my attraction for him. Weirdly that same night I couldn't get an Uber home, which forced me to ask reception to book me a taxi. The lady at reception wasn't there, but Teddy was, so I asked him for a taxi home. But they were taking cash only, and that night I didn't have any on me, which was really annoying. Teddy could see that I was annoyed, so he kindly offered to pay for it. I knew that was his way of saying "I like you." I was beyond happy, my charms were working. This was the beginning of my little story with Teddy…

The second man who was in my head, or shall I say "still" in my head, was Sebastian. Ever since that night we spent together in August, I kept thinking about him constantly. We only saw each other once after that: he invited me to one of his launch parties the day after my audition at the club. I was so excited to be finally seeing him again; I was really hoping for some chat, something more than the last time, but the place was crowded and he was busy entertaining everyone. As I left the party, I received a call from him asking me to join him in his hotel. Even though I felt a bit like a booty call, I didn't really care, I wanted to spend time with him. As I was nearly at his hotel, Sebastian called me back with some nonsense bullshit: apparently a girl had his jacket, he was pretty drunk and I couldn't understand anything; all I knew was that I couldn't join him. I knew he had another girl probably waiting for him already. He kept texting me how sorry he was, even the following day, which I appreciated, but this is when I put an end to Sebastian in my heart and my head. If I was going to let myself like him even more, I would end up hurt; he had no time for a relationship, and neither did I. It was better to just forget about him…

Then I met Sean, a regular client at the club. I met him on my first Monday night at work. Mondays were so dead, no one wanted to work then. I remember experiencing something so surreal that night. On my first night of work I'd been so busy that I didn't stop dancing, so I had no idea what a quiet night would be like. As soon as a client or a group walks in, as soon as he or they have their drinks, the girls are allowed to go over, talk and obviously try to get private time. Imagine twenty, forty, fifty girls rushing to one group or guy to try their chances: it was a human wave! The first time I saw the girls doing this, I thought a really important client must have walked in; but no, the girls were just desperate to make money, and be sure they were on the front line. You have two types of client when this happens: the one who gets scared, which I can understand, so he ends up not talking or else just leaving; then the one who gets arrogant, thinking all the girls are interested in him, whereas the only reason the girls are on your case is for your wallet and not for your "amazing" personality and looks, honey.

So that Monday night, Sean walked in and went downstairs. All the girls stood up and followed him, so I did too. He sat down by the stage downstairs and looked at all of us. I felt as if I was a tomato in the middle of the vegetable aisle at the supermarket, sitting ready to be picked. As soon as he saw me, he asked me to join him. I started to do my usual chat, but he then stopped me straight away, saying that he never paid. Err, cheap, but even though he never paid for dances, that night was so dead that I didn't mind staying and talking to him anyway. We just clicked: we chatted so much, laughed and flirted! Funnily enough, I didn't know who Sean was: apparently he was a famous singer in England. What a coincidence that I was meeting a singer at the time I was trying to be a performer myself. I could feel that the universe was sending me key people for my journey. After a few hours of talking, we realised we knew people in common; and one of them was Sebastian! What the fuck! I was intending to go on a date with Sean and talk about the world of performance, to see where things might go, but I couldn't sleep with two friends, could I? I still took Sean's number so we could arrange a date – which we never had time to do, because something else bigger and better than a regular date was planned for us… I mean, that's what I thought.

And then I met Alfonso, who I would classify as my first sugar daddy, I guess. Monday 4 November was as usual a quiet night at work, like every Monday, but a slow night doesn't mean a non-lucrative night. I realised that the nights when I make the most cash are the quiet nights like Mondays or Wednesdays, because wealthy clients are making deals during the week and come to the club to celebrate on Fridays and Saturdays. That's when we also get the cheap clients or tourists, who stay for hours with just one beer, sitting by the stage and perving until closing time without booking any girls in private, not even for one dance. Ewww, we all disliked this sort of client. That Monday, two clients walked in; they sat down straight away at the table by the stage in the restaurant area; they seemed to know the club, probably some regulars that I didn't yet know. They ordered food and didn't even look at the girls; they were very much into their conversation, probably about work.

"And now on stage, Satine… " So here I am on stage, dancing for literally no one, that is the most boring thing; being on stage while there are no clients and just the other girls staring at you. The only two clients there were those two guys eating and talking business. After my three songs I came off stage and went and wash my hands; yes, I think I do probably wash my hands ten times per night. If you think about it, touching that pole that everyone is holding, and being close to all those men when we don't know where they're coming from, is quite disgusting. I didn't want to get sick all the time, so I became even more of a clean freak than I was before. Hands clean, I came back to the bar area and sat at one of the little tables by the stage. None of my girlfriends were there that night, so I was hustling on my own. I mean, there was no one to hustle really, apart from those two guys who were finally talking to one of the girls. It seemed that they knew each other already. I was half looking at them, half day dreaming, when suddenly one of them looked at me and pointed at me. I looked behind me in case he was pointing at someone else, but no, it was definitely me and he made a sign for me to come over.

Great, let's go! I sat down next to the man who'd called me over, Alfonso. He was really tall, broad shoulders, silver hair with blue eyes, a man in his late forties; my type, the daddy-looking type. People never believed me when I told them that I liked older men, with a hairy chest and a belly. They clearly thought that a girl like me would go with the typical young-looking guy. But no, I wasn't into the wax chest, fake tan, baby face sort of guy. I like men, real men! Was I maybe into this type of guy due to my daddy issues? One day another stripper told me that we were attracted to men who looked like our dads. That sounded a bit gross, if you think about it, but human psychology can be fucked up sometimes.

Alfonso was definitely my type. Next to him, I felt so small and innocent. He was the typical New Yorker: Italian from Brooklyn, who came from having nothing to having everything. I love people with success stories like that, people who know what it is to struggle. It's inspiring, and made me hope that one day it would happen to me! We started to talk straight away about the universe, energies, the law of attraction, which is obviously my favourite subject to talk about. Not many people can understand it, or they just think I'm crazy, so it was nice to connect with someone who had the same mentality as me. After a good twenty minutes of talking at their table, we all moved, Alfonso, his friend, the other girl and myself, to the "Glitter room" where we had a sit-down for two hours! Yay! That was the guarantee to have £400 for myself, minimum! Well done, Satine, amazing Monday for you! Alfonso and I talked non-stop for two hours. I even ordered food; I wasn't that hungry, but when I knew a client wasn't a cheap ass, I took as much as I could. The fact that I knew he wouldn't say no made me want to order food. It is the same concept as a Chinese buffet: even when you're not hungry any more, you still go back a few more times, because you feel that somehow it is free. Another human psychology trait that I couldn't explain!

During our sit-down, we didn't even dance, they weren't

interested. I think men that age have seen a lot in life, they don't really get obsessed about seeing boobs and ass, they'd rather have good company and talk. At the end, he asked for my number and asked if we could see each other outside work before he flew back to New York. I was a bit hesitant as I knew the other girl was watching, and I didn't need someone to bitch about me to management and get me fired, so I had to be discreet. Alfonso could see I was a bit hesitant; he knew I wasn't allowed to do that. Out of nowhere he asked me for my bank details, which I didn't know, so he asked me if I had Paypal, which of course I did. I could see him on his phone to the Paypal app. He then asked me discreetly to tell him my phone number, and after less than a minute he looked up at me and said to look at my phone once he was gone and text him back a confirmation to see each other outside. We all hugged goodbye and they left.

I straight away went downstairs to look at my phone. I had a notification from Paypal saying a payment of £500 had been made by Mr Alfonso. What the fuck why? I mean, I was over the moon, but why did he send me money? Then I looked at my text. Alfonso had already messaged me saying that I was really special, he was happy we'd met and he had sent me a little something for the next time we would meet, because if I was taking a night off for him, it was only fair for him to compensate me. I couldn't believe the world I was in: a man paying to see me, how crazy! The only time that had happened to me was with my regular from the bar when I was a hostess, but I mean he was old, so I thought he needed to do that to get girls. But Alfonso was charming and still kind of young; he didn't need to. I discovered that some men love to spoil and provide for the girl they like. Alfonso was the first to treat me like this, but not last…

It was Wednesday 6 November, the day Alfonso and I

finally agreed to meet each other before he flew back to New York. His friend who was there the night we met at the club was also coming along as they had some business deals to talk about, so I asked Alfonso if I could invite a girlfriend, which he of course accepted. I called Jasmine and invited her. She accepted of course! We met them at 9.30 p.m. at a luxury restaurant in Mayfair that I'd suggested. This restaurant was so expensive that I had to get invited if ever I wanted to eat there. The restaurant was beautiful, really heavy on decoration, everything looking expensive and luxurious, the music loud and entertaining. As we walked through the restaurant, we could see that more than half of the room was men, businessmen, and they were all staring at us. I knew what they were thinking: two young girls with older men, must be "gold diggers", "escort girls", but I didn't care. The more you look embarrassed and uncomfortable, the more you look stupid and guilty. Anyway, I wasn't guilty of anything; I was happy to be out with Alfonso. I really liked his vibe and personality.

We sat at the table by the stage area and enjoyed the shows while we were eating. They let us order anything we wanted: Caviar, Truffle, Sushi, Burrata, you name it. It felt so good not to be budgeting and not feeling guilty at ordering something expensive. Alfonso and his friend, named Youssef, were a bit quiet that night, probably stressed because of work. Unfortunately, I realised that dating a rich businessman comes with few downsides, including not always having the attention I wanted. Most businessmen are always preoccupied or constantly on their phone, which is annoying, but is the price you pay to be with someone successful who can offer a luxurious lifestyle. My problem was that I wanted everything: someone with success, money but also there to give me love, affection and deep conversation. This is probably why I was single for so long; no man I met could match all those criteria, so I didn't know if I could ever meet my Mr Right.

After dinner we went to the Box, my favourite nightclub in London. The Box is a private members' club where no phones or cameras are allowed, due to the high-profile clientele and the naughtiness that happens in the club. At 1 a.m. and 2 a.m. the club turns into a cabaret where freaks and sex shows are shown on stage. I loved those shows, so well choreographed and beautifully done. Once again, I felt in my element. We didn't even queue, we just walked straight in and entered the club without any trouble. Alfonso knew everyone, and I loved that sort of treatment! I love to feel special and privileged. We had a table booked for us, ready with Champagne. Lord, this is what I call life! I wanted every day to be like this one! That is what I was meant to live for! A life full of abundance, privilege, fun and money. The boys kept drinking but also going to the bathroom every ten minutes. I wasn't stupid, I knew exactly what they were doing, but I wasn't questioning. As long as no one was forcing me to do anything, I wasn't one to judge on someone else's lifestyle. I had nothing to drink as usual, and Jasmine wasn't a big drinker either, which upset Alfonso a little. They had ordered all this Champagne for nothing.

I could see Alfonso getting a bit upset, so I went to sit on his lap and give him a hug. I think he appreciated it and started to kiss my neck while I was grinding on him. I love flirting and teasing, but my tease didn't seem to work. How come? Usually if I grind on someone, I can feel their boners straight away! Not this time. But after thinking a bit, I remembered how much Alfonso and his friend went to the toilet that night. Can you follow me? Yes, another thing with businessmen… drugs! I wasn't a big fan of them, and especially if I wanted to have sex. I don't understand why men want to take cocaine when they're with a girl. That shit can't make you hard. What is the point? With time and experience I could see the difference between having sex with someone healthy, and someone who drinks and take drugs all the time. Not the same hard one, trust me! And not the same cum! So I was a bit upset by his soft thing, but then when I remembered the £500 in my account, it made me forget about his soft thing straight away. I was on top of the world, I'd had an amazing dinner, had a cheeky dance at my favourite club and on top of that I'd made money! I was loving life. We finally kissed towards the end of the night. At 3 a.m. we decided it was about time to leave. Alfonso gave me £30 for a black cab, we kissed goodbye and we went home like two good girls. I decided to not sleep with him that night, as I felt that if I gave in straight away, he wouldn't bother seeing me again…

I didn't end up alone that night, though. After a month of teasing, arguments and making up with Teddy, the security boy from the club, I finally gave in. It was his birthday, and I decided to live a little and stop over-thinking. I fancied him a lot and I needed sex. As soon as I got home, I texted Teddy to come over. Thirty minutes later he was at mine. I have to admit I was happy to see him and his stupid face. We went upstairs to my room. For this special occasion I wore some sexy lingerie and my silky robe. Even though he sees me naked every night, he still appreciated the effort. We started kissing and touching, and as I told you before, guess what happened? NO HARD ON! And why?? Because this idiot had been taking drugs the whole night! I was so annoyed! I needed to be fucked, fucked hard, not fucked by a semi-hard! I still managed to get him hard, and we finally had sex! To be honest it wasn't all that. Lucky for him to have a massive dick so I could still feel something, but foreplay-wise I gave him just 4/10. You know when those guys promise you the world, telling you how they will go down on you for hours and finger you until you squirt everything you got? Yes, you know that sort of text. Well, I didn't even get half of what he said. He went down for probably two minutes and fingered me with one finger for another minute. Dude, do you really think that is going to build my pleasure? I swear some men are delusional and simply lazy. We still managed to do it twice, and it still felt nice to be close to someone and kiss. He left my house around 6 a.m. and I went to bed feeling pretty content about my night.

ELEVEN

I Will Follow My Dreams

> *If you can dream it, you can do it.*
>
> Walt Disney

After just over a month working at the club, I still found it great, even though autumn school holidays make it hard for us to make money as all the men, especially the rich ones, are away with their family. Sometimes you don't make money at all, not even to cover your house fees at the club. Those nights are hard mentally, because it makes you over-think everything: "Is it worth it?" "Am I actually good at doing this job?" "Is the industry going to survive?" "For how long will I have to do this?" But then comes the night when you make £400, £500, £600 and more, and then you feel on top of the world. It is a constant battle with your brain.

Within a month I had managed to get back on my feet financially. I could finally afford to pay for singing classes, dance classes and all the beauty treatments necessary to keep me young and fresh. As previously mentioned, my main dream and goal was to become a singer, a performer. It might sound vain, but I have something special about me; I'm not talking about looks, it's just something inside me, my soul, that feels the need to express itself artistically. I think I'd heard it enough times from men and women that I started to believe it. What comes back the most is: "You have a beautiful aura, this *je ne sais quoi* about you." I know that I am the sort of person who walks into a room and everyone stops and stares. Even the other strippers would classify me as "not a basic bitch, but a bitch who belongs on the red carpet". Everyone compared me to Catherine Zeta Jones or Audrey Hepburn. Maybe because of my long neck, dark voluminous hair, deep dark brown eyes and high cheekbones? I had no idea, but I wasn't complaining about being compared to those talented and beautiful actresses.

When I was little, I was always performing: either at family gatherings, being silly and making jokes, or dancing. I studied modern jazz and ballet from the age of four for about ten years, until my parents decided to split. Their separation literally broke my heart and made me terribly negative and lazy. I just stopped dancing and believing in any of my dreams. I shut myself away completely. As a child, I was very confident, funny, happy, always entertaining people somehow; but as a teenager, after my parents' separation, I lost all my happiness. I became very shy, very self-conscious, angry, hurt and even suicidal. I didn't feel any love from anyone any more. But I am a fighter, and it took me years to build the confidence and maturity that I now have. With life experiences, *The Secret, The Magic* and the love from my friends, but mainly from learning to love myself, I managed to feel good about myself. But stripping was the biggest confidence boost for me; making me so confident that I was finally ready, mentally and financially, to pursue my dreams. Even though, let's face it, being a stripper is really draining mentally and physically, most of the time I just wanted to rest my brain and body. But I really had to kick my ass twice as hard to go out and get what I wanted. I couldn't afford to be lazy, I had no excuses any more, I had the time, the money, the confidence to be who I wanted to be and invest in myself. Being a stripper was helping me with my confidence, and surprisingly also helping with my singing and dancing. Every night I got amazing compliments, which boosted my self-esteem, but what also helped was talking to strangers every night, so I did not have time to be shy or care about what they were thinking. I was putting on my best act and that was working; I was performing.

What I was also really enjoying about working in a strip-club was that I was meeting a lot of interesting people, either clients or dancers. I know that the most common cliché about strippers is that "strippers are cockheads", "sluts", "easy girls", "trashy", "always drunk" – but not at all. Of course you have few of those, but I mean in any jobs or any social circle you have this type of woman and man, right? But because we have our tits out, we get more judgements. But to be honest, more than half of the clubs employed really respectable girls who just needed to earn some cash quickly and easily while studying, trying to clear their debts, actresses, models who needed to finance their lives while waiting for a big contract. I liked being surrounded by the same type of person as me: girls who were pursuing their dreams and were hustling for it, and being surrounded by people with similar interests to mine was a really good motivation for my success.

One of the girls that I was very close to was Amber, who was pursuing TV presenting. Just like me she was a Taurus and very much into the Universe, the law of attraction, and believed in the benefit of living a positive life. She was so generous with her contacts from the music industry. I was very grateful to have someone so similar to me in my circle of friends, but getting tips and contacts wasn't enough for me. I wanted to be out there, I had to do more than the odd photo shoot here and there.

Then, something really strange happened out of nowhere. A few months before I'd started to work at the club, around the month of August, I'd been going through all the social media of the big influencers: reality TV celebs and singers in the UK, to see who was looking after them in terms of management. After a little research, I decided to message some management companies. I probably messaged about fifty of them. I was just trying everything to get noticed by someone. I was done with the French market, so I was determined to try my luck one more time in England. Even though I tried everything and messaged so many agencies, none of them responded to me. What I didn't expect was that the universe would give me a response to my messages. It brought the response to me..

One random night at the club, a really tall guy in his early fifties walked in. He was clearly a regular, shaking everyone's hand, talking to all the girls. I didn't know who he was; his face was so familiar, but I wasn't sure from where. My gut instinct told me to go downstairs to the changing room and check my phone. As I was scrolling through my direct messages on my social media, one message caught my eye. I opened it: it was one of the messages I'd sent to a celebrity agent; the agent had never responded to me, but there he was, it was him, upstairs on the floor! How crazy! Due to his big following, he'd obviously never seen my message, but there he was in front of me! That was so much better than a response via messaging. I'm telling you, everything happens for a reason. I went back upstairs and didn't hesitate twice about going over to him and introducing myself; and he did the same.

"Hello, beautiful lady. I'm Charlie, very nice to meet you."

"Lovely to meet you too."

Pretending I didn't know who he was! Charlie was known to be a predator for the new girls. He loves women, but never pays for dances. Clearly the sort of regular we didn't like, but I didn't care as I was on a mission. Becoming his friend, being as close to him as possible, and trying to get something out of him was my new goal. Yes, I am definitely an opportunist. We started to have the usual chat that I have with every client: "Where are you from?" "How old are you?" "What brings you here?" He then asked me the same questions in return. I explained that I'd participated in TV shows in France, which didn't work out for me, so he naturally mentioned his job as an agent. When he did, I acted as surprised as possible, pretending I didn't already know his job title. A few minutes later, I put on my best act and started to look at him slightly confused. I said, "I'm not sure where from, but I have this feeling that I've seen you before… Of course! I messaged you months ago on your social media, but you never saw my message."

He then looked at his phone, shocked by what I'd just told him, and went through his messages to find mine. He read my message, congratulated me for my well-spoken English and apologised for not seeing the message earlier. We then started to follow each other on our respective social media, and he told me that I had the look and personality to be on stage. He would definitely hook me up if anything good was coming up! I was so happy, I felt that I was getting somewhere. It was a small step, but one step closer to my dreams. But once again I was to be disappointed…

TWELVE

The Tricks and the Fake Millionaire

> *Never perform card tricks for the people you play poker with.*
>
> Anonymous

It was 16 November 2019, time was flying by at the club, and I was now making more money than ever. When I started to understand the tricks of the trade and the Dos and Don'ts of approaching clients at the club, I made better money and it was way easier than when I'd started. I had a better approach, better conversation, I was becoming a master at manipulating their mind to spend more and more time with me, and so more money. I was already good at this before being a stripper anyway. I knew how to trick men to get what I wanted from them… gifts, money, trips, but now I was becoming a professional. A good thing I was doing was going to luxury night clubs in

Mayfair, having fun and studying the crowd, seeing who could be a potential client for the club. I would go out with Amber and Jasmine. My London club promoter, G.O., would put us on a VIPs only table, telling us who were good clients, meaning who had money, and then we would take it from there: have a chat, tell them about our jobs and see if they were interested to come and have fun with us at the club some time.

One night G.O. introduced me to this really tall dark guy, called Nathaniel. We said hello to each other and talked for a bit. I told him straight away I was a stripper, which didn't bother him at all. It's weird, because usually when I tell people that I strip, they find it really cool and congratulate me. If I was telling people in France, I don't think they'd be that kind and open-minded. Nathaniel and I exchanged numbers and I went back home. Once home, Nathaniel and I kept texting. I really didn't expect to text so much with a potential future client. All I had in my head was to get him to the club so he could spend money on me, but after texting him for a while it wasn't just about that. For once I didn't have to stroke some stranger's ego, he was the one asking all the questions about me, my past, my life, my desires, and that felt really refreshing.

After two days of texting, I managed to get him to come to the club to see me. But I was getting tired of the club taking 50% of the money I was earning. I then had a brilliant idea: I suggested he pay me directly in my account, and then just pay for thirty minutes at the club, but I would obviously spend more time with him. We were both winning: he was spending less and I was earning more. He agreed straight away, we arranged for him to send me £400 to my account, have dinner at the club and then just spend thirty minutes together in one of the VIP booths. I was over the moon. I was making £500 for sure that night, before I even started work.

On top of this amazing arrangement, a friend of mine, or I should say someone I'd once worked with in Belgium, the previous year during an event, messaged me out of nowhere informing me he was coming to London and was looking for great nightclubs and fun. I didn't waste any time, I arranged a VIP table for him at one of G.O.'s clubs, which I knew would pay me a commission, and I also suggested he have more fun after the club and come along to a well-known gentlemen's club... you follow me? Yes, the stripclub. He asked me straight away if it was where I worked, and I said yes. I told him that if he came, that would be his way of paying me a commission, for me to organise everything for him. I thought he was going to tell me to fuck off, but no, he agreed. I couldn't believe it, everything that I was asking for was happening. My energy and vibration must have been at an amazing level. That night was going to be a great night.

At 11 p.m. Nathaniel walked into the club, still very tall, well dressed and charming, but my excitement about him had tailed off a bit. I always do that: I get really excited and passionate about someone, and then a few days later it wears off. Anyway, I still joined him for dinner, we talked about anything and everything, but more about how he became rich, how he was the CEO of a tickets company, how he just bought his £5 million house in Mayfair, and how much he liked me and that my life was about to change. He said that he would invest in my projects, that I wouldn't have to take public transport any more, especially at night time, he would always arrange a chauffeur and treat me like a princess. I was blown away: my life was about to change; finally I was going to have the life I deserved, live somewhere luxurious, have my own businesses, concentrate on my singing lessons and I wouldn't have to strip any more.

I was so happy that life had brought him to me. I didn't really fancy him that much, but after being with many guys that I fancied who still managed to break my heart and leave me with nothing, my mind had changed: I would rather be with someone who could take care of me, even if I didn't fancy them that much. On top of being so excited about my future, he paid for one hour of my time instead of thirty minutes as we'd originally agreed. By 1 a.m. I'd made £600 for myself. I was on my little cloud dreaming away, but it was time for him to go. We hugged goodbye and he left. Overall I'd had a great time with him, but as soon as he left, I could feel something odd in my body, like a bad feeling; something didn't feel right. We women have definitely a 6th sense that men don't. It's called female instinct, but mine, oh boy, with all the liars and bastards I'd had in my life, that sense had developed a hundred times over. Everything we talked about was too good to be true. I kept this feeling and my worries in the back of my head, and made sure I would dig a little bit more about him before going any further.

Around 2 a.m., my friend who was visiting London arrived at the club with another friend of his. Lord, were they wasted! And when you don't drink yourself, handling drunken people is the worst thing ever. As planned, I spent an hour with them, and Jasmine was also with me in one of the VIP booths. It was the hardest sit-down of my life: they did not understand the words "NO TOUCHING", they kept begging us for more, but we could do nothing. The hour finally finished, they were even more drunk than before, so we took advantage of the situation. I asked them to tip us, which they did. He asked me how much I wanted, so I randomly said £300 each. As asked, I received. Well done, Satine. I ended up making over £1,000 that night. They kept asking us to go back to their hotel, but no chance was I was going to. I knew exactly knew what they wanted, and I was so drained from all the talking and pretending that I just wanted my bed. Trust me, the dancing part is the fun part in our job; the talking part is so tiring, because even if it is genuine, let's be honest, hearing people's personal issues or their life story for hours can be tough. I seriously don't know how therapists do it. I always felt as if I was acting; being constantly smiling, bubbly and chatty non-stop is really draining.

It was 5 a.m. when we finished, and we were starving, so we thought why not? We could do with a 5* hotel breakfast. I texted my friend and asked him to send us an Uber to their hotel. Ten minutes later we arrived in front of a beautiful hotel in the heart of Mayfair. We felt so privileged and lucky that we were able to go to this kind of place. We went to their room, ordered breakfast, ran a bath while we were waiting for our food, ate and left. They kept trying to get us to touch each other or have sex with them, but we were having none of that. They kept calling us boring, but clearly we didn't care. We made money, we were fed, life was good. Thank you, but bye-bye!

As soon as I got home, I couldn't stop thinking about Nathaniel and that bad feeling I had about him. I then decided to search online for his name and his company. Nothing came up, and it wasn't a big shock, to be honest, but why would he lie like that? I would find out eventually that he wasn't a millionaire, or not the one he pretended to be. I didn't tell him straight away. I wanted to see how far he would go with his lies. I was meant to go to his the next day to watch a movie in his cinema room, and as expected he came up with some bullshit excuses that he had to go out of London for the day as he had a family lunch. He would let me know later on when he was back home, which of course he never did. Silence radio for the whole day. Since that day, one thing after another was a lie. If he ordered me shoes, they did not arrive. If he was meant to order me a cab, his account was acting up; the same thing with bank transfers. At some point I'd had enough and told him I knew he wasn't who he was pretending to be. He read my message and never responded. That was the end of my two minutes' hope and dream of becoming a millionaire's wife. But just as every time I had to let go of something or was feeling negative, something brand new and positive would appear out of nowhere.

On Wednesday 22 November, I was home on my phone, scrolling like a maniac, like we all do nowadays. Suddenly I saw an article about Sean, the singer I'd met a month ago at the club, being part of a brand new series on television. I knew it wasn't a coincidence that I'd met him at the club, and then a few months later seeing this article about him being part of a TV show; and only a few weeks earlier meeting Charlie the celebrity agent, who had access to all the castings for TV, films and commercial. I knew he would have access to the casting director's numbers and details. It was way too many coincidences for me to ignore them. I didn't waste any time and contacted both of them to see if they could put me forward in the casting process, as I knew they needed new talented faces for this series. They both messaged me back and agreed to help me, as they thought I would be great on television. They both had my details, photography and everything they needed to put me forward in the casting process. All I had to do now was wait for an answer. I was praying every day to be taken, as I really wanted to be on British TV. It wasn't the biggest opportunity, but it was something, and a step forward in my career.

THIRTEEN

Is It Worth It?

> *Will it be easy? No. Will it be worth it? Absolutely.*
>
> Anonymous

Already I'd been working two months at the club. Time literally flew by there, and I have to say I was really enjoying my time there. Who wouldn't enjoy working with their friends every night, chatting, laughing and making money? I was also loving being on stage, and I was getting better and better at it. I loved all the attention on me, the clapping at the end of my performance and the way men looked at me. I was comparing my payslips from October to November and I could see a massive difference. In November I made £5,000 for myself; I know this isn't a crazy amount, but we're not on the same level as the strippers in America, the culture is totally different. Also I was working only three days a week. Most people earn this salary while working more than 50 hours per week.

It was the last night of November, the club was busy, we were all working hard, making money, when suddenly the favourite regular walked in with his group of friends: the regular I'd had my first ever night of work. As soon as they walked in, all the girls gathered around him like he was God! I was looking round to see if Valente was part of the crew, but no signs of him. I was so annoyed, because if he was here, it was my entry to two hours sitting down, for sure. Everyone headed downstairs to the Glitter Room, where we knew the guys would pick the girls. A wave of us followed them, hoping to get picked. One of the guys was obsessed with Jasmine, and picked her straight away. None of the other guys wanted to pick me. Damn it! I didn't want to be left out, I wanted to make money! Jasmine begged her guy to take me as well. It took him a couple of minutes to decide, but then he chose me too! I was beyond grateful for her help. That is why you need to have friends in the club: to make sure you push clients to take them with you, or be taken with them.

I went into the Glitter Room with them, which I was happy about, but I had no one to entertain. Everyone had a girl, and Jasmine's guy was only interested in talking to her, and not me. He even called me plain and boring! Thank God I have a strong mind and personality not to take it personally! Trust me, if you aren't strong, this job can kill your self-esteem! But why would I listen to a guy who needs to pay a woman to get attention! After fifteen minutes, Valente appeared. I was so happy to see his little Norwegian face! I stood up, walked towards him and he straight away grabbed me and lifted me up, as he was very happy to see me too. He was drunk as usual, which was annoying. But I was happy to have him all to myself, and we drank, flirted and talked the whole night.

At some point we looked at his private folder on his phone. Private folders always means naughty pictures and videos. And there we were, watching all his pornographic photos and videos of him and his wife. I couldn't believe it. I was getting so turned on, and for once I'd had some booze, so the devil inside me was out! I was so horny that I asked him to finger me, obviously discreetly as we were not allowed. We took a pillow to hide ourselves. I opened my legs and put my thong on the side. And there he was fingering me! I was so wet, due to all the alcohol, the teasing, the pictures and the fact that I was doing something that wasn't allowed. After a while of him seeing me getting pleasure, he offered me to have sex with him and his wife. He wanted to do me so bad, but he always had one rule: never cheat on his wife, she had to know everything. That made me like him even more. He was crazy and naughty, but still somehow honest and respectful towards his wife. He wanted me, but wanted to share it with the one he loved. I found it so beautiful.

The night ended, I was happy, I'd had a good time with Valente, but once home I couldn't stop questioning whether this job was worth it. I'd had a good week, but was it that good, though? I was tired mentally and emotionally. Every time I had an OK or bad week, I would question everything. January was also just around the corner, and we all knew that January is a really bad month. No one spends money after Christmas. I clearly didn't want to go to the club, pay my house fees and taxis, and then not earn money. I had to find a solution, I had to find a rich man that I liked or that I could deal with, who would look after me. I was getting stressed about my singing and dancing. Sometimes I was so tired that I didn't had the energy to go to classes. It was also very expensive. All I wanted was to have the money to be able to buy as many courses as I needed, but also time, time to rest and feel 100% focused, and with stripping I had a hard time. I could start to feel the late nights getting to me. I would wake up really tired, and I just wanted to rest. The more I was stressed about money and time, the more I was down mentally, and the less I was making money.

But once again I could feel the universe being on my side. Another advice I could give you is that you cannot appreciate the good without the bad, the bad without the good, everything in life is balance. If the universe was giving me everything that I wanted straight away, would I be truly grateful and appreciative ? Would I be humble? Ask yourself the same question.

FOURTEEN

An Unpredicted Meeting with a Music Producer

> *The universe works its magic in mysterious ways. All you need to do is let it.*

On 4 December 2019, one of my days off, I decided to spend time with my friend Julia, one of my long-term friends I'd met during my hostessing years. Julia and I had remained friends all these years, even though it's hard to maintain a friendship in London; everyone is so busy that you barely have time to see people. So we'd not seen each other that often, but when we did catch up it was always amazing! That day we just went for a few cheeky drinks to celebrate her birthday. I also made her some vegan chocolate cake, and she was simply the happiest! The older I got, the more I appreciated simple pleasures. Simple as having a laugh and seeing my friends smile, it really made me happy. Don't get me wrong, I was still craving for adventures, luxury and excitement, but I understood that in order to appreciate those, I needed a strong base and to stay humble, having a good time with friends, which was precious to me.

I loved spending time with Julia. She was always so much fun to be around, and always had some crazy story to tell. When I was with her, I was obviously listening to what she was saying, but I was also thinking how grateful and lucky I was to have the friends that I had. As I wasn't too close to my family, friendships were really important to me. The older I got, the less I spent my time with people who didn't matter, which meant I wasn't hanging out with a crazy number of people, but I didn't care; it was quality that was important to me. Sometimes I tried to open up to new people, but it didn't feel the same. It felt like a task, like I was playing a role to be around those people. This is why I decided to stop hanging out with people just for the sake of it. I was happy with my small circle, I was happy to talk to people who got me and had stories to share, and weren't just consumed by their phones and fakeness. My job was fake enough that I didn't need my real life to be that way too. Growing up and being a stripper truly made me understand that time is precious and the importance of the people you surround yourself with. Life advice: keep your circle small. I'm getting carried away with the emotional stuff, but I wanted to express the importance of friendship and who surrounds you, as it also reflects who you are.

Going back to my time with Julia. After a few drinks at a bar called Termini in Soho, we decided to walk around a little in Covent Garden and have a look at the Christmas lights. I was a big fan of Christmas decorations, lights, shiny bubbles, anything pretty for the eyes. One restaurant caught our attention as the decorations outside were fabulous. We went in there to take a few pictures and at the same time take one last drink. No tables were available, so we sat at the bar. I ordered a Grasshopper, my favourite cocktail, and Julia ordered a glass of wine. She didn't stay long as she had to meet other friends. I was still halfway through my drink, so I told her I would stay, finish it and go. We hugged goodbye and she left.

I was actually enjoying the time by myself, looking around being happy in my own world, but it was time for me to go as I was also meeting another friend to go to Winter Wonderland in Hyde Park. I asked the bartender for the bill, but he kindly told me that my drink was on the house. I was flattered, I hadn't even spoken to the bartender, so it was a really nice gesture from him. I'm telling you, vibration and energy is everything. When you feel your best, people can feel it; and small or extraordinary outcomes can result from it. I thanked him and gave him a tip. I was ready to leave when a couple behind me started ordering drinks and were looking for somewhere to sit. I turned round and told the gentleman that I was leaving so he could take my seat if he wanted. The gentleman politely declined, but stared at me for a second and suddenly asked me if I was an actress!

In my head I thought "What the fuck!" So many people kept asking me if I was, but I told him I wasn't, but that I was pursuing singing and dancing to become a performer. He said that I had a very particular face and amazing cheekbones, again something that I hear all the time. He then told me he was himself working in the music industry as a producer. Again, big shock in my head. After ten years living in London, I've never met someone from the industry and now that I was taking singing lessons and putting messages out there in the universe that I wanted to become a performer, I run into a music producer, a singer and a celebrity agent, just like that, out of the blue. We spoke briefly, about my time in reality TV and the lessons that I was taking. I showed him briefly some videos of me dancing and singing. He said I should definitely pursue it, as I have talent and a very distinctive look. He gave me his card and I left. I felt full of life and happiness that day. My life was so crazy! Everyday I was meeting new people, interesting people, and key people for my success. I was high on life!

I really started to feel like a manifestation beast, and believe in the law of attraction. I did believe that if I really wanted something, I would work hard for it, visualise it and anything could happen. Dreams do come true. Just have fun with life, do what you love, what you are passionate about, what makes you laugh, that's the best way to get your vibration high! Then simply visualise, ask, be grateful and you will see how magic happens.

FIFTEEN

Positive Mind, Positive Life

“ *Even if you stumble, you’re still moving forward.*

Victor Kiam

After feeling so high for a few weeks, making good money and getting so many signs from the universe, I suddenly felt really low. I don’t know why, but I’m like that sometimes, it’s part of my personality. Live everything to the fullest, feel every emotion, and unfortunately my emotions do change a lot. One day I can be over the moon, happy feeling full of life; and the next day I could wake up overthinking everything and feeling down. And with this job the highs and lows were getting worse, due to not knowing when I was going to make money, the empty promises from men and simply a whole fake world. Thank God I don’t touch any drugs and barely drink. My personality was already so extreme that no drugs were needed. And when you are feeling down, everything else is down too: your mood, your energy, your aura, and no one wants to talk to a miserable stripper. I wasn't shining as much as when I started, so money was slow. I wasn't sure I wanted to carry on. The hustle was getting harder, it was so tiring to have to repeat the same shit to those fuckers every night and waste my time.

I actually remember now when it all started. After meeting that music producer, I was so high and so happy, I went to work the following day feeling full of good energies. That night a famous retired footballer came to the club with a few friends of his. As soon as he walked in and saw me, he couldn't stop staring at me, touching me and grabbing me. Let's face it, he wanted to fuck me real bad. Anyway, all good, I knew that was my ticket to a long sit-down. I finally got picked for an hour and sat down with them. As we were walking to the Glitter Room, some other girls who had been working at the club for ages chased us. Apparently they knew the boys and didn't want to let them just be with us.

One of the girls started acting very jealously towards me. She couldn't handle that he'd chosen me, she was trying everything to get picked too. That's how the girls who had been there for ages behaved: extremely pushy, persuasive, almost aggressive, but it was actually working. That wasn't my tactic at all! I always believed that no matter what happened in life, you needed to stay kind and humble. Clearly that isn't everyone's state of mind. After ten minutes of negotiation, he also picked her. I mean, I didn't care as he'd picked me too, but the competition didn't end there for her. She had to be all over him and make me feel extremely uncomfortable. I couldn't even speak to him or be near him. I was literally a standing wallflower, which I don't like at all. It was the worst sit-down ever. I don't understand why she was doing that? She got picked, so why the need to be mean and competitive on top of it? But I couldn't be bothered to fight for a guy, footballer or not. I had my dignity to keep up, and that has no price. After that hour, the footballer kept this girl and I had to leave the room. I am usually good at separating my emotions at the club in terms of rejections, but this made me feel so rubbish that I couldn't be bothered for the rest of the night or the rest of the week. Night after night I was making shit money or no money at all.

I really wanted Satine to be back, the real Satine, the sexy, sassy, bubbly one… On the bright side, Christmas was around the corner, which meant the club was closing, which meant holidays. I think that is exactly what I needed. Some time off. I'd worked for three months straight, three to five nights a week. I was drained, I needed to recentre, sleep, have time for myself and concentrate on what truly matters: my singing career, my creativity and well-being. On the bad side, January was also just around the corner, and we all knew that January was a bad month for the entertainment and hospitality industry. I really didn't want to have to come back to pay my house fees, taxis and get no money. I had to find other options.

Many years ago, I tried this Sugar Daddy website. But it was never successful, as most of the men on the site were looking for escort girls to sleep with, and it was clearly not what I wanted. I wanted someone to spend time with and look after me financially, so I could have time to concentrate on my studying. I was a bit worried for the future, but not too worried. Until now, all through my life, I've always managed to be fine financially. Every time I thought I was going to struggle, something came up. I just had to have faith and trust in myself and the universe. Being positive and believing in the law of attraction is not about pretending to be positive all the time; it's about accepting the negative times and letting them be without making it worse. We are only human beings; of course bad times will happen, but the key is to acknowledge it and deal with it in the most loving way possible: no hate, no anger, no sabotage. I knew I had to break that circle and change something in my attitude, but I wasn't sure how and what.

One night I was talking to Amber. I loved our time together: we were both on the same page spiritually and creatively. We were always talking about work, obviously, and how those men were driving us crazy; but mostly about how we wanted to be creative and successful. I was an aspiring singer and she wanted to be a presenter. We were both helping each other with our contacts, giving each other tips, books to read to motivate us, of which our favourite was our reading about the universe and the law of attraction. When I told her I was feeling down and negative, she helped me to lift my mood. She told me to be more chilled about money, to stop feeling anxious about it, and gave me tips about meditation, to help attract what I wanted. It might sound weird to you, but strippers do meditate or pray to bring about a good night at work, full of success and abundance, to make sure we are in the best mood and energy possible before work. That is the thing with spirituality and well-being: it has always been associated with hippies, but you don't need to be vegan or a monk to be spiritual and a good person. I applied Amber's rules: I chilled, I tried not to worry about the future but enjoy the present more, to meditate, to relax and be visual; and it actually worked. I was so grateful to have her around me. You see, the more you worry about an outcome, meaning the future, the more you will block your manifestation. I know it can sound hard to do, but worrying is the worse vibration to have, and it will only fuck your vibration and aura, meaning you won't manifest shit.

On Friday 13 December, I got up, meditated and prayed. I asked the universe and my angels to make me happy, bubbly and earn £1,000. Meditating and praying helped me to feel so well and happy that I could already see the money and success; I felt on top of the world even before I'd even started to earn the money. As soon as I arrived at work, it was my turn on the list to approach a client with two other girls. I got picked straight away, only for thirty minutes, but it was already a good start. Those thirty minutes were so long: this client was in his early thirties but so freaking boring. After ten minutes, I didn't know what to tell him any more. You know, when you talk to someone and they barely reply, and on top of that don't ask you any questions, well that was him. One of the reasons I like older men is that they have much more conversation and life experience than someone younger. I kept pretending I had to use the bathroom or get a drink at the bar, just so I could have two minutes break from him. I went to the bar for the fourth time to get water, when suddenly a familiar face appeared right in front of me.

My most annoying client ever was there at the bar chatting to a girl. I'd only had one sit-down with him before, around a month ago: we'd stayed together for two and a half hours; I could have stayed longer with him, but I had to put a stop to it as he was giving me a headache, I could feel he was taking my soul out. Not that he was rude or anything, he was just very annoying and convinced that we were going to get together. He was just weird in general and not charming at all. His name was Ron, fifty-six years old, consultant for God knows what, I never really understood and didn't really care. He was short, round like a balloon, grey hair and very wrinkly, bad breath and bad humour. The good thing about him was that, first, he spent a lot, and second, he did all the talking. I didn't even have to dance that time: all he wanted was me to be near him and pretend to be his girlfriend. He was talking about how good he was in bed and how he wanted to go down on me. Let me tell you that I wanted to throw up my dinner at that moment. I was so good at my job and at acting that he was convinced that I truly liked him. He gave me his business card, which I threw away as soon as our time together was up.

But when I saw him again at the bar that night, I was the happiest. He was my money maker for the night, my wallet, my cash, my everything. He was already chatting with another girl, so I approached the bar. As soon as he saw me, he stopped and stared. I gave him a little wink and a cheeky smile, then went back to my boring sit-down. Fuck, thank God those thirty minutes were over, and now I had to pray for Ron to be still here and free! I ran upstairs and there he was. So many girls were trying to get with him, as we all knew he was a big spender, but as soon as he saw me he rejected all the girls and stood alone by the bar so I could approach him. I put on my best smile, my personal attitude, I approached him, and said, "Ron, darling, how are you? It's been so long! I've missed you! I was praying every day for you to come back here. I lost your card and I was scared I'd never see you again."

He believed every single one of my lies. He invited me straight away to go to a private booth with him. We ended up staying two hours together, which to be fair went quite fast. He was annoying, but I could talk with him, and he had conversation. He was still convinced I liked him; he kept repeating he could see it in my eyes... How can you be so stupid and desperate? Another funny and stupid thing he said: he asked me for my real name, which I didn't want to give of course, so I told him "Emilie", which was obviously not my real name. He then turned around and said, "Emilie, yes of course, you did tell me last time. You see, you can't lie to me, you can't fool me, I have the best memory."

I stood there amazed at how much he believed himself. I was laughing so much deep inside, but in a way that was what I was here for, what all the girls were here for: we were meant to be there to make them feel good about themselves, make them believe what they wanted. Those men were frustrated, misunderstood and probably lonely, and they were paying to have the attention of beautiful open-minded ladies. So even though he was annoying me, I still felt a little sad for him, but happy that somehow I could help make him feel happy for an hour or two. When he left, I had few other sit-downs and dances, and at the end of the night I'd made £1,000, which was what I'd hoped for.

Monday 16 December 2019 was the last week of work for everyone before the club closed for Christmas until 2 January 2020. I still had no plans for January, but I still wasn't worried; my mood and energy were at their best.

Thursday 19 December, two days before holidays began. I was so excited I would finally get some rest, but a little sad, to be honest. I knew that even though this job was draining and mentally hard, I was going to miss the buzz I get when I'm on stage every night, the hustle and the crazy stories and the fun times with the girls. I was more chilled this week about money, less stressed; I was doing my meditation every day, so I was feeling more calm and less pressured, and it was working. The calmer you are, the more genuine the clients think you are. I was becoming Satine again. I felt so good. I was ending the year with new knowledge. I was getting better at my dance classes and progressing each time. I'd started to sing, managing to fight my fears and get more confident. I was healthier than ever, more mature, I knew what true friendships were, I had real friends by my side, and I was richer than I'd ever been, but also richer in my heart. Overall, I was happy and feeling blessed.

I walked into the club that night feeling great again. I had my last singing class of the year. I did amazingly so my mood was really high. That night I was wearing a mini leopard-printed dress, golden hoop earrings and black high heels. My style was very Latina, very wild. The list was still on when I walked in. I sat at one of the tables with the other girls. I probably waited fifteen minutes and then it was my turn to approach the next client. As usual I was with two other girls. I knew this client was for me. I was so relaxed, happy and smiling, everyone could feel it and my positivity was spreading around me.

His name was Paul, forty-nine years old, a property lawyer. He was average looking, not very tall, blondish hair, very geeky and goofy. As soon as we approached him, he smiled as if he was fifteen years old. We could tell he was shy, embarrassed but very happy to be here. Paul was glowing, smily and welcoming. Trust me, it is not always like that! Some clients are petrified or simply rude and just ignore us when we approach them. He ordered Champagne for the four of us, how nice of him, even though I couldn't stand Champagne or wine: it gave me such a bad headache and hangover the day after. We started the usual chat: "Where are you from?" "Where do you work?" "Are you here on business?" "iis it your first time here?" "Do you know how it works?" After ten minutes of chatting, we finally asked him if he wanted to spend time with one of us, and if so, who? He was nervous, not in an awkward way, but he was just looking like a child who was doing something wrong. After a minute of thinking and looking embarrassed, he looked at me and said: "Satine". He was actually blushing really badly. We both left to go to a private booth. He did mention to me that he was very nervous about staying with me privately and seeing me naked. I told him that I didn't have to get undressed if it made him feel too uncomfortable, and we could just talk for now. We started with thirty minutes, but ended up staying together for an hour and a half. I did end up dancing, but probably only for about three minutes. Considering all the clients, I had never had someone kinder and more optimistic than Paul. Like the others, he kept saying how beautiful and fantastic I was, but I could tell it wasn't in a sexual pervy way like the others. I think he had a genuine crush on me. Every time I put my legs on his lap, he would almost faint. He actually took my hand to make me feel his heartbeat, and it was crazily fast.

He couldn't believe I didn't have a boyfriend or someone to look after me. As soon as he said that, I didn't think twice and asked him if he would be happy to do so? He blushed even more, but accepted straight away. The thought of him spoiling me was making him so happy. He was just grateful to have me by his side and have a good conversation with a pretty girl. I asked him if he was married, which he confirmed. I then asked why he needed to come here to spend time with a stranger. He explained that he would never cheat on his wife, but that after long years of marriage things get a bit boring, and as a human being he wasn't feeling so important for his wife any more and needed to feel that way. Work gets in the way, kids also and he simply did not feel like a man any more. He loved his wife very much, but he needed to talk to someone else and escape his routine for an hour or two. He was really happy to find me, because he felt he could talk about anything and everything.

I actually enjoy making people happy. I mean not everyone, but kind people, people who deserve it; for once you feel you're doing something right. Trust me or not, but many depressed men managed to handle their depression or marriage issues simply by talking to strippers. We are a bit more expensive than a classic therapist, but we are more fun, and sometimes more efficient. He gave me his business card and promised to take me out for drinks and shopping. Who would refuse such nice treatment? When our time was over I hugged him goodbye and wished him a merry Christmas. He promised to think about me every time he heard "Last Christmas" by Wham, as this song had been on loop in the club during our sit-down.

After that the night was slow. I did one dance for a guy who tried to tell me he was going to pay at the end of the dance. Dude, do you think you can choose your own rules here, and that you're the king of the club? You give me money straight, don't try to act like a boss with me, or else get out! We were getting these weird guys who wanted to feel that they had the power. It was very strange to see how they acted as if they couldn't handle not following their own rules. Very weird. They felt inferior, so they had to act rude and arrogant, probably because they knew that if they didn't pay, no one would be interested in them.

Then I danced for a lovely lady. It is quite rare that I dance for couples or women. I find it very uncomfortable, as you're never sure if the woman wants to be there and actually enjoys it, or if she's only there to please her man. But for once I had a great time with this woman. She congratulated me for my performance on stage. Once I was done dancing for her, I went back upstairs to check what was going on. It was dead town: the only person there was Charlie, you know, the celebrity manager. He was sitting by the bar as usual, chatting to the girls, making them waste their time as he never spent money. I still went over to say HI, as I wanted him on my side for any potential TV show. We spoke briefly, flirted a bit. I liked him, kind of; he was cool, chilled, a bit pervy, but I didn't mind.

It was my turn on stage again. No one was there, no client apart from Charlie, so I decided to give my everything. I danced more sexily than ever. I knew he was watching. That night under my dress I barely had anything, no bra, no suspenders, no extras, just the smallest G-string ever, I was almost naked. I could see Charlie staring at me, almost saw him drool. Even Leo, our manager, was laughing at him as he looked as if he'd never seen a woman before. I got off the stage and went downstairs to chill on one of the sofas.

I was actually dreaming away when Charlie came downstairs and walked past me without a word. Then he walked back to give me a little stroke on the cheek. That actually made me smile a lot, and I looked at him differently. A connection had happened between us. I needed so much affection, and I'm not sure if it was the Christmas spirit, but I was full of love and joy. I went over to him, hugged him and flirted. He was surprised that I was being so needy and affectionate. He grabbed me by the waist, held me really strongly, and that actually turned me on a lot. Bear in mind, Charlie is extremely tall and big; next to him I am the size of a stick. All we did was talk about sex. He was more than twenty years older than me, but who cares. That night I fancied him. I needed that daddy feeling, that father figure that I didn't have, that feeling of someone who can look after me, someone who has enough life experience not to judge me, someone who's also a bit fucked up so he could understand me, someone who could talk. Charlie had it all. He was successful, rich, fucked up, older, tall, charming, everything that I liked. I really wanted to finish the night with him. He kept holding me by the waist, but for once I had control and decided to be a good girl and go home. If he had me that night, that would be it. I didn't want to be like all the others.

I left the club and went home. Once in bed, we kept texting. I was falling hard! I simply needed someone to call me Princess, to get me off my feet. He kept repeating how he was looking forward to seeing my pretty face again, how he would treat me like a princess. He kept asking for a voice note so he could hear my accent! I was so into it. I was gutted that I had to wait till after my Christmas in France to see him again! That night I had two dates planned for early 2020. The New Year sounded so promising, if only I knew…

Friday 20 December 2019 was a day to remember, a memorable day that I will never forget. I woke up in a very good mood, still thinking about Charlie. I was so horny: that week was full of love, sexual tension, flirtations, my sex drive was hitting the roof! I kept texting all day with Charlie: "Your pussy is mine", "I'm your daddy, I will take what's mine, and if you're disobedient then you will be spanked", "I can't wait to taste that juicy pussy", "I will slide my penis inside you once you're dripping wet and ready to be fucked." Very romantic, isn't it? But that's exactly what I needed just then: a dirty gentleman.

Later that day I met Julien for our annual Christmas evening. Each year we go to watch a ballet or a musical. That was our little tradition. This year we decided to watch *Les Miserables*. I can't believe I'm French and have never read the book, watched the movie or the musical. *Les Miserables* clearly didn't catch my attention enough for me to stop texting Charlie during the evening. While Cosette was going through the Revolution, I was texting about being tied up, spanked and fingered. The play finally finished. I kissed Julien goodbye and wished him a merry Christmas and happy New Year.

I went to work around 10.30 p.m. I walked in and never

saw the club so dead. Nobody was there, no girls, no clients, nothing! All the businessmen were already away, and we were left with all the cheap ass of London. You know, the sort of clients that talk for ages to get you nowhere; not even once dance, this is how cheap they are. I didn't have any of the regular girls I hustled with that night; everyone was away on holiday. One girl I'd chatted with before was there; we weren't close, but she was cool, Francesca. She and I had started talking the week before, when we'd both tried to get this really young guy to get the two of us for a dance. I remember it took us about twenty minutes to convince him, and when we finally convinced him and went down the stairs, Francesca felt really bad and hurt her foot. She had to go to the hospital that night! Since then we'd hustled together. She was just so easy-going and funny. I was almost pissing myself laughing every night because of her.

Going back to our Friday night: Francesca and I approached every single client, which I don't usually do because I can spot who's cheap, and I don't deal with cheap guys. But that night we told ourselves to stop being divas and do as many dances as possible. She and I finally got a client each, only for once dance. We were in a separate booths but next to each other. The booths were separated by curtains, so you couldn't see anything but you could hear. I was sitting waiting in the booth alone until my client got his cash out.

While I was waiting, I could hear a repetitive spank, then Francesca saying, "You like that?!" and her client saying on loop, "HARDER!" Francesca wasn't even dancing; she was spanking her bum cheek for the whole song. I was laughing so hard, I again almost pissed myself. Imagine hearing for three minutes your friend saying, "You like it, yeah, yeah", and the guy saying, "Yeah! Harder, harder!" I have never witnessed anything like it! You do get weird requests from time to time!

Lord, what we have to deal with! I'm telling you, if we could show videos of those drunken men to their wives, they would be so embarrassed. They act like lunatics, as if they're transforming themselves into weird creatures, and none of them are charming or making sense. I couldn't stop laughing, and my laugh was pretty loud, so Francesca obviously heard me and started laughing too. Once she was done she joined me and we carried on laughing. I cherish my job for those moments! A lifetime memory. If she ever gets married and I'm invited, all I will be picturing is her spanking herself in a Gtring with an idiot behind her screaming "HARDER!"

My client then came back. He was a total dickhead: he gave me £30, and I asked him if I could keep it all (one dance is £25). He turned round and said in the most arrogant and ignorant voice, "We'll see at the end of the dance if you're worth it." What the actual fuck! If I'm worth £5 more for real? My usual clients tip me a minimum of £50. He was just disgusting. You know the type of man who hates women for some weird reason. I started dancing, and asked him what was his type of woman. He just said, "Something like that", talking about me. "Something?" Am I a thing? He didn't have any respect. He was probably frustrated that he had to pay to see some tits. I didn't even finish the dance. I just left, and he naturally asked for his £5 change. Cheap.

Once I was done, I was back on the hustling with Francesca, we went up to this guy again, another disgustingly cheap one. He was sitting at one of the restaurant tables, so we sat with him and started to chat a bit. After a while he decided to order fries, and Francesca kindly asked him if she could have a chocolate cake as well. He said OK, let's all share a cake. We looked at each other, confused. He cancelled his fries so she could get her chocolate cake. He was that cheap that he didn't want to order both! We looked at each other, and we knew exactly what we were thinking. If he couldn't spend £6 on fries and £8 on a cake, God forbid spending £50 for a double dance.

At that point a group of guys walked in. I looked at Francesca, conveying that they were our last chance and we had to leave this cheap guy. We thanked him for the chocolate cake and left. We followed the group of guys downstairs: they all sat on a booth by the stage downstairs and ordered two bottles of expensive vodka and Champagne. That was a good sign. A better sign than just buying fries! We sat with them and started talking. They were from Canada and Switzerland. After ten minutes chatting I had to go on stage. Lucky me, I was on the stage right in front of their table. While I was dancing, I kept looking at the guy I'd been speaking to: he was hypnotised. I came off the stage and we finally started to talk business. We explained how everything worked, and meanwhile I took an ice cube from the ice bucket as I was really hot and sweaty from the dancing. They all found it sexy; I wasn't trying to be, but they liked it. Francesca saw an opportunity to turn them on. She also took an ice cube but started to play with it. She was sucking it, licking it, rubbing it against her nipple, it was so funny for me to watch, but for those men it was such a tease. Those ice cubes got us to sit down with them for the rest of the night. As they were from North America, they weren't interested in talking, they wanted a show! Not that they were rude or anything, they were lovely, but they wanted fun. Francesca and I were in such a good mood that we gave our all to them!

My client was a bit more shy and conservative; he felt bad for liking me and appreciating me. He was newly married and felt very guilty. I had to explain it was all a show and nothing else would happen. The problem was that he was liking me a bit too much. On the other hand, his friend who was paying was a happy bunny and kept asking for us to dance and have fun. We kept calling him Daddy, as he was the one looking after us. For an hour Francesca and I played with the ice cube, pretending to touch each other with it. We twerked, faking playing with ourselves, we were screaming, laughing, grinding on them. We actually got scared we'd get fired, as we were not allowed to do half of what we were doing, but we didn't care. It was Christmas, the spirit was there, it was the last night and we wanted to create an amazing memory for them and for us. I could see my client had a boner and he kept going to the bathroom. Poor him, but it was actually cute and funny to witness. I couldn't stop laughing with Francesca, and then imagining if our parents could see us. But we were happy, no one was forcing us to do anything, we were enjoying ourselves. We were acting, this was just a crazy performance to us.

I know most of you won't be able to understand that I compare this to a performance, but that's what it is. We were getting paid to dance, to perform, to act for people. Like actors or dancers who get paid for a role, we were getting paid to be someone else. We were selling a fantasy, and then when the job is done we are back to our real self. We are all performers: different types of performance, for sure, but it is still all one thing. When I was thinking of my family at that time, I think they'd be disappointed in me. They didn't know about my job. I knew they'd never reject me, but I don't think they'd understand. My world was so different from theirs. I didn't really get along with them, and didn't want to add another reason to the list of why they'd find me weird. Anyway, I wasn't thinking about them too much during my job. There was no point in doing that.

I could see my client's guilt getting worse. I stopped dancing and sat on his lap to give him a hug and reassure him it was all fine. I didn't want to be too aggressive and pushy. I could see he needed a break, so I calmed him down, but Daddy didn't want any of it. He told him to man up, shut up and enjoy the show. I could feel his boner, so I started to grind on him. I know, bad Satine, but Daddy wanted a show, so here I was giving him one. I was twerking on him, going up and down with my ass pretending no trousers were in the way. I could hear him breathing loudly, his heart beating so fast. I loved it, I was the biggest tease you could imagine, but weirdly I don't think I'd be able to do the same outside the club in a regular bedroom with someone I'd dated. I think I would get embarrassed. How weird is it that I was always very confident when I had to play a role, either for reality TV or at the club, but if for example I had to go on a real date with someone that I fancied, I would be petrified and get really shy.

The club was about to close so we decided to give Daddy one last show. Francesca and I went on stage, just her and me, to perform the dirtiest dance just for him. We were all having a ball, laughing, shouting, singing. Best night ever. Then the lights went up. That is something we strippers don't appreciate. We'd been dancing for hours, and shouting, we were so tired that, trust me, our faces weren't the same as in the dark. But anyway, they were so drunk that their vision was probably blurry. The last song the DJ played was "Shameless" by The Weekend. We were all singing together and hugging goodbye. We were so happy: it wasn't just about the money, but the good time we'd just before Christmas. We'd done a good job, our clients were happy, we'd had a laugh, we'd made money, life was great! I was so grateful for that last week at work and the way the year was ending.

Once they'd left, we got changed and came back upstairs to order a taxi home. It was hard to get one as London was busy that night. Francesca managed to get an Uber but I couldn't. After fifteen minutes waiting, I decided to head to the casino to chill until 6 a.m. so I could take the Tube home. People would be going to work by then so it would be safer. As I walked into the casino, I ended up face to face with Teddy. Universe, why are you doing this to me? Teddy and I hadn't spoken for a month. I'd stopped talking to him as I was getting tired of his childish, disrespectful attitude. He was young and immature, and thought he could treat me like an inexperienced girl. He was the typical fuck boy, talking sweet to get me into bed, and then acting like a dick, ignoring me for no reason. I do forgive people and always give them a second chance, but Teddy had had way too many second chances. At some point I'd had enough and simply stopped giving him credit. He'd realised how pissed off I was when I blocked him everywhere on social media. Weird that nowadays people react when you block them on those platforms. He kept calling me, harassing me, texting me and begging me to answer. But dude, once I'm over, I'm over, there's no coming back. Something that I don't like is people taking my kindness for granted. I didn't want to speak to him, but I felt I had no choice. I didn't want to, but I was in a positive vibe and thought why not, maybe this would be the occasion for him to apologise for his shit attitude towards me. It was about time to stop hating, I would forgive but not forget.

"Look who's here! Princess Satine!" We laughed and then hugged. I told him to shut up and to carry my bags. I was so drained from my sit-down with Francesca, I had no energy left. We headed towards a table, and he ordered a few drinks for us. After a while, with him getting drunk, he finally apologised. I couldn't stay mad at him, I have a hard time holding grudges, but like I said, I will forgive but not forget. This is the best advice I could give you: never hold grudges. Grudges are ugly, they weigh you down, they make people miserable. Even if people do hurt you, the best thing is to acknowledge that clearly the person did you wrong, but simply don't give credit to that person. It's not about being weak and being a doormat, but it will only do YOU wrong to have so much hate inside you. Let bad people be bad people, karma will look after them, just move on and next time be more careful. Everything life throws at you is a lesson in life, and until you learn each one, life will keep throwing the same type of people or relationships at you until you truly learn. Trust me, I had the same lesson thrown at me a million times because I kept making the same mistakes.

After a few drinks we left and took the Underground to go home. He walked me all the way to my door. During the whole journey, he tried to kiss me and be near me as usual. Teddy and I are like magnets when we're together. There is no intellectual connection whatsoever, but a very strong physical one. It was 7 a.m. when we arrived at mine. He tried so hard to get in, but no chance was I going to let him. This time I'd learned my lesson and I was exhausted. All I wanted to do was sleep. I hugged him goodbye, we looked at each other, kissed and he left.

SIXTEEN

Happy Ending

> *The only way to get rid of temptation is to yield to it. Resist it and your soul will grow sick with longing for the things it has forbidden itself.*
>
> Oscar Wilde

On Saturday 21 December 2019 I woke up exhausted! No surprises after dancing all night, screaming, laughing, drinking a little and going to bed at 8 a.m. For once I wanted to listen to my body and do absolutely nothing! I'm the sort of person who finds it hard time just to sit at home and do nothing; I'd feel I was a loser or wasting my day. Some people can lead a routine, normal life with the same things happening everyday. I simply cannot; I've never had a stable life and stability is scary to me, stability is associated with boredom. But getting older and more mature was helping me to understand it was fine to relax and enjoy my own company, and that my own thoughts were not bad. When I'm alone, I always have the tendency to over-think and end up feeling negative and anxious. But stripping had helped me to appreciate my own company and take care much more of my body and mental health. I was becoming a master of separating work from normal life. After many years of battling with low self-esteem and anxiety, I was finally getting over it, and I was loving it. Trust me, it does feel good to get confident, simply happy and more comfortable with yourself.

So my only plans for that day were to watch box sets all day long and eat crap food. My body was really hurting though, all my muscles were sore. I am a big fan of body massage: I usually got a massage twice a month. If I wasn't going to a spa, I was ordering massages at home via a famous app. How crazy that nowadays you can order anything you like from the comfort of your own home by a simple click! I'd been keen on this app for probably the past four years, and it had always been great. I loved the fact I could stay in the comfort of my own home, no need to get ready, no need to take public transport and go out in the cold. I could just relax and enjoy the moment. I booked my massage for 8 p.m., but I was so turned on by such an exciting week at work that I was wondering if any of my guys could give me some pleasure after my massage. I was so horny after this week of talking about sex, flirting and teasing that I simply needed to be fucked.

As I scrolled down my phone and looked at my contacts, no one looked appealing to me any more. I'd done them, seen them, the fantasy was gone. I wasn't on the same level as the guys I used to deal with before. I needed something else, something new, something I'd never done or seen before. Those guys were still the same, no changes in their lives, nothing exciting, no deep conversation, nothing interesting to say, they were simply not exciting to me any more. I couldnt just fuck to fuck, I would rather touch myself, that was much better. So me and my frustration got along with it, and we were fine with just getting a relaxing massage.

The doorbell rang at 7.45 p.m. I quickly ran downstairs to open the door to the massage therapist. His name was Steve; he was very tall, dark hair, blue eyes, young, not the usual male masseur. I'd had so many massages in my life, and never had I had a male masseur that good-looking. As soon as our eyes met, something happened; electricity was in the air, but even worse, we were both somehow shy and embarrassed for no reason. I couldn't look at him without smiling, and nor could he. I think my sexual frustration was so high that he could feel it. I showed him into the living room for him to install the table; we couldn't stay in the bedroom because I was sharing my room with another girl. Yes, at twenty-eight years old I was back living like a teenager. I had no money when I got back to the UK after staying in France for six months, so I had no choice but to share a room until I was financially stable enough to get my own apartment. You see, a stripper's life ain't always so glamorous, and sometimes you have to make sacrifices to get where you want and reach your top priorities. My goal was to become a singer, a performer, so I had no interest in spending my money on designer bags and a beautiful apartment.

Steve installed the massage table. How amazing that it was heated, that was also a first for me. The oil was hot too. He gave me five minutes to get ready and make myself comfortable while he was washing his hands in the bathroom. I lay on the massage table, under my towel with just a thong on and no bra as usual. He came back to the room and started my massage. He began with my legs very gently, a bit too gently I thought. My muscles are always really sore from working out, dancing and stress. I like my massage to be firm. He was also very talkative. I guess he wanted to be nice and polite, but the last thing I wanted was talking. I just wanted to relax, no talk, no interactions, just me time. I gently informed him that I like this time to be quiet, which he understood. After my legs, Steve started to massage my back, and oh my gosh, that was just perfect. The pressure, the movement he was doing with his fingers, I literally started to feel high. He then went down to my lower back. He politely asked me if he could tuck the towel under my underwear, and I gave him the green light to do so. He tucked it in a bit lower than a usual masseur would, but oh well, I wasn't a shy person, so I didn't really pay attention. He was massaging me slowly but really strongly, up and down, but also lifting slightly my lower abdomen.

At that exact moment my heart started to beat extremely fast. We both knew that something happened at that precise moment. The massage wasn't an ordinary massage, it was something else that I couldn't explain. His energy was going through my entire body and vice versa. I knew that on his side the way he was touching me wasn't professional; but it was like my body gave him the authorisation, without being verbal. Our bodies were talking. The more he rubbed my lower back, the lower he was going. My thong was now halfway to my bum, but again I didn't say anything. The sensation I was feeling was too good, too extraordinary. I don't think I'd ever felt like that since the first time I'd experienced someone touching me. Sex is sex, right; this wasn't sex, it was something else. It was such a big tease, such a slow and intimate rubbing without actually rubbing any of my private parts, it was too much to handle. I didn't want it to stop.

Steve asked me to turn over, to massage my front. I was so relaxed, feeling so good and happy, I could feel my underwear was wet. He started to rub one of my legs, and this time the pressure was perfect. The hour was almost over, but I didn't want him to stop. I was on a perfect sexual good vibe cloud, I didn't want to come off it. As a stripper, I know the frustrating feeling of someone taking a percentage off your earning, so I offered to extend the time and pay him cash. We were both winners: cheaper for me and more money for him. He accepted, and we extended the time by another thirty minutes.

He carried on rubbing my legs, but this time he was going higher and higher up my inner thighs, really close to my lips. This sensation of being touched without being touched felt like reaching Nirvana. Only ten minutes were left, so he kindly asked me which part I wanted to be massaged again. I didn't hesitate and asked him to do the back of my legs and lower back. I turned over, lying on my stomach, and Steve put more oil in his hands and started to rub my legs again. The oil was so hot and his hands were so soft, I was melting away. He started with my feet, then my calves and thighs, to finish with my bum. The more he was massaging me, the more he slowly and subtly touched my lips. I couldn't breathe, my body was so hot but cold at the same time, my head was spinning around, my heart was beating so fast, my whole body was convulsive, my breathing was getting louder and deeper and I knew he could feel it and hear it.

He then sat down on the massage table, lifted one of my legs and put it on his lap. I could feel his erection and that turned me on even more. He spread my leg a little bit more and he carried on rubbing me, going back and forth, up and down my thigh to then discreetly touch my vagina. At that point I was dripping wet and close to the most intense orgasm of my life. He then stood up and massaged my lower back again, and let me tell you, my thong was clearly not at an appropriate level, it was under my bum cheeks, not even half way down my bum, my thong was totally gone. The whole time I was thinking, is it me who's just dreaming away, being turned on by nothing? Am I imagining things? Maybe it is appropriate, and I just like what he does so that I get turned on? But no chance that pulling my thong all the way down was appropriate. I finally had my answer: he was teasing me on purpose, the whole massage was not professional. One part of me thought this is crazy, he could be a serial killer, a pervert who enjoys massaging women, I'm mad to let him touch me. But the naughty side of me didn't really care, and I was letting him do just what he wanted. I was shaking like a virgin, my legs were so tense and my blood was boiling inside me. I was so ready to be fucked. I couldn't believe that I, the experienced stripper, the one who people paid to get time with, was paying to get pleasure. Not that I intended to at first, but when I extended the time, I knew exactly where this was going.

Then it all suddenly made sense in my head. I thought of my job, my clients and this whole weird world we live in. To be honest, I'd been judging my clients sometimes and looking down on them, feeling sorry for them that they needed to pay to spend time with girls. But during this massage, this is what I was doing too. I was like my clients, I was paying for a good time. Those men who come to a stripclub or simply pay for escort girls are men with no spare time, men who are lonely, or simply don't want the headache of a relationship due to their hectic work schedule. They also get the adrenaline of being close to a stranger without any sex involvement, which for some people is even better than sex. Teasing builds your sexual tension to a higher level. My whole mindset was changing, the way I was seeing life, relationships and men.

If you think about it, you pay to eat out in a restaurant or get a take-away when you could actually cook yourself. Sometimes we enjoy the luxury of not having any hustle and being able to pay for something that is just great and easy. Well, I guess it's the same with relationships: some people don't have time to cook, and some people don't have time for a conventional relationship. It works the same way. When you're concentrating on your career or yourself, you simply don't have time any more to go through the classic dating process, which most of the time fails anyway. If a man goes to a regular bar and tries to chat to a "regular" girl, he will probably get rejected and be classified as a player or annoying. And trust me, I'm the first one to ignore men who chat to me in a club or on the street. So obviously why not come to a place filled with beautiful and fun girls who are there to listen and chat to you?

For the ones who are married, well, it's not that I agree with cheating or coming to a stripclub, as I am myself very jealous and possessive and I think it would hurt me really badly if my husband was doing that. But growing up and doing the job that I do makes me understand that life isn't black or white but a big grey journey. Marriage and relationships take a lot of time and effort. They're not like they show us in the movies, in Disney and on Instagram. This whole #couplegoals is a killer to our society and puts a big pressure on people to pretend to have the perfect relationship in life. But life, REAL life, real relationships are not perfect, that's a fact. After a while you forget each other, you don't talk that much, but you still care for your partner. And do you really want to ruin everything that you have built together? This is why men like strippers and or escort girls, this is their getaway from their everyday life to stay mentally sane and stable without throwing everything away with their wives and families.

Don't get me wrong, I'm sure that many powerful and successful women do the same thing! But again it's something we don't talk about, it's not as socially accepted as for men, unfortunately. I know a woman would be ten times more severely judged for paying for a male escort than a man paying for a female escort. At the end of the day, we are all humans we all have needs, fantasies, desires that we can't share with everyone. Not everyone is open-minded and free as a "sex worker". I am not trying to normalise and make escorts, affairs and strippers a glamorous thing, not at all, but all I can say is that I do now understand why it can happen. But once again life is not black and white, and what might apply to someone doesn't to another.

On my side of things I was becoming this woman: I was too busy trying to balance work, social life, singing, dancing and resting too. I had no time to date; I'd never really liked dating anyway, always finding it so awkward to meet someone via an app, or someone you barely know. I was more the old school type: meeting someone through a group of friends, or work, and gradually getting to know each other until you realised you like them. But on the other hand, no dating, not meeting new people meant no sex, and I needed sex so badly. But there was no chance I was going to pay for sex on a regular basis. I am the one who people pay for my time, not the other way round. I wasn't going to play his game for a long time. Who the hell did he think he was playing with? I'm a stripper, I know all the tricks.

When the massage finally ended, I put my clothes back on. I was a bit shy, to be honest. We were both shy actually, and embarrassed, but we acted like nothing had happened. We exchanged numbers so I could book him again directly, instead of paying him at the rate on the app. Trust me, as soon as I was back from my Christmas holidays, I would call him straight away and put an end to this game. I wanted to fuck him and I was going to. He texted me an hour later to thank me for today. I replied back in no time asking him if he did this sort of massage to every client. He completely ignored it and acted like nothing had happened. I was so annoyed at him carrying on playing the innocent "nothing happened" game. Anyway, fine! Don't you worry, mister, I'm going to get you no matter what. Now that he was in my head, I wasn't going to let go this crazy amazing fantasy. I asked him straight away if he was available on 28 December when I was back from my holidays. He obviously was. I couldn't stop thinking about this massage. I became obsessed. I'm not a big fan of porn movies, but all I was watching was tantric massage porn and touching myself for hours. I was counting the days until I could see him again. I didn't like him really, but I was obsessed with what he did to my body, and that was all I needed at that time: sensuality, adrenaline, something new, something exciting.

There I was in Corsica, where my dad lives with his new partner and her kids for a few days over the holidays. My grandmother was also there; I love this woman, I could tell her anything. We were talking about anything and everything; I could even talk to her about sex. She was never judgemental. She and my other grandmother, who'd unfortunately passed away, are the only ones who always believed in me. Since I was little, they'd always wanted me to be on stage. I never really listened to them, or I was simply afraid, but I was happy that some people from my family were mentally supporting me.

I actually had a good time at Christmas with everyone. I do tend to become a bit claustrophobic when I am with my family for too long. The differences between us are too big: different mentality, lives, tempers that it makes me feel uncomfortable and anxious to be in France. And this time on top of everything I had to lie about my own life, how I was making money etc. I know they would never reject me and they would always love me, but I don't think they would understand my choice. When you don't work in a stripclub, you can never really understand the mentality and what is really going on. I didn't have the energy to explain how to me this was normal, how it was all fake and just entertaining. I could already hear my sister: " How can you call that a job? How can you make it sound like it's fine to show your tits and that it is a healthy place to work in?" So for now I decided to lie.

Finally the 27th arrived and I left Corsica to come back to my dearest London. I was exhausted from travelling and being sick. I get sick every time I go back home for Christmas. I end up with the worst vomiting and cold, not sure why. I guess even my body doesn't like it when I'm with my family. I came back home, ran myself a bath, went to bed early and watched "YOU" season 2 the whole night. How lovely to watch a series about a psychopath stalker, knowing I'm meeting strangers all the time who easily get obsessed with me.

I woke up on 28 December as fresh as a daisy, unpacked my suitcases, worked out, cleaned and got ready for my massage. This time I wasn't going to receive him in my shitty joggers, messy hair and non-shaved legs. This was the state I was in the first time we met. This time I took my time, I showered, I shaved my legs and my lips to make them extra smooth, I applied cream on my whole body, even on my butt hole, sprayed the whole bottle of my vanilla body spray from Victoria's Secret, put my hair in a high bun so my face and neck were showing, applied some tinted cream on my face so my skin looked glowing but still natural, and finally I wore a silky black robe and no underwear. I was totally naked, ready for Steve.

At 8 p.m. the doorbell rang. My heart was racing so fast that my stomach was hurting. I opened the door and there he was. We were exactly like the first time: embarrassed and shy to look at each other, but we couldn't stop smiling. We went to the living room, spoke briefly about our Christmases while he was setting up the table. I finally told him that I was a stripper. I was so convinced that he was an escort and that massaging was a cover job for him, or a way to get clients, but he kept denying it. Oh well, not my business, as long as he was touching me, that was all that mattered. I lay down and we started.

At first it didn't feel as good as the first time, maybe because he wasn't a stranger any more and this time I knew what was going to happen so I was less surprised. Towards the end of the first hour he finally started to gently touch my inner thigh. Maybe he had remorse or maybe he wanted to be more professional? I didn't give a shit, I wanted my fantasy and I was going to get it! When we went over the hour, he asked me if I wanted to extend the time, and I obviously accepted. The little fucker, teasing me towards the end, so I would ask him for more time. He started to massage my front first. He was clearly massaging my breast. He then asked me to turn over to do my back again. I was getting fed up with his mind games and I said, "OK, now are you going to tell me that this is massage is normal?"

He denied it again and said, "I didn't touch your breast, I was massaging your muscles." Fuck off, dude, what are you playing at? You can't play a player. He really started to get on my nerves. He even mentioned that I shouldn't worry about being fully naked because he couldn't see anything with the towel there. Liar. I knew that the way he was placing the towel could let him see everything. This time I wasn't going to let him win and carry on pretending it was all normal. This time, when he started to rub my inner thigh, I deliberately opened my legs even more so he could see properly my entire vagina.

As he was getting closer to my lips, I started moaning and tensing my body. No man can resist a woman moaning. And there I was winning, and he completely lost it. As my hand was hanging from the table, I could feel his erection through his trousers while he was standing next to me. I could feel his grip becoming stronger and more intense. His breathing was getting louder. He even started to moan himself. He was totally rubbing my vagina this time, not just the side, he was properly rubbing me. As he touched me, I was lifting my bum up so he could get access to my clitoris easily. As soon as he did, I screamed and squeezed the towel with one hand while I grabbed his arm with my other hand. I was dripping wet, so horny and tortured. I kept moaning, swearing in French, moving my body with pleasure. He was also moaning, everything was so intense. I'd never experienced something so good in my life. I was on another planet, like drugged, high, my heart was about to explode, my head was confused, it was a mixture of pain and extreme pleasure.

I couldn't handle his rubbing any more, I literally grabbed his hand and pushed his fingers inside me. We both moaned loudly at the same time. I think at that time he lost more control than me. While he was fingering me, his other hand kept caressing my neck, back and bum. It got too much for him: he suddenly stopped and asked if he could use the bathroom. But I wasn't finished with him. I let him breathe for a second and when he came back I asked him to massage my front legs again, just for ten more minutes, and promised him we'd be done. That's what I wanted him to believe. He did it straight away: it didn't take long for him to finger me again.

I threw the towel that was covering me on the floor and finally looked him in the eyes. His face was so tense with pleasure, but so happy at the same time. He couldn't believe what was happening. He kept repeating how I was driving him crazy. I turned my head towards his trousers. I could finally see his erection, and I started to touch him. Just the feeling of my hand on him was so intense that he looked in pain. I asked him to pull his trousers down so I could give him a blow job. I couldn't believe that I was in my living room, naked, on a massage table, having sex with my male masseur. If you have the chance to have this experience one day in your life, please go for it! You won't regret it. I barely sucked him; every time my mouth touched his gland he stopped me. I think he was ready to come at any minute.

I then quickly stood up, ran to the bathroom to grab a condom, came back and bent down on the massage table, my legs open and bum facing him. He was standing behind me and said out loud "Wow", which made me laugh. He put the tip slowly once, twice then his full erection inside me. I thought I was going to faint. He suddenly stepped back and stopped everything. I turned around and looked at him, confused. He looked so troubled and lost, a mixture between pain and pleasure. He kept saying that we had to stop now, but we'd see each other another time. I was so confused by this guy: he was doing everything since we'd met to tease me and drive me mad, and now that it was the real deal he was backing off. What could I do? I wasn't going to force him, so we got dressed, he put away the table, packed his stuff and kissed me goodbye.

Later on that night I messaged him to ask what was going on with him. I also made it clear that if he wanted to carry on seeing me, there was no chance I was paying. I do not pay for sex. He then later explained that he'd just broken up with his fiancée, so everything was a bit confusing for him. But he agreed to come back to give me a massage for free, and have sex in exchange for a dance. A bit of a weird request, but why not? I was getting my two favourite things in the world for free and without effort: a massage and sex.

Curious and nosy girl that I am, I decided to look for Steve online to see what he was about. It didn't take me long to find him and also his ex on Instagram. She was the opposite of me, blonde, blue eyes, athletic body but not thin, pretty but nothing special. She had very much of a "Daddy's girl" look about her. Every single picture of her by herself or with him looked so staged and fake. She always had this stupid fake smile on that made me cringe. She was clearly the sort of girl men present to their family, the sort of woman that men settle for but always end up being bored with after a few years. She was just so vanilla. Let's face it, I didn't like her. I had no reason to but, I don't know, her face was just annoying. I mean yes, I'm not going to play the perfect positive spiritual person here, I was probably jealous because I was terrible at relationships and she was probably much better at them than me. I was being envious and that is a very ugly trait to have and I'm still working on it. Meaning I still needed to work on my self-esteem, I needed to truly love myself much more. Envy is only a lack of confidence and self-love.

Steve and I planned to see each other the following week, and I couldn't wait for it!

SEVENTEEN

2020, I Am Ready for You: Happy New Year

> *Stay true to yourself and listen to your inner voice. It will lead you to your dreams.*
>
> James Ross

While I was obsessed with Steve's tantric massages, I was also obsessed with Charlie. He and I were texting everyday during the Christmas holidays. It did feel good to have someone to message me everyday and ask about my holidays and just care a little. When I got back to the UK I was meant to meet with him, but I ended up cancelling twice. The first time I was still too sick to see him and didn't want an uncomfortable situation of me throwing up everywhere on our first night. The second time I cancelled only because we'd scheduled a day that I didn't think was working for me due to one of my beauty treatments. He then got so upset with me for cancelling twice on him that he stopped texting me. I think Charlie had a massive ego and wasn't used to having a girl cancelling on him. After a few days, we finally came to an agreement to meet on Saturday 4 January 2020. I was finally feeling better and ready to make 2020 a very productive year! I didn't want to wait around, and I wanted to take every opportunity to be out there, making money and being successful at my dancing and singing.

After having two dinners with Yoan, the music producer I'd met one evening before Christmas, I decided to follow his advice and organise a photo shoot and video shoot for my portfolio. I'd start to film myself on camera and post the video on Youtube to start getting noticed a little. Yoan was impressed by my performances at school: I'd managed to get short video clips of exercises we were doing during singing lessons and he pushed me to continue. He promised that once I got better, he would help get me out there. I was so happy to have the criticism, help and confirmation that I had talent from a professional. I had doubts because I never knew if a man was genuine with me or if he was just being nice to get me into bed. But a really good friend of mine, a talented singer and actress who played many roles in the West End who I'd met during my hostessing years confirmed that I was talented. She was amazed how good my short clips were, and pushed me to pursue when I had doubts.

I followed the advice from both of them and organised a photo shoot, a video shoot and wrote my resume so I was able to send some material to agents. As Charlie booked a hotel for us for the night we were meant to meet, I didn't hesitate in asking him to use the hotel room for my photo shoot and some footage for my video shoot. He kindly accepted and told me I could have the room for myself from 2 p.m. until 6 p.m. until he got there. Perfect, I just needed to find a photographer/videographer, which didn't take long. Amber knew so many, so I contacted one of them and boom, in a few hours the shoot was organised.

Saturday 4 January 2020, I woke up feeling good, healthy, full of energy, pretty, clear skin; everything was on my side for an amazing day. I met with the photographer at a boutique hotel in Soho where I was meeting Charlie later on. The lady at reception knew that I was coming; she gave me the key and we started working. I was so proud of myself: I was getting better and better at posing, even with portraits which I usually hate! My body was also better than ever; I was going to be twenty-nine years old in four months, but I looked more like twenty-two. For the very first time in my life I was proud of myself, and thought I'd come a long way. We finished the shoot around 4.30 p.m. Once the photographer had left, I ordered room service, with the bill of course being put on Charlie's account, and then I decided to nap. At 6 p.m. the door buzzed, which was Charlie. I got up still half asleep, and there he was… tall, well-dressed as usual, big smile. I was so happy to see him, and I think he was really happy to see me too. He gave me the biggest warm hug and that really turned me on. He had such an effect on me, we just couldn't stop touching each other, hugging, being close and smiling and staring at one another. We lay on the bed, talked for a bit, laughed, it was a really good time, to be honest, not even awkward as it was the first time I saw him outside the club.

Within minutes, Charlie started kissing me, which felt amazing. He slowly started to remove my top and lick my nipples. They were so hard and ready to be sucked. As mentioned before, Charlie is a foot fetish, so it didn't take him long to touch my feet, look at them and start to lick them. No one has ever licked my feet before, it was such a weird feeling. Suddenly he put all my foot in his mouth and started sucking it, exactly the same way a woman would suck a man's penis. Let me tell you, it felt really good. After taking care of my feet for a good while, we simply started to have sex. We were both very passionate and not shy. I couldn't believe I was having sex with a fifty-year-old man, my first ever real "daddy". At some point we were both lying down on our sides, facing each other in 69 positions. Charlie was licking my lips at the same time that he was touching my feet, I was licking his penis and then went down to his balls. I could see that he was spreading his legs more and lifting his bum up. The lower I was going down his balls the more he was moaning. I'd only licked one anus in my life, Gabriel's, my first ever boyfriend who I'd stayed with for two years when I was sixteen years old. Since then no man ever wanted me to do that; how stupid of them when you know this is the best point of orgasm for them. Probably they were scared of liking the feeling too much and being classified as gay.

But I could see Charlie enjoying it, so I started to lick his anus… he loved it. He literally put himself in doggy style, opened his bum cheeks and he was just waiting for it. I couldn't believe I was in a hotel room with this famous guy, in doggy style and licking his butt hole. I was loving this little freakiness. It was fun to be with someone who had no shame and who enjoyed sex as much as I do. While I was licking him, I also decided to tease him with a little finger there. He couldn't stop screaming my name and how much he liked it. I felt like I had the power and that I was "fucking him". I was almost calling him my "little bitch", but I didn't want to push it too far. I loved to be the submissive one in bed as I'm such a control freak in my everyday life. I'm always in control, so it feels good when someone else is in charge in bed. But feeling like I was the one dominating him felt great too. He said that he would have loved it if I'd had a vibrator with me so I could fuck him with it. That made me laugh inside. I am very open sexually, but some stuff still intrigues me and makes me feel weird. I was sure I could have fucked him with a toy or a strap-on, but I don't think I'd have looked at him the same way after. After an hour of intense sex, he finally came. We were both drained from so much passion that we decided to have a nap before our date night. When we woke up from our nap we were both horny still and had sex again.

At midnight Charlie and I went out for drinks. We didn't really know where to go, so we decided to go to a stripclub, a different one from where I was working. I'd always wanted to go to a stripclub as a client. I remember asking my former colleagues all the time to take me, but they always refused, I never understood why. Luckily Charlie had no issues taking me there. We went to another well-known stripclub on Leicester Square. As soon as we approached the club, Charlie shook everyone's hands, he was a regular at this club as well. How many stripclubs did he need to go to? We walked down the stairs and reached the reception area and left our coats. The club was such a joke compared to mine. The place looked cheap and far from glamorous. It felt like I was back in Spain or Turkey at some random club on the beach. The girls weren't wearing dresses, they were walking around in underwear which made the place look like… well, a typical stripclub. It made me realise how much I liked the place I was working.

We sat on a sofa and enjoyed our drinks. All the girls were coming by one by one to say Hi to Charlie. I wasn't surprised, to be honest. After a while I got hungry, so we decided to leave. As we were leaving the club, the security told him how extremely beautiful I was and he should look after me. Charlie responded that I was his future ex-wife; we both laughed and headed towards the casino, as it was the only respectable place to grab a bite at that time. Once there, Charlie decided to gamble, so we played for a while. By the end Charlie had won £400 and gave me half; I was pleasantly surprised by his gesture. We decided to grab one more drink before heading back to the hotel. As we sat down near the bar area, some random man walked past us with his wife and insisted on buying us a drink as I was so beautiful. Charlie politely refused; he felt a bit uncomfortable for the gentleman's wife, so he politely said that his wife was pretty too.

When they'd left, Charlie turned and asked me if I was paying people to give me compliments, as he couldn't believe how many people had come and tried to talk to me. I knew he was jealous, which I liked. After that we took a black cab back to the hotel, had sex and slept. The morning after we also had sex. We were two horny fuckers, but Charlie was sweet. To be honest, I didn't feel I was with what we call a "fuck boy"; I knew he probably had sex with half of London and was always hunting out new girls, but when I was with him he was a gentleman. That is exactly what I needed: I loved being with someone like him, someone who was established, who had no issues with money, someone who was able to pay for a black cab, who held doors open for me, was able to hold a conversation, and had a lot to teach me.

I knew at that time I could never date someone my age with a regular job. I am not judging anyone: some people are happy with a regular life and a classic conventional relationship, which is fine, but I knew this wasn't matching my personality, my needs and dreams. I needed to feel that I was with someone who could upgrade me, mentor me and help me improve in my life and projects. I'd struggled enough in my life,but I was now making really good money and pursuing my dreams. I couldn't be with someone who wasn't established itself, it would feel as if I was downgrading. Also, let's be honest, I was loving having this sort of father figure next to me, feeling that I was looked after like a little girl. I just needed someone to protect me, to be there for me and tell me that everything would be fine.

Around noon Charlie put me in a cab, that he'd paid for of course, and I headed home. As soon as I got home my gut feeling told me that it was already over with Charlie and that he would never really help me with any castings either. Overall we'd had a good time, a great time, but men like Charlie are hunters, and once they get what they want, the game is over. Once again my gut instinct was right, but I wasn't going to let it put me down.

The year 2020 was already starting really well for me: I'd had my date with Charlie, got money out of it without even asking, managed to organise a photo shoot in a beautiful hotel, got great pictures and footage for my portfolio, and I'd started sending out my resume and headshot to agents. I was productive and felt great about it. I was missing the club, those crazy nights, the hustle, but I was enjoying the freedom I had, not being tired due to late nights and being able to choose what I did with my days. A break from time to time also felt good. I was much more proactive and focused on my goals. I was also less tired for my commercial dancing lessons. After a few classes, I wanted to dance more and started commercial heels, which I was loving. One thing though, I needed shoes for this class: real, comfortable high heel dancing shoes. I could afford them easily, but I didn't want to pay for them. When you become a stripper, you have the tendency to think you can get anything paid for: dinners, clothes, shoes, rent, cars, you never know the type of men you meet and what they are ready to pay for you.

At that point I remembered Paul, my really sweet client

I'd met before the Christmas holidays. I knew he wasn't rich but not an asshole either, so I didn't want to play mind games too much to get what I wanted. Some girls have no heart and would rip someone off without feeling any guilt, but I wasn't like that. I'm not here to pretend I was an angel either, as I was still trying to get something out of him. But I didn't want to be a piss taker. As I thought about my new dancing shoes, I texted Paul to arrange our date we'd spoken about before the holidays. We arranged to meet on 7 January at City Social, a beautiful restaurant with one of the best views of London.

As soon as I walked in I saw Paul. He was still the same: shy, goofy and bubbly. His vibe was so good. We started with a few drinks sitting by the window, and then moved to the restaurant area for lunch. We had a really good time: service was impeccable, the food delightful and Paul's company just great. He didn't try once to lay a hand on me or make a sexist comment. He was just really enjoying my company; I was making him laugh and that was all that mattered to him. During lunch we spoke about my goals and what I was up to, so I explained to him how singing and dance classes were expensive, especially now that I needed shoes, but money was tight at the minute so I couldn't get them. I could afford them, that was a lie, but he didn't need to know that. As he felt for me and loved the fact that I was pursuing what I loved, he straight away offered to pay for my shoes. I was so happy he'd offered to get them for me, even though I'd made him offer to pay for them without him realising. We ordered the shoes that I wanted online while we were having our last drinks. I could see he was beyond happy to spoil me a little. He kept saying he wished that he could buy me designer shoes; I reassured him that I didn't need them, but I was grateful for him to invest in my dreams. When we left I gave him a big hug goodbye. If you could see his smile and happy face, you would have melted. In a way, yes, he paid for my shoes; and yes, I got something out of him, but so did he. For more than two hours I made him forget about his routine, his stress at work and I kept making him laugh. We both left happy and winning.

The next two weeks were pretty simple: I was just enjoying my time off, going for walks, bike riding in Hyde Park, going for lunches and coffees with Julien, Amber or Francesca. Those times were the best of times for me: I was enjoying my true friends' company, talking about anything and everything, having a laugh and being far away from random men. We always promised each other to make sure we kept having those simple times, staying humble and still appreciating simple pleasures. In a way, after a while of going out, dining in expensive places, I was realising that quiet and simple moments are the real luxury. Don't get me wrong, I was still going out, but you realise that everything is about balance: going out too much is never good, being surrounded by shallow people, luxury and superficial stuff can be harmful, you can lose track of reality, but being at home all the time, alone, never seeing anyone and having a "poor" state of mind wasn't good either. I needed to have both in a reasonable manner to stay mentally healthy, humble but still retain my go-getter mentality.

Lucky me, every time I went out would yield some beneficial effect. There is no logical explanation to this, but every time we went out we met men who wanted to spoil us. I have been living in London for ten years, I've had a few people here and there who wanted to look after me, but not as frequently as now. Was I better looking than before? Could men tell that now if they wanted to spend time with me they would have to make more effort than just paying for dinner? Was my aura so good that men were just happy to please me?

I don't have an answer to it, but I wasn't complaining. I didn't work for a month, so technically I didn't earn any money, but I wasn't spending any. Overall I managed to get my rent paid for two months, my singing lessons paid for an entire course, dance classes also paid for and some online shopping here and there. Technically I saved more than £2,000 that month, just by meeting the right men who were willing to help me out. That was a great bonus for me when I wasn't working.

My life was great, I was concentrating on my goals, I was free, I was saving money, I was healthy and I was seeing Steve once a week for our weekly sex-massage session, which each time was better than the last. The only issue I started to have with Steve was him wanting more than what we had at the time. We would message every single day, all day, which was fine with me, I wasn't complaining to have someone to text. But every time Steve came to mine, he asked to kiss me and stay over, which I didn't want, and he would then get upset. You know how things are when you let people stay over: you get attached, you start to act more like a couple and things get complicated.

I knew Steve wasn't someone for me: apart from sex, we had nothing else. The conversations we had were very plain and basic; he was content with that, but I wasn't. I felt awkward once we'd finished the sex: nothing was there. It didn't seem to bother him. He was much simpler than me, and staying silent didn't make him feel uncomfortable. I'd be trying to talk to him, asking him questions, but the return wasn't great. I'm not saying I wasn't attached to him, that would be a lie, but I was probably just getting used to him, used to have someone to text to every day and have amazing sex with once a week. One day he even said he would love for me to be his girlfriend, but only if I had a "regular" job such as being a beauty therapist. That actually hurt me really bad.

I didn't want to be with him, but the fact that someone would tell me that I wasn't good enough or respectable because of my job really hurt my feelings. That was another reason why I wasn't attracted to him: I needed to be with someone who was mentally strong and confident enough to understand my job and understand that it was all an act and nothing was real. It would probably take me a while to find that man, but I knew I would. I wasn't going to settle with the first guy who gave me a bit of attention and good sex. My last relationship didn't work because my ex was so simple compared to me. I couldn't repeat the story again. I had to be strong and keep our relationship the way it was: purely sexual.

EIGHTEEN

Only You Can Make A Difference, No One Else

> *Things may come to those who wait… but only the things left by those who hustle.*
>
> Abraham Lincoln

On 19 January 2020, after one month off work, I decided it was about time to get back to work. I was fine financially, but I didn't want to get too comfortable and spend all my money. I was not really looking forward to going back: I was feeling a bit lazy after such a long time off, but I had a little adrenaline inside me that got me excited at the thought of being back and seeing all the girls again. There I was back on the floor, the lighting, the music, the lingerie, the stage, the girls… God, I'd actually missed the club and the hustle. Amber and Francesca were there. I was so happy to see them at the club again. As we were all sharing the latest gossip and life stories, Francesca started to tell us how before

Christmas she'd got paid by Charlie to touch her feet: yes, Charlie had a foot fetish and they were planning to go on a paid date the following week for him to touch her feet again.

As soon as she said that I felt sick. I felt a pain in my heart. How could he? I wasn't stupid, I knew he would have sex with other girls or whatever; we'd even spoken about it, but we'd also had this conversation where I asked him if he was dating anyone from the club and he assured me he wasn't. Francesca wasn't just any girl at the club, she was my friend and he knew that. What a fucking bastard! I wasn't annoyed at Francesca at all, of course; she didn't even know about him and me, she clearly didn't care about him. She was doing it only for the money. No wonder he scarcely texted me after our first and only date! Luckily Amber knew about Charlie and his tricks, as so many girls from the clubs went out with him, and we all knew he was a cheap ass who didn't pay anything. We didn't try to change Francesca's mind about him, but we did tell her that it was obvious he wasn't going to pay and that she was going to waste her time. She understood that and texted him straight away to cancel their date.

As soon as she'd texted him, I received a text from him asking me if I was free the following week, the exact same day he was meant to go on a date with Francesca. What the actual fuck, he didn't waste any time! I didn't even respond. I was too annoyed with him. On top of being a fuck boy, he hadn't done anything for me regarding the casting for the new show Sean was in. It was the end of filming, and I'd never received a call back. That day opened my eyes: I realised that no one I met at the club would ever help me with my singing or TV career, and that I could only count on myself. Men at the club wanted one thing: SEX. They didn't care about my drive, my goals and aspirations; that didn't interest them, they were just seeing me as a stripper, they don't see the hustler, the dreamer and the hard worker that I am. But I wasn't going to let Charlie, Sean, Sebastian, or any men who pretended that they would help me, kill my drive. It was actually the opposite: I wanted to prove even more to the world that I could be a stripper, be naked every night, but still be clever as fuck and achieve my goals.

One week later, after I'd started at work again, my new singing course began. I could see I was getting better and better at it; I was understanding the techniques and the work to put behind it to be a great singer. On top of enjoying my course, I received good news. During my holidays, when I was sending my portfolio to all the agents possible in London, I also applied to an singing/performing course that was taking students only on audition. They called me back and asked me to audition for them, which I did. I had to send them a resume, my portfolio and a video of me performing. A few days later, I received a call from the manager of the school to congratulate me: if I was still interested, I could be part of the next course starting in May.

I was so proud of myself, succeeding in everything I tried. Paying for a regular course was one thing, but being accepted onto a course that took students only on audition proved to me that I was doing something right there, and that I had potential. Never let anyone or any situation make you feel worthless. If you know you have something great in you, go for it, even though life can be disappointing at times.

NINETEEN

Sapio... What?

> *Confessions of a sapiosexual: I want someone to fall in love with my poetry. Someone who celebrates my ideas, who debates and tells me how his thoughts are different. I see myself as more than a pair of boobs and vagina. Any girl has them. But there's not a single person who has my thoughts.*
>
> Tracy Ossment

On 28 January 2020 I received a text from Alfonso, randomly out of nowhere. After months of us trying to meet each other either in New York or London, I simply stopped texting and asking him to see me, so I was pleasantly surprised when I received a text from him that day. He was informing me he was in London for a few days and would love to see me. I was beyond excited to see him again: that meant time off work for me, getting spoiled and having an amazing time.

The night before seeing him, I was meeting with Steve for our weekly sexual massage. I was clearly addicted to it: I couldn't imagine myself having sex in any other way for the time being. As usual he came late at night, set up the table, massaged me for two hours at least and finished by having sex. When we finished, we actually lay down and talked for once. This is when I felt 100% sure this wouldn't go anywhere; the conversation wasn't flowing, he wasn't funny or deep, he was really simple and that didn't attract me at all. I could let him massage me and have sex with him as no talk was needed, but I could not picture myself sitting in a restaurant for hours with him. That thought was really scary to me. When he left, he begged me to kiss him; yes, we were sleeping together, but I was refusing to kiss him. To me a kiss is really intimate, the same as staying overnight. He was always begging me for it, and I never wanted to. He got really annoyed that night with me, and I could feel something ODD when he left.

Wednesday 30 January 2020, the day I was meeting Alfonso, I was so excited and for once we were planning to meet just the two of us, no one around to disturb us. I got ready and then Jasmine asked me if she could join us for dinner only, and then she would go out after and meet some other friends. I accepted, why not? She would be there just for the dinner. I asked Alfonso, to check he didn't mind, and he didn't have any issues with it. We met around 9.30 p.m. at a famous luxury hotel in Knightsbridge where he was staying for his time in London. This hotel was so luxurious, I loved it. I was wearing long boot-cut split black trousers, a long-sleeved black top, my hair down and straight and a long white coat. I felt like a princess walking into this hotel. I knew this was the life that I wanted and deserved.

We saw him in the lobby straight away, we all hugged and went for a drink at the hotel bar before heading to a new Latin American restaurant that had just opened in Mayfair. We all had a great time, we talked, laughed, ate. I had really missed him, even though he was as stressed as usual about work, constantly getting up to take calls. But again that is what you have to accept if you date a rich businessman. At some point during dinner Jasmine looked really upset and started to cry. Unfortunately she had caught with feelings for a fuck boy who was messing with her head. He'd told her that he wasn't happy that she was out with me and Alfonso. How ridiculous, he'd never made the effort to see her outside his bedroom, to take her out on a proper date, but he was always complaining and trying to control her. I didn't like the way he was treating her and the mind games he was playing. Alfonso felt really bad for Jasmine and told her that if she didn't want to be alone she could stay with us. I didn't really mind, but I was a bit annoyed as I wanted time alone with him. But in a way that would make him have to wait another night to have me in bed.

We all went back to the hotel after dinner. The bed was big enough to fit three people – I couldn't believe I was going to sleep in the same bed with Alfonso, who was much older than me and I'd met only a few months ago, and Jasmine as well. What a life! I went to the bathroom to remove my make-up, shower, put on one of Alfonso's T-shirts and go to bed. Alfonso kept repeating how I was much better looking when I was natural. That felt good to hear. When it was Jasmine's turn to be in the bathroom, he tried straight away to have sex with me, but no way was I going to fuck while my friend was in the same room. He was begging me for it, but no chance: I didn't care if he was rich, that he'd paid for dinner and let me stay in a luxury hotel. No matter how much money you throw at me, if it's not *what* I want, if it's not *when* I want, if it's not *where* I want, it's not happening. Men have a tendency to think that because they're paying for things for you, it means they owe you, possess you and can control you. But no. Girls, let me be clear, even if you agree to go to a guy's house, bedroom, car, whatever, No means NO. I never felt guilty letting a man spend a lot on me and not giving him anything in return. I wasn't anyone's property, and a woman should never ever feel bad for refusing what a man asks, even though he's spent on her.

After trying to explain to Alfonso that nothing was going to happen, he finally understood and we all went to sleep like three good people. The next day we woke up and ordered the biggest breakfast ever. I loved hotel life, I mean luxury hotels. We felt blessed. I was looking at everything around us, and I was so grateful that I was living the life that I was in. How many people could say they'd stayed in so many hotels, dined in so many good restaurants and everything paid for? Alfonso was already on his phone like a maniac, and not enjoying breakfast with us. I begged him to relax a bit and enjoy the morning with us, but he had too many meetings scheduled and had to go. As Jasmine and I were still eating, Alfonso approached me and apologised for being a bit pushy the night before. I told him not to worry about it. He smiled at me, kissed me on the forehead and told me to check my account. I looked at my phone: Alfonso had just sent me £1,000. I had no words. I asked him why? He said that it was his way of apologising for being a jerk, and that he also wanted me to take a night off during this week so we could all go out again before he flew back to New York. He then kissed me and left. Lord, thank you, Alfonso! I couldn't believe I had just received so much money by doing nothing! How do some people have so much money to just throw it around like that? I mean, I wasn't complaining, I was on a cloud, I was feeling like Julia Roberts in *Pretty Woman*, except that I wasn't a prostitute.

I was so happy until I received a text from Steve. The night before, while we were all out, I was still waiting for Steve to text me as I'd not heard from him the whole day and evening. I was mad because the last night we'd slept together, he'd kept wanting me to open up to him and ask to stay. And now he was ghosting me! It didn't make any sense! So when we all came back from the restaurant, I texted him and told him that I hoped he enjoyed fucking me and thanks for disappearing. He finally responded back that morning with the shittiest text ever: " Yes, I did enjoy [fucking me] but we cant carry on like this. Have a good day, babe." "Babe?" "Yes, I did enjoy. Have a good day?" Are you for real, Steve?

Sometimes I as wondered if he understood what I was saying; if he was just a pure player, or simply completely stupid. I left the room, walked down the corridor with my baggy T-shirt and one of Alfonso's joggers and tried to call Steve a thousand times. Who the hell did he think he was? Trying to get me to open up, have sex with me, then ghost me like I was trash. He finally responded and straight away I asked him what was wrong. He said that nothing was wrong, but he didn't want to carry on like this, as he wanted a relationship. I played his game and said OK, let's have one then, let's try. You never ask me out, so what are you waiting for? And as expected, he didn't want to, saying that he wasn't rich enough for me. I hated when men used that excuse. I just found it so lame, so lazy. I hung up, as I could feel that I was very loud in the corridor. I then started to bombard him with texts, begging for a better explanation. He then said that he'd had a great time with me, but what we had was just sex, nothing else. I felt sick that I'd been played by such an idiot, by someone who didn't even pay for one dinner. I'd let this guy touch me, and then he'd ghosted me like that. As soon as he'd sent those words, I deleted his number and moved on with my life.

I was sad, I mean I think my ego was hurt, but if the universe decided to remove Steve from my life, that was probably for a good reason. I probably needed to concentrate more on what truly mattered and feel more available for the right person. I left the hotel around noon with Jasmine, making sure we took all the hotel samples with us, even toilet paper. Don't ask me why, I guess when you aren't born rich you want to save money anywhere you can, even though we were making money. I arrived home and went for a nap straight away. I wanted to feel rested before going to work, as Alfonso was planning to come with his usual friend Youssef to the club that night. Great money was already guaranteed before we'd even started working.

1 February 2020, Alfonso's last night in London. For the occasion we all decided to go for dinner: him, Jasmine, Youssef and me. We'd all spent the night before at the club: it was pretty chilled, nothing special, but for our last night we wanted to have a great dinner and go to The Box. That was our little tradition. Jasmine and I dressed up for the occasion. I had a short white tight dress, see-through high heels and my hair up in a ponytail. Jasmine was wearing a long tight orange cocktail dress. We looked Glamorous and Fabulous. When we joined them at the restaurant, Alfonso was out of breath; he couldn't stop staring at me and kept complimenting me on my look.

We started dinner, everything was fine, until I started to be a bit short with the waitress: she had a really bad attitude for no reason, and I wasn't having any of it. Alfonso didn't like my tone, and kept telling me to shut up. He hated when people were rude to staff, which I totally agree with as, let's not forget, I'd done all those hard jobs for a few years and I know that customers can be rude and demanding, so I always make sure to be respectful towards staff. But if you give me attitude, I'm not having it. I was trying to explain to Alfonso why I was short with her, but he didn't want to hear anything and kept telling me to stop as if I was five years old. I was fed up with his attitude, talking to me like I was a child and not having a proper conversation with me, so I decided to ignore him. I really didn't care that he had money, it didn't give him the right to patronise me. He was probably used to his other girlfriends who said Amen to everything, but I wasn't like that, I was not having it.

I then decided to turn to my right and pay more attention to Youssef and try to get to know him. As soon as we started speaking, I felt electricity through my body, my eyes couldn't stop looking at him. The way he was speaking with so much passion and so many interesting stories, I felt possessed by him. Youssef was short, definitely overweight, a big arabic nose, glasses and messy dark hair. He wasn't the type you could call "good-looking". I didn't mind a bit of a Daddy's look and a guy having a few extra pounds, but Youssef wasn't my type at all. However, his personality was so intriguing and full of life that I started to get turned on by him. I left the table as I had to use the bathroom. As I was peeing, I was thinking to myself, "What's with me that I keep being attracted to random looks and people? Who am I really attracted to? I can't pin it down. Am I attracted to intelligence and depth?" I came back to the table and said to everyone, "I think at twenty-eight years old I finally realise that I'm sexually attracted to intelligence, people who have depth and passion, but I can't pin it down." Youssef straight away told me that I was Sapiosexual, a word that I'd never heard before, but it felt good to put a word to who I am.

The whole night, I couldn't stop talking to Youssef, looking for his attention. I was completely ignoring Alfonso, which he noticed. Once we headed to The Box, Alfonso grabbed me and asked me what I was up to. I simply told him that I couldn't tolerate the way he spoke to me. Money or not, he still had to respect me, that I wasn't his little thing. He understood and apologised, which I appreciated, but that didn't change the fact that I wanted to be with Youssef now. I even asked Jasmine to keep company with Alfonso, as I was busy flirting with Youssef. We finally left the club around 2 a.m. They were both so drunk, I didn't like it. We took a black cab back to the hotel. Things started to get heated in the cab. Jasmine was still busy flirting with Alfonso, and he also started to be very flirty and touchy with her, and I was getting more tactile with Youssef.

We came back to the room. Alfonso pushed Jasmine onto the bed and started to massage her while I was busy sitting on Youssef's lap and trying to figure out if he liked me or not. We put some music on and I started to dance for him. He was trying to resist, as he'd promised his wife never to sleep with anyone else in London. She knew what he was doing; they both had an arrangement. I guess she also had her toyboys on the side, but weirdly they had a rule of not having sex with other people in the city they lived in. At least I wasn't feeling so guilty for liking him, but I wanted him so much though. He then pushed me onto the bed so I was lying next to Jasmine, who was still getting massaged by Alfonso. It clearly didn't take him long to move on. Youssef was also massaging me now, and it felt so good. As he was massaging my lower back, he suddenly put his little finger inside my anus. I didn't expect that, but the surprise felt good. He then rubbed himself against me. Again, I was picturing this scene and couldn't believe what Jasmine and I were doing. But I thought, we were young, free, and could do whatever we liked as long as it made us happy and we were not hurting anyone.

Youssef stood up and told me to join him in the bathroom. I stood up and followed him. He closed the door and just grabbed me by my waist. We didn't kiss or have sex, we were just pretending. He'd made a promise to his wife, and even if it was hard he was going to maintain it. For about two minutes, we just rubbed each other, hugged and told each other how much we wanted it. The bathroom had a huge mirror. At some point, Youssef grabbed me, held me tight against him, showing my front to the mirror. One hand was holding my waist, the other my neck which he kept kissing. It felt so good to be controlled by him. He kept saying to look at myself and see how I was such a pretty princess, and one day he would fuck me. It was a mad scenario. After a while he decided to leave, as he couldn't control himself any more. I was so sad. He texted me straight away to thank me for this perfect evening.

As soon as Youssef left, Alfonso stopped massaging Jasmine and came to the bathroom to talk to me, telling me he was only with her because he had no choice. I was confused. He then explained that Youssef was his boss and that if he liked something, he couldn't tell him no… meaning he liked me and Alfonso had to leave his place. He kept repeating how Youssef was an important person, more than I realised, and Alfonso was just here to serve him. I was really confused about what he was talking about. I don't think I realised who I was dealing with. He then tried to have sex with me, but no chance was I going to after he'd tried to go all the way with Jasmine, and clearly I was still caught up with

Youssef. It was already 6 a.m. Alfonso had to go, as his driver was downstairs to pick him up to take him to the airport. The way we said goodbye was weird, and I didn't feel good about it. I still liked him. I didn't have feelings, but I was attached. I was exhausted by those three days non-stop of partying. He left and we finally went to bed.

I woke up not feeling well. Steve had stopped our arrangement, Alfonso was gone and not on the best terms, I was getting money but I wasn't feeling happy, none of those guys made me feel really good about myself. I'd always felt that something was missing, but what? Jasmine and I woke up, had breakfast, and left.

TWENTY

The (Very) Expensive Dates

> *He asked me what is your favorite position. I said CEO.*
>
> Anonymous

When Alfonso left, I was even more determined to find a man who would look after me. I was still working at the club, but I didn't want to work as many days. I had too many classes to attend to waste my energy and time at the club. It was also getting harder and harder, to be honest; we could even hear rumours of the club closing. Thankfully some weeks are really good, due to worldwide events taking place in London such as the Casino week.That week was the event of the year. Everyone in the Casino industry from around the world was meeting in London to attend the biggest Casino show of the world. During the day Casino owners and suppliers would meet at the Excel exhibition centre, and at night-time guess where they were going to party? Stripclubs. I had a very good week that week; I probably made £3,000.

One night we met these two French guys, casino owners on Mauritius. They were really not my favourite clients, but they were loaded. They booked Francesca and me for the entire night, and wanted to see us the next day for lunch, which we agreed to. My client offered me £500 for lunch to compensate for my time. The first time I'd ever gone for lunch and actually got paid for it! Getting paid to eat delicious food, having my clothes on and talk… I say YES! I was less and less a stripper, I was becoming more a platonic companion who men would look after, and that is what I was after. We met at The Shard. What a view! The day was beautiful, all sunny, bright blue sky. Once again I felt blessed and lucky, even though their company wasn't the best. One of them was so arrogant and self-centred, and my client was just so negative all the time. All they talked about was the issues France was facing with security, people being unemployed and obviously this new virus that had come out of nowhere since January… Covid-19. I was not paying attention to this virus that had come straight from China. People were acting mad about it, all these posts on social media about washing our hands, but as a normal clean human being I was already doing all that, especially in my job environment. Cleanliness is a must to stay healthy. Never mind, Francesca and I were together, having the best view and food in London and I was getting paid for it. What else could we ask for?

The lunch ended, I went back home and allowed myself a few days off, as the previous weeks had been very successful. During this time I enjoyed simple moments, such as low key cafes and restaurants with friends, walks in the park, bowling, gym, meditating. I was loving it. That's what I really liked about my job: the time I had for me, and doing things that made me happy. Those times were better than the fancy restaurants or clubs. I was also practising my singing and rehearsing, as I'd managed to put together a team to help me out with a showreel for my portfolio. All the money I was earning, I was investing back into singing or dancing. I really wanted to have my showreel ready before heading to Miami, where Francesca and I had decided to spend the entire month of March. Francesca and I were planning to travel to the States to get a break from London, enjoy some sun, network and work. A few girls at the club kept saying how they'd heard stories about strippers making a minimum of £10,000 a month, that stripping was way bigger in America. It sounded so appealing, and Francesca and I wanted to escape the winter in London and make that £10K, so we could come back better than ever to London, get our own place and not work for a while. I really thought that going to Miami would bring me a lot of money and an amazing network for my singing career. Until then, I decided to join a famous dating site for sugar daddies and sugar babes who want to meet. I had tried this website before, but most men online were using the site as an escort platform. That was fair enough, but that wasn't my purpose. I felt my best luck was with me, life was great, I felt good, everything I asked for I got, so one night I tried my luck and started to look for a potential new boyfriend who would look after me. That was when I found Kevin.

Kevin was a trader, thirty-seven years old, English, divorced, looking for an easy relationship with no headaches, and happy to provide for the right girl. We clicked straight away! As soon as we started talking, we couldn't stop. We spoke constantly for a week about anything and everything. It didn't feel like an arrangement any more, but more like a potential boyfriend who wanted to help me out. As he really liked me, he offered to take me out on Valentine's Day, and asked if it was OK to give me £500 as a Valentine present. That was the best Valentine present I ever had! I am always alone for Valentine's Day. I was actually imagining myself with him, his house was my dream house and he wasn't bad looking either, I would even say charming. We were talking so much, laughing, it was just perfect. Until we met, I was just having normal days, waking up, meditating, gym, cooking, enjoying my time alone. But you know what they say… when you're happy and feeling good, that's when the old flames come back.

And guess who came back one week later… Steve! What did he want? He had the guts to text me to ask if any of my rich clients were looking to get massages, and if I could hook him up with them. Once again, I didn't know if he was really dumb, or if he had no shame at all. I think I did insult him at some point, but I usually don't stay mad at people for too long. He apologised for his attitude last time. I accepted his apologies, but that was it, I still didn't want to have anything to do with him. He begged to see me and give me a massage, and guess what, I gave in. I simply cannot resist a massage. So on 13 February 2020, Steve came to mine. I wasn't really happy to see him, as the little feelings I'd had for him were gone. I think he didn't realise that for a girl like me, things move fast, really fast, and I'd had many opportunities to forget him. I wasn't going to wait for his ass or feel sorry for myself. He was trying to be all nice, cuddly and affectionate, but I wasn't having any of that. I just wanted my massage.

I was about to lie on the massage table when he pulled out a box from his bag and gave it to me. What the fuck what was this? He wished me a happy early Valentine's Day. I opened the box and found a long thin gold chain. A chain that I immediately wanted to use to hang my crystal around my neck. I was surprised, I really didn't expect him to make such a nice gesture. I thanked him, but that didn't change my feelings towards him. During the massage he still tried to go beyond, but I didn't allow him. Anyway, we had only one hour this time, as I'd decided to go to work that night.

I did go to work, without much motivation. It was the night before Valentine's Day so the club wasn't busy. Half of London, I mean men, were probably too busy running around trying to find a last-minute present or a florist who still had a decent bouquet. Amber, Francesca and I were sitting together at one of the tables waiting for clients to arrive. Before work I'd texted Kevin to wish him a good evening. That night he was out watching a comedy with one of his friends, which happened to be right next to my club. I never told him where I was working, for security reasons. All I said was, "Oh, you're near me tonight, we ain't far from each other." I didn't think he'd guess where I was working, as two other stripclubs are in the same area. He texted me back asking if I was working at this club, meaning mine. I didn't respond, as I didn't want to take the risk of seeing him turn up.

I went on with my night, trying to get clients, but I clearly couldn't care less. My mind was with Kevin, to be honest. As the little girl I am at heart, I could already imagine myself being married, living in a luxury home in Kensington, walking around with my dog and kids, and having the life that I'd always wanted. Suddenly something, or shall I say someone, took me out of my daydreaming. One client looked very familiar. I studied him and – how embarrassing! This client was a guy that I'd dated probably about three years ago. I remember a Tinder date, my only Tinder date ever, that my former work colleagues forced me to go on as they were worried that I was never dating. I remember, the date went well but nothing more. I didn't have any butterflies, I was also having really weird dreams at the time I was seeing him, his vibe just didn't feel right so I ended it. He'd tried many times to ask me out again, but I wasn't interested. Why was he here, seriously on his own? How embarrassing. I pretended that I didn't recognise him and carried on with my night. All the girls were trying to get time with him, but he was just staying there, sitting by the bar and looking at me out of the corner of his eye. I knew he recognised me, but he wasn't making a move.

Suddenly the worst thing happened: I was with the girls, chatting around, when I saw Kevin coming into the club, by himself. He walked towards the restaurant area, sat at one of the tables, facing the wall, his face away from the stage. I was mortified. What was I meant to do? Go and say Hi? Pretend not to see him? I was about to go, but that didn't feel right. How could he come to my workplace when we'd never met (except by photo)? And my workplace is not the usual place, let's remind ourselves: I don't have many clothes on at work! I didn't want him to see me as a stripper for the first time, and on top of that not paying me for my time would be so unfair from him. I went and hid downstairs in the locker room and checked my phone to see if he had texted me. Of course he had: he'd informed me he was there and asked me to come over and say HI, which I refused and explained why. The way he was texting was a bit weird; he seemed drunk. He was saying things that were a bit much for someone I'd never met: very dramatic, a little disturbing.

"You are the only person in the world I want to see right now."

"Please don't block me. I'm such a piece of shit for doing this to you. I'm so dumb."

"You are the most important person in my eyes, I want you so much."

I mean, for someone that I'd never met, not even once, his personality seemed a bit extreme. I am an extreme person, but that sounded as if he was out of control. I knew a few bipolar people in my circle, and this is exactly what it looked like. We'd had many conversations about how he was depressed before, and how he was in a very dark place. So to me it looked as if he had very high moments and very low moments. I am not a judgemental person, I work everyday on my own mental health and I have seen many therapists throughout my life to talk about my jealousy, low self-esteem and anger, due to my parents' separation and men treating me badly. But facing someone I barely knew and who I'd only met on this sort of platform, I had to be extra cautious. I told him that he had to leave, that I couldn't work if he was there. He agreed and left. Thank God I could finally work! I then had a sit-down for an hour and a half.

I was happy when I came out of it: my Tinder date was still there at the bar waiting! Jesus Christ, why?! One of the girls came and informed me that he didn't want any other girls, and that if he had to spend money it would be on me. Obviously! I didn't know if I should go and talk to him, I was way too embarrassed, but like the girls were telling me, should I just take his money and go? Well sure, I am a stripper, that is what I'm meant to do, it's my job. Let's go.

I went over and said, "Hey, I guess we know each other."

And with the worst acting, he looked at me, pretending to be confused, and said, "Hold on a second… Are you… Lo… ?"

I stopped him before he said my real name, and said, "Yes, it's me."

He knew exactly who I was, why pretend? He was a man

in his forties, a grown ass man, why pretend? I found it so pathetic. We spoke for about five minutes and then I told him that if he wanted to carry on speaking, we had to go private. I think he thought I would give him a discount or something, because I knew him, but no chance. We went to one of the booths, sat down and started talking. After two minutes I was so bored, I just wanted to get out. He had nothing interesting to say apart from how he was in a bad relationship, he didn't love his girlfriend but didn't want to leave, as he didn't want to be alone at his age. Was that meant to impress me, or make me feel bad for him? That was such a turn-off for me. To lighten up the mood, I asked if he thought I'd changed and if I looked good? He simply said, "Yes, you're OK." I'm OK? Really? Wow, what a way to impress a girl!

And then he suddenly tried to kiss me! Are you for real? First we're at my workplace, second you don't even ask or receive a sign from me that I want that too, third you're telling me I look OK, and then you think I'm going to let you kiss me? Some men are so confused. If that usually works for you, well good for you, but that doesn't work with a girl like me. His excuse for his attitude was the fact that we knew each other, so he thought I was allowed to kiss him. Dude, this isn't a dating site or a regular club. Finally the thirty minutes were over and I didn't try to extend the time. I just left. He ran after me, asking for my number. I simply said no and went downstairs. What a loser. I was thanking the universe every day for being single and never settling with any of those guys from the past. I was alone for a reason, probably because someone better was coming my way…

When the night ended, Leo our manager called me into the office. I wondered why. He told me that a client had asked about me earlier on during the night, but didn't want anyone to come and get me to come and talk to him… I knew it was

Kevin. He then told me that he'd asked to be left alone, no managers or girls to come and speak to him. He apparently ordered a really expensive bottle of Champagne, some truffle pasta and spent the whole time on his phone. I knew why, because he was texting me. But what Leo told me after freaked me out a little. He said that he'd then started to cry, proper crying, paid for his food and the untouched bottle of Champagne, ran out and left. Leo asked me if he was an ex-boyfriend or something. I said no, I knew him but I'd never met him. Everyone in the office was shocked. How come a guy could cry over a girl he'd never met in his life and only spoken to for about a week? I have to admit I was sceptical about his attitude. I wasn't going to judge him and let him down because he cried. I was always trying to understand the other person, but at least this told me he had a bit of an extreme personality and I should be careful.

Friday 14 February, Valentine's Day, I woke up with ten messages from Kevin apologising and begging to still meet me tonight. I was hesitating because of what had happened the night before, but it was Valentine's Day and I didn't want to be alone. I still liked him, and let's face it, I needed the money. Anyway, what could happen to me in a public place? I texted him back saying it was all good, but that it was the last time something like that could happen. I obviously didn't tell him that I knew he'd cried. I got up, carried on with my day and got ready to meet him. I didn't really dress up: I wore jeans, a black long-sleeved top and some heeled boots, my hair straight and natural make-up. I felt pretty and confident. Kevin, here I come.

At 8 p.m. I arrived at the restaurant in the heart of Mayfair. Kevin was already downstairs waiting for me. I gave my coat to the hostess and headed downstairs. I was nervous, I have to admit. I have no issues meeting strangers every night, but as soon as I like someone I become shy. The good actress that I am knows how to put a brave face on and the biggest smile to hide my nervousness and shyness. I recognised him straight away. He stood up and smiled. I walked towards him and we kissed on the cheeks. Kevin was really tall, approximately 6'4", broad shoulders, beard, my sort of guy. He wasn't as charming as I thought face-wise, but he wasn't unpleasant.

From the minute we sat down, we didn't stop talking. I mean he didn't. Usually I am the one talking and always asking the questions, so it was quite refreshing to have a man who could talk. But for someone who kept saying that he wanted to find out about me and my story, well, that was a bit of a failure. I was having a good time, don't get me wrong, but I felt that it was forever me coming up with the questions and him answering and never asking anything in return. After a few cocktails, and when I say a few I would say at least six or seven amaretto sours, we started to flirt a bit. But the more he drank, the more I observed that his behaviour was becoming a little ODD. I know when a man is looking at me with desire; I see that every night, but the way he was looking right at me and biting his lips was disturbing, like he couldn't hold himself in place. It was almost like the first time a teenager sees a naked woman. Another thing that made me question his intentions was the way he constantly repeated that he was going to treat me like a princess and do X, Y and Z for me. Let's remember that I'd experienced that before, and it had never ended well. I was enjoying my time with him, but I wasn't going to be naive and dream away this time. I was also in the back of my head visualising him crying at the club the night before.

At some point I actually asked him if he was bipolar… he stopped for a second and said No, but for sure he had

ADHD. That was explaining a lot. I wasn't feeling threatened by that, as we all have our past and reasons why we are the way we are. I mean, look at Kim Kardashian: she is married to Kanye West, who has been diagnosed bipolar, and he is one of the greatest artists of our time. The same with my dear Britney Spears. Having a mental condition does not classify someone as being bad, depending on the severity. I obviously had to be careful as I didn't know him. Before we left, he begged to see me as much as possible before I left for Miami. Business-minded as I am, I thought straight away about him coming to the club the next day, which was a Saturday. Weekend nights are dead, full of cheap people, so I thought it could be good for him to come, with my authorisation this time. He straight away accepted and promised he'd turn up.

We took our coats and left. He transferred me my Valentine present via PayPal, gave me £60 for my cab back home, and kissed me on the cheeks like a gentleman. I mean, I warned him not to even try kissing me as I wasn't doing that on a first date. Bullshit, who was I fooling? I could do that within the first minute if I wanted to. I just didn't feel like it. I came back home full of hopes. Had I finally met the perfect arrangement? That's what I wanted to think at the time. I got back home and went straight to the kitchen to grab a bite to eat; all this alcohol had made me hungry and thirsty. I was not used to drinking so much, I was feeling dehydrated, I needed water and some greasy food.

As I came in the kitchen, I saw a beautiful bouquet on the table alongside a parcel and a card with my name. Jesus, a necklace, £500 and now flowers and presents! Life was definitely better single than in a relationship. The flowers were my favourite, Pink Lylis. I opened the card: "Hope you like my favourite masterpiece, it is finally finished. Happy Valentine, Frenchy, Alex". I was so excited to open the parcel, because I knew what it was. A few years ago an artist had come across my profile on social media. We'd been talking for a while now, we'd never met, but out of nowhere one day he decided to make a painting from one of my pictures. I opened the parcel and discovered a painting of me. The painting was stunning: the background was bright pink and just as on my picture, I had a bright yellow top and an extremely high long ponytail. I was so happy: that was such a cool present, my first piece of art, and on top of that it was of me. How crazy to receive such a gift from someone I'd never even met once. I was beyond grateful. Everyday I thanked the universe for my life, even in the down time, and I knew how privileged I was: talented, successful, lucky, with a financially good, exciting life. I went to bed that night with a big smile on my face.

On Saturday 15 February, I woke up not so fresh after all the drinks I'd had the night before, but I still felt on top of the world. Just as every day for the past week, I was texting Kevin all day. We still agreed to see each other at the club after his dinner with friends. As we were talking, I joked about how this time he needed to ask questions about me, as on our first date I'd been the one with all the questions. Well, that joke didn't go down well. He immediately got defensive and told me I'd made him look like a dick. I told him that wasn't my intention at all, that he was just very passionate when he was talking, which was great, but he shouldn't forget about the other person in front of him. I could feel a little chill and awkwardness between us after that. I really didn't think that would be such a big deal, but in a way, coming from him and his personality, I guess I had to get used to sudden changes of mood. I usually don't like people who change their mood from one minute to another, but I thought he was worth it.

On top of that, that day a famous British TV presenter was announced dead. She had killed herself due to the pressure of social media. We are living in such a weird era. I'd experienced hate on social media when I had my two minutes of fame in France, and trust me, reading bad comments about yourself every single day can be damaging. I wasn't even that famous, I couldn't imagine how out of control it can get when it happens to a big celebrity. As for myself, I decided back then never to read the comments, either good or bad, because I didn't want it to affect my life. Why would I read comments from people I'd never met in my life and who probably had a brain the size of a pea? I am much happier when I avoid bad energies. It is hard to, but trying was the best decision I'd made, and that was how I was living my life in general since working as a stripper, never listening to people's comments. The death of the TV presenter really affected Kevin much more than I expected. I think he knew her to some degree, and felt for it, as it has to do with mental health.

I have to say that 2020 started strongly in terms of dramas around the world: Australia's bush fires, the spread of the new virus Covid-19, Kobe Bryant and his daughter's helicopter crash, more deaths due to social media, the world was going mad. On my side, 2020 was my year. It started off more than right and I knew it was the year when everything was going to change for me. But I didn't know that one world tragedy would change my life…

Kevin was on a low. I didn't know which was easier to deal with: when he was high or low, and I didn't know if I could cope with it all, to be honest. I knew I was enjoying a financial benefit, but at what cost? I was feeling his emotions so strongly that they were getting to me, and I was scared of getting drained by his change of moods. Feeling empathy is a blessing but also a curse; you probably know what I'm talking about. I went to work that night and waited for him to text me. Nothing from him the whole evening. I couldn't believe that after just one meeting he was already acting so cold. On our first date he kept repeating, "Actions speak louder than words," "I will prove that I'm not bullshitting you." Well, he was clearly proving that he was all talk and no actions. I couldn't believe he was not even texting me to let me know what was going on. I was so angry, first because I couldn't believe that because I'd said one little thing the guy was already turning cold; and second, the club was dead and I wasn't making any money.

At around 2 a.m. I finally received a text from him telling me he wasn't in the mood to come to the club. Fucking idiot of me to believe even for one second that he was maybe different. I should not have cared and just gone with the flow as this was purely an arrangement. This is how I was meant to see it, not acting like he was my boyfriend. But as usual I fall for people, especially if I feel they're in pain. I liked him, let's face it, and if I had an arrangement, I would have preferred to be with someone young and in a situation more like a real relationship than something dead cold and fake. I felt played with. Was it going to be like that with every rich man? Every time I said what I thought, would I get the cold shoulder? Couldn't they handle a woman who speaks her mind? I didn't even bother responding, and I went back on the floor trying to make some money somehow.

At around 2.30 a.m. a group of guys walked in. I felt that they had money. I told Francesca to go to the bar straight away and not wait for them to have their drinks. None of the girls were making money that night, so we were all hovering like bees around a hive. I don't think that made them feel comfortable at all. Imagine twenty girls surrounding you. No doubt that feels overwhelming. One of them had his back to me, and I was trying to say Hello, but he was clearly ignoring me. How rude! Francesca managed to get herself in front of him and started speaking to him. He seemed very pleased to see her, because at least one of us was the client's type: Francesca looked Egyptian, with beautiful caramel skin, long curly hair and deep dark almond-shaped eyes. If one of your girlfriends is picked by a client who is part of a group of guys, there are good chances you will also get picked. After talking for just a few minutes, we told them they had to pick quickly if they wanted to have fun with us as the club was closing in just over an hour. They all picked their girls and that didn't include me. Fuck. One of them couldn't decide, though; he was so afraid of hurting our feelings that he simply left, went outside for a cigarette and asked his friend to pick for him. Luckily for me the main guy that had to decide was Francesca's guy, so she naturally told him to pick me, which he did. Yes!!!!! Thanks, Francesca. She knew I would have done the same for her. We were definitely a good team and looked after each other's back.

We all went to the Glitter Room, about six of us. Everyone was there apart from the guy who couldn't pick. I felt a bit stupid to be there on my own, so I decided to join Francesca and her guy and join in their conversation. His name was Liam, forty-five years old, an Irish investor. At first I thought he was a bit weird and stuck up, but the more we talked to him the more we liked him. He was actually very cool: he told us he'd had a really long day and he was just tired. So was I. I couldn't stop yawning. Their friend finally came back, and I could finally speak to him. Jesus, he was so weird, he kept telling me I shouldn't be here, I should be a model and I shouldn't have to deal with this shit. They make me laugh when they give us that sort of comment. Yes, man, I want to be a singer, but sorry my parents aren't rich and can't provide for me while I'm studying. I have to eat and make money, and sorry for not wanting to work in a regular job that doesn't give me as much freedom and money.

He then turned around and looked at Liam and said, "Do you know some agents that you could introduce to Satine?" He was finally saying something interesting. He then left again for another cigarette. I'd never met someone so uncomfortable around a stripper. So I ended up the whole night talking to Liam, and obviously I wanted to know more about this mysterious friend of his who was an agent in Ireland. The sit-down was almost over, so he asked us our number and offered to see us both for lunch or dinner in a couple of days when he was back in London for business and I could meet his agent friend. Bingo! So happy. We exchanged numbers and he tipped us both £500 each without us even asking for it. Francesca and I both looked at each other, shocked, we had no words. We'd never received so much money in tips. We both hugged him and kissed him on the cheeks and thanked him. He said we could at least enjoy ourselves with the tips: go and buy something nice to wear for the next time we would see each other, and that it would also compensate for our time with them next time we met. Liam was so generous, chilled and cute. He didn't even ask us to get naked and dance; we only did it because we wanted to tease him. He was such a gentleman. I was grateful that my Saturday turned out that way after starting off so wrong. Again, I thanked the universe for all the abundance in my life. I'd really started to get used to those paid dates. Some girls charge way less and offer their bodies; whereas I was there enjoying the best restaurants in London and getting paid for it, how amazing.

On Sunday 16 February, as soon as I woke up, I checked my phone: no message from Kevin. I mean, I'd never responded to his last message, so it was technically normal for him not to message, but I thought he would try a bit harder. I did what I do best: I tested him to see if he really wanted me, and if everything he'd said two nights ago was real. I simply said that I couldn't be bothered to be with someone who was all talk and didn't keep his promises. I do that all the time at the early stage of a relationship: I try running away to see if they are willing to go on the ride. It usually works and they usually beg me to stay, I mean until they have had enough, because I usually go on and on all the way throughout the relationship. Well, that didn't work with Kevin: he simply agreed to end things there and then; he couldn't be bothered arguing with me. Wow, for someone who was meant to be so into me, that felt harsh. In a way, that proved to me he was all talk, like the others, so I shouldn't be that surprised. How could they be so demanding? Those guys have the guts to act like they are the big deal, only because they have money. They are not even good-looking or most of the time interesting, and they act as if we are the one doing them a favour. No, dude, we are doing you a favour by allowing you to walk around with a beautiful woman, which is why you need to put up the price. How arrogant. I texted back to say that no matter what happened, I'd really enjoyed my week talking to him and wished him the best. He didn't even respond. Bastard! I was way too nice, seriously.

As soon as I saw him not responding, I went back to the dating site, which I was really annoyed about. That website was full of pervs and freaks, and I just wanted someone normal, or as normal as possible, like Kevin. Why did I open my mouth? Why do I always let my emotions talk? I got too much into this, as if it was a real relationship; I should not have, I should think of it like a business, the same as the club;

this was the best way not to get hurt and to do the job properly.

That day I went for afternoon tea with members of my family who were visiting London for a few days. It was nice to show London to people who'd never been there and have quality time with family members. But every time someone asked me a question, I had to lie. I was so tired of lying, I wished I could tell the truth, but I really couldn't be bothered to explain the non-explainable and change people's beliefs and opinions that had been in their heads since they were born.

Wednesday 19 February meant an exciting day ahead for Francesca and me. After texting for days with Liam, we'd finally managed to arrange a time and place to meet him and his friends for lunch, perfect! Surprisingly, I was also talking to Kevin again. After a day of non-talking and researching potential sugar daddies, I decided to put my pride aside and text him to apologise and say that I was missing him. I genuinely missed him: after trying to talk to a few men on that website, it made me realise that Kevin was great. Thank God his response was positive; he also apologised and asked to see me again. I felt a bit bad about going for lunch with Liam and his friend; I felt that I was lying to Kevin, but he was so unsure and unpredictable that I couldn't totally count on him yet. Until I was set with him and sure about his feelings, I still had to hustle.

That day, I woke up fresh as a daisy and full of energy. I dressed up smart casual: in a long knitted grey dress with black over the knee boots. The dress was so fitted that I wasn't able to wear any underwear. I never wear a bra for sure, and from time to time no knickers if the clothes are too tight. I reckoned underwear marks were cheap and not elegant. Liam asked us to join them at a well-known brasserie in South Kensington at 2 p.m. We walked in, gave our coats to the hostess and she then walked us to our table. I saw Liam first; it was so nice to see him, he was such a genuine nice guy, you could tell just by looking in his eyes that he was kind. I gave him two kisses on the cheeks while Francesca was saying hello to Liam's friend. I then went over to him also to say hello and introduce myself.

As soon as our eyes met, something very warm happened, such a good vibe and energies. His eyes were so blue and sparkly, I felt lost, like I was in another dimension. So lost that instead of introducing myself as Satine, I said my real name. What an idiot. I never say my real name ever, that is a number one rule, but right now I couldn't do anything about it. He then introduced himself: "Hi, I'm Connor, nice to meet you." He had the cutest Irish accent. I was pleased because I usually have a really hard time understanding the Irish accent, but his and Liam's were fine. We all sat down. Francesca was on my left, Liam on my right and Connor across the table facing me. We all started to talk about what sort of business they did, how they'd met and obviously about our life as strippers. I realised that Connor wasn't an agent as Liam had mentioned to me. He had once invested in a talent agency, but that was about it. However, he knew many people in the industry, so it was still good to have him in my contacts. We all had a very good time and fun conversation. At some point Francesca was not making that much effort with the conversation, and Liam was simply not the biggest talker. Connor and I couldn't stop talking, we were drawn to each other, laughing, talking, flirting with our eyes, he was just so interesting, so intriguing. I was getting so turned on and I know he was too. We were not near each other but I could feel the sexual tension across the table. I could feel how kind he was too, just like Liam. I'm not sure if it's an Irish thing, but the energy round this table was so good and positive, I was having a really good time. For the first time in a long time I didn't feel that I was acting or putting on a fake smile. My conversation, laughs and smiles were very genuine and real, maybe that's why I naturally introduced myself as Lola and not as Satine, because something inexplicable and real was happening between Connor and me.

At some point Connor and I were talking about my experience as a stripper, so I shared a few funny stories and a few less serious ones. He naturally told me I should write a book. Connor was like a mind reader, everything I was thinking or about to say he was also thinking it too. I said that I was keeping a diary and was hoping to publish it one day. I always mention that to my clients when they ask me my goals in life, I always say that I want to become a singer and also publish my stripper diary, which they never really bother asking about. They probably think "Oh, she's cute thinking she will publish this one day." Connor was properly into it and started to ask me questions about it: "Who was going to read the book?" "Would it be male or female?" "How would the book end?" He had so many questions about it. That made me so happy that someone was truly interested in my diary and my story. Which made me want him even more. I could even feel my nipples getting hard, and I could see him trying to be discreet but sneaking a look.

Something really magical, beautiful and sexual happened at that lunch between Connor and me. A lot of it was sexual, but I could feel something more, as if we knew each other already. I felt such a strong connection, something so powerful, deep, I felt so secure talking to him. We finished lunch around 5.30 p.m. I couldn't believe how long it had lasted. I didn't even realise the time, I was just in my happy bubble. Liam and Connor had a business dinner in a few hours so we all had to leave. When we left, Connor grabbed a black cab for us and gave me cash to pay for it. When I looked at how much he handed me, I saw it was way more than I needed. I told him that I didn't need £200 for a cab home, but he told me to keep it and just get myself something nice with it. When we said goodbye, I felt a pain in my heart. I was sad to leave him, I didn't want the afternoon to stop. We exchanged numbers so I knew I was going to see him again, but when? I knew he was attracted to me, but did he feel what I felt? I'd had a few crushes on my clients before, I mean yes a lot, I admit it, I was easily falling for men at the club, but this time it felt very different.

I jumped into the black cab home. On my way home, I was looking outside at the beautiful streets of London. It was winter so it was already dark outside. I was dreaming away in my own thoughts, and then I realised I hadn't checked my phone all day. I looked at it and saw a few messages from Kevin. I'd completely forgotten about him. I responded, but my heart was not with him any more. All I could think about was Connor. Once home, Connor messaged me thanking me for this amazing time, and he would definitely message me the next time he was in London. I returned the compliment and told him I would be more than happy to see him again. We texted throughout the evening, even though he was having a business dinner. We couldn't stop messaging each other. I then asked him what time his flight was in the morning. He told me it was only in the afternoon. I jumped in straight away and suggested I come and meet him at his hotel once his dinner was over. He accepted straight away.

At 11.30 p.m. I was back outside on my way to South Kensington again. I was so excited to see him, even though I'd seen him only a couple of hours ago. I arrived at his hotel, walked towards the entrance and entered the lobby. I saw him straight away, sitting on one of the sofas waiting for me. As soon as he saw me, he stood up and walked towards me with the biggest smile. As soon as we were close enough we hugged and didn't leave each other for one minute. He took my hand and we headed towards the lift. We were not alone waiting for the elevator. A group of three women were also waiting. Once the lift arrived we entered first so we could be at the back of the lift. I'd changed my outfit since lunch, I'd showered and put on fresh clothes. I was wearing a beige knitted fitted jumpsuit and no underwear at all. As he was holding me by my waist he could feel that I had nothing on. His eyes were more than shining.

We arrived at his floor and walked to his room. We first sat on the sofa and talked a bit about dinner and life. At some point he looked at me and told me how fascinating my life was and how smart I was. That was a first: I hear from time to time that I am street smart, but more from friends than from men. He was loving the fact that I was so independent, driven and passionate. He said that the way I was speaking at lunch about my singing career, my book and my life in general with such passion was a real turn on. I felt so warm in my heart and happy. Maybe I was wrong, but for the first time in a long time, I felt that someone cared about me. We started kissing and moved to the bed. Connor was not selfish. He started to kiss my neck and remove the top of my jumpsuit to discover my small hard nipples, which he loved. He kissed them and sucked them while rubbing my vagina. He then removed my jumpsuit completely and went down on me. The way he was going down on me was so beautiful, he was kissing my pussy the way he would kiss me. He then put his tongue really deep inside me that made me scream.

He then looked at me, his bright red face dying of pleasure, and said: "Princess is so naughty for Daddy she is going to get spoiled. I know what you want, you want to be a spoiled princess, but to get treated like a slut in bed. You deserve everything, and I'm going to give it to you."

Could he read my mind? We hadn't even spoken about sex during lunch, but what he said was so accurate, as if he could read my mind. I always had this fantasy of having a man spoil me, respect me, love me, care for me and be the sweetest with me; but once in the bedroom be totally dominant and treat me like a complete slut. I know it can sound wrong and not very understandable, but that is what my body and mind needed. I needed someone to treat me with a lot of respect, to love me unconditionally for who I was, so I could feel reassured all the time, but also be treated badly in bed, so all my life's frustration and pain could be externalised. I have tried many times during my past relationships to explain this concept, but none of my exes really understood. Either they treated me well but were boring in bed, or they were simply bad with no respect, so I couldn't show my true self in bed, as they would take advantage and think I was an actual slut and treat me with even less respect. The fact that he pronounced those words turned me on even more, so I let myself go and did act like a slut. I wasn't thinking, I was being myself, my true self, not thinking what he would think of me, and the more I let myself go, the more he was looking at me like a princess. Every time he called me by that name, I would get wetter. He kept telling me how much he would spoil me and treat me right. I know I'd heard that many times, and it had always been a lie, but this time I believed it. Something inside my core was telling me I could trust him. He fingered me for so long without asking anything in return, but the fact that he was such a giver made me want to give back. I pushed him on his back, stood in front of him and started to lick his body and touch his penis.

I put all my heart into it, I wanted to please him so much and he loved it.

"Princess is so good to daddy."

After a while I wanted him inside me. He grabbed a condom from the bedside table and put it on, but like many men Connor wasn't a fan of condoms and couldn't handle it. The condom was too tight for him, so his boner kept going down. No chance I was going to sleep with him without it, I had just met him and didn't have his medical records or anything. I decided to wank him again. I asked him to sit on the edge of the bed, I went on my knees and started the job. At some point he grabbed my face, held it really tight, which hurt me a little, but turned me on at the same time. He looked right into my eyes, his eyes got dark, they were not as blue any more, he looked at me and said how much of a good girl I was and kissed me really deeply. I felt that my soul had left my body. His face, his eyes were so different from during lunch. I felt that I was with a different person, but in a good way. He was exactly what I needed. He finally came on my breast, screamed with pleasure and then kissed me on my forehead. He went straight to the bathroom to grab a towel and cleaned me up. So many men just throw tissues at you and let you clean yourself, which I find so disrespectful and lazy, knowing that it is their sperm and mess. When a man cleans his own sperm off you, that means he has education and he respects you. Once I was cleaned, he grabbed me, held me in his arms and lay with me. His soft face was back and his eyes were smiling again.

I asked him if I could order food, which he obviously accepted. As I was ordering it, I could feel his eyes on me. When I hung up the phone from room service, I turned around and he was there staring at me. He said, "What are you doing to me, Lola?" I smiled and went back into his arms. I felt so good and safe. Then I asked him if he'd ever had this sort of relationship, "daddy princess" sort of thing. He told me he hadn't, but looking at me made him want to spoil me so much, but also treat me like a slut as I was so sexual. He explained that he found me very complex: he felt that he had to protect me, that I was so adorable and special, but also so sexy and sexual that he couldn't hold his perviness towards me. I appreciated his honesty, and I was totally fine with it. Until my food arrived, he touched me again, he couldn't stop himself. "You have the prettiest pussy i have ever seen, princess."

I left around 2 a.m. Connor put me in a black cab and kissed me goodbye. He once again gave me £200 for the cab, which I didn't need. I tried to give it back, but he wouldn't hear a thing. I was on a little cloud, but I was also worried about my strong feelings after only a day. It wasn't the time for me to think about being in a relationship, I still had to continue my job, which is not an easy one when you have a partner. I also wanted to concentrate on my career, my book and going to America. It was really not a good time. I thought that I should embrace it for now and live one day at a time and see. I was meant to go to the States in two weeks' time. Would I see him before I left? Would these feelings be gone as fast as they came? Only time would answer those questions, but I'd been gone only twenty minutes and I was missing him already.

By 22 February I'd known Connor for three days, and for three days we'd been texting non-stop. I knew I shouldn't entertain this and act as if it could go somewhere: I was a stripper, he was a businessman; I was twenty-eight years old, he was forty-four years old with four kids. I wasn't even sure if he was married or divorced; he'd never mentioned anything about being married, he wasn't wearing a ring when we met and I didn't ask. I was probably too scared to hear the truth and wake up from my dream. He was living in Ireland, me in London. What was the point? But the pull was stronger than me. The way he was making me feel was so good, I hadn't felt that way with someone since Filip.

I was completely honest with Connor. He obviously knew I was a stripper, but I also told him about sometimes meeting my regulars outside for lunch or dinner. He also knew about Kevin, and the fact that I was looking for someone to look after me financially. He even knew about Steve. I was so transparent with him, I didn't lie once about what I was doing or where I was going. He was extremely jealous, but the fact that I was so honest reassured him. He didn't like me dancing much and being so tired because of the club. He wanted me to concentrate on my singing, dancing and writing. I think it was also the fact that he didn't want men around me. But I wasn't going to stop what was feeding me, which he understood. But to avoid me going too many nights to the club and help me concentrate on my study, he offered to pay for my dancing classes, a whole semester of singing lessons and my rent. Connor was simply amazing. He was so supportive of what I was doing. I felt for once that someone had my back and I could rest on him.

That night I was meant to see Kevin for our second date. Connor knew about it, and wasn't very pleased, but he had no choice. Kevin had already paid for my plane ticket to Miami, so I couldn't cancel the date. Anyway, I had a feeling it was probably the last time I was going on a date with him. I loved money and all the treats I was getting, but I couldn't fake liking someone for too long, and if I was playing my role of the perfect girlfriend with Kevin, he would at some point want sex, and I simply couldn't. First reason: I wasn't attracted to him; second reason: I was already so emotionally involved with Connor that I couldn't imagine myself sleeping with someone else. When I am really into someone, I am the most loyal person you can meet. If the person in front of me is respectful and treats me right, I give as much back.

I was on my way to see Kevin before work, which was my excuse not to stay too long. I met him around 8 p.m. at a restaurant called Beast. As usual he was there before me, and I met him at the bar. I put my act on and went for it. I saw him straight away sitting there, I put on my big smile and went to hug him. It was nice to see him, but I didn't know if my character-act was happy or if I was truly happy. Sometimes I got confused between the role I was playing and my real self. We had a few drinks and ate some dinner. He apologised for his behaviour of running away from arguments, and promised again to treat me like a princess and never shut down as before, even if I was saying something he didn't like. I wanted to believe this, but I didn't, and to be honest It didn't really matter any more. All I had in my head was Connor. I couldn't wait for the dinner to be over. The date was exactly the same as the first one: all he was doing was talking about himself. Around 10 p.m. I could finally leave and headed to my last night of work. I wanted a whole week off to prepare for my trip. As soon as I shut the door of my black cab, I knew I was never going to see Kevin again, and it was only a matter of time before we stopped talking.

I arrived at the club, went downstairs to get changed, paid my house fees and waited upstairs. Guess who was sitting by the bar, hunting for new girls? Charlie. I wasn't pleased to see him at all. He tried a few times to have a go at Francesca for telling me about him and their dates, but with me he knew he couldn't have the power. He knew he'd done something wrong. At some point I had no choice but to sit next to him, as all the other chairs were taken. He was trying to make eye contact, but I wasn't giving it. I was looking straight at the stage and ignoring him. He then said "*Bonjour*" with his English accent. He thought he was being funny. I turned round and looked at him with the most disgusted look ever: my left eyebrow was so high, and my eyes were scanning him from head to toe.

"Someone's moody today," he said.

I love how men always have the excuse to call a woman moody just because she doesn't agree with his attitude. That is way too easy. I wasn't going to let him make me think I was the one in the wrong here. I told him everything I was thinking about him, and that what he'd done was wrong. He was trying to speak over me, but I made him shush each time. I didn't give him one second of opportunity to speak over me. This guy was so used to having his own way, someone had to put him back in his place at some point. That wasn't going to make him rethink or change his personality, but I just wanted to show him that not every woman will put up with his shit and beg for him and let him get away with his attitude. Once I'd finished, he apologised and asked me for a hug, which I refused. When I did, he tried to play with my soft spot and say "Someone is going to be punished for being a bad girl." He thought that kind of talk would still work. Did he really think I was that weak? It clearly didn't work. What some people don't understand is that to have some sort of submissive–dominant relationship you need good respect and communication with the other person; if not, it doesn't work. I wasn't getting turned on by him any more, at all. That was the last time I spoke to Charlie and never saw him ever again…

That month I made over £3,000 by simply going on dates. This was clearly my new way of making money, and I was loving it. #levelup

TWENTY-ONE

Feeling Like a True Princess

> *Chaos is an angel who fell in love with a demon.*
>
> Christopher Poindexter

From 23 February, I was finally off work for at least a month. I'd made it. I had time to concentrate on being productive, creative and getting ready for the States. I had so much to do that week before flying to Miami, Florida. I had to pack, organise my showreel: extras for my video, singing rehearsal, director and videographer. I had to write for my book as much as possible, dance, meet with Paul for a lunch date, meet with Yoan the music producer, attend to all my beauty appointments and of course meet with Connor.

I was so happy that Connor and I managed to schedule a quick meeting before my departure. The more Connor and I were talking, the more attached I became. I'd never met anyone who was so into me for everything that I was. Ambitious, sexy, very sexual, curious, very demanding and straightforward: all those traits that I used to apologise for. I'd always heard that my standards were too high, that I was too sexy, that I was dancing inappropriately, that I was speaking my mind too much, that I should calm down. Why do we always teach girls and women not to be themselves? Why was I too ambitious? Why was I too sexual? Why was I too demanding? What does that even mean? Connor loved those things about me, and naturally I wasn't as demanding and moody as in my previous relationship. He understood me sexually, he wasn't blaming me for being sexy, he was pushing me to be even more ambitious, he was listening to me, I didn't feel frustrated with him once. Nothing was missing. He was so perfect and on top of things, always romantic and full of surprises. In one week, he offered me a microphone so I could record myself, a new computer to write as I didn't have one, flowers and beauty treatments. I was so spoiled, loved and appreciated, I felt that I was living a dream, a dream from which I really didn't want to wake up.

That week I also met up with Paul, my regular from the club. I hadn't seen him for a while so it was nice to see him. We met for lunch on 28 February 2020 at Rules, the oldest restaurant in London. As soon as I walked in and he saw me, his face lit up and blushed. I was genuinely happy to see him, it felt like seeing an old friend, a friend who buys me gifts but is still a friend. During lunch he asked me if I needed anything in particular, which I did. I'd broken my phone a week before, so I was left with an old phone and in desperate need of a new one. He didn't waste time: he asked me which one I wanted and we ordered it. Thank you, Paul. Once we'd finished our lunch, he texted me straight away thanking me for my positive attitude and helping him to feel better. That's what I loved to hear: obviously I loved the gifts, the money, but I felt that I was doing something good for him too.

Even while I was an executive assistant, everyone used to come to my office to speak to me about their issues. I always had this ability to listen and help others. The only thing that was different now was that I was wearing a cocktail dress and sexy underwear at night, or going for lunches or dinners. I was happy to help people to feel better, so why stop? That was what I was trying to explain to Connor: I was telling him that my job helped me to feel more powerful, more in control, more confident than in any other job, and on top of that I was my own boss and making more money than I ever did. So he opened his mind and understood. He liked me too much to make me stop doing anything. He'd had a hard time, but he was proud that I was earning my own money and not just counting on him. I knew that if I wanted to, I could just ask him for an amount to be sent to my account every month; that would be ideal, that is actually what I wanted to do before meeting him, but because I was real with him, I was Lola, not Satine, I didn't want to take advantage of him. I was really seeing him as my lover and not as a client or a guy from a dodgy website. Of course I was accepting his gifts and financial help for my dance and singing classes, but I didn't want to count on him and take him for granted. He might one day wake up and completely forget about me, so I always said to myself that no matter what, I should have my own money and never just count on a man.

In the meantime, while I was having the perfect relationship with Connor, I was still texting Kevin on the side. Not that much though. I felt that we had nothing to tell each other any more, and what I thought might happen again, did happen. One day he seemed sad and distant; all I asked him was if everything was fine, or had I done something wrong. The other side of Kevin came out, and he literally just blew up and said he'd had enough of me always questioning everything, he couldn't play this game any more. He blocked me without giving me the chance to respond. I was shocked. I didn't even get the chance to explain myself, but in a way it was good that he was out of the picture. He was too weird anyway and too demanding.

Saturday 29 February 2020, the day of my showreel, I'd prepared everything for a week beforehand. I had my extras ready, my music, one director/videographer. I was so excited to finally show my talents and have real material to send to agents. I felt amazing doing what I loved, but also exhausted. I truly understood that day the hard work of being a performer, an artist, but I had so much emotion inside me, so much depth to let out, that singing felt like therapy to me. Everyone was really impressed, and hearing compliments was the best feeling ever. Everything I was working towards was successful. I couldn't wait to get the video and send it to agents. The day finally finished at 6 p.m. I was so drained, I went to the bathroom, ran myself a bath and went to bed.

Tuesday 3 March 2020 was the day I was finally seeing Connor before I left for Miami. I have to say I was very excited, but also very stressed. I had met him only once, and since then we had been speaking like a real couple, talking about our feelings, desires, the future. I was scared that we'd just got carried away by this one-time fantasy, but once we were face to face again it might not be the same. Sometimes people create a virtual bubble: you drown yourself in your imagination, and when you face reality you can feel really disappointed. What if I didn't find him attractive any more?

What if we didn't have anything to say to each other? What if sex was shit? All those questions that I always get in my head usually make me cancel a potential date. But this time I wasn't going to let my insecurities and doubts take over. I was going for it.

Connor had a meeting in Cambridge that week, a business dinner planned for 3 March and a board meeting on the 4th. He usually went to Cambridge straight from the airport, but for me he flew in earlier that day so we could get a chance to see each other, even if it was only for a few hours. He asked if I wanted to be picked up from somewhere, or go for lunch with him, but I'd already promised my best friend Julien to meet with him that day. London life is so crazy, having a social life is as hard to organise as a professional agenda. I had the lunch with Julien at 1 p.m. at Oxford Circus: it felt good to meet with him before seeing Connor, so I got the chance to tell Julien all about it and hear his thoughts on the situation.

Julien's opinion did really matter to me. He was always very supportive of my choices, but if he felt something wasn't right, he was always very honest about it, but never in a negative, judging way. Julien was always so kind and full of humour: one of the only people who liked me for who I truly am. I always felt very calm around him. Julien advised me to just go with the flow, to always be careful, but that everything seemed fun and genuine so why not keep going. He was trusting my gut instinct, as it had always done me good in the past so I just had to follow it. I left Julien around 1.45 p.m. as he had to get back to work. He wished me a safe trip to Miami, gave me a big hug and thanked me for lunch. I was so proud and happy that I was able to pay for my friends from time to time. I'd had a really good month, so I felt that being generous and giving back was my way to thank life for making me so blessed and lucky.

At 2 p.m. I reached King Cross St Pancras where Connor had booked our hotel for the afternoon. I walked towards the Great Northern Hotel, as confidently as possible, listening to Halsey's "Not Afraid Anymore" to give me confidence and push my adrenaline to the edge. I was wearing black faux leather trousers, ankle-heeled boots, a black sleeveless body top and my big black faux fur. All black everything. That was always my look if I didn't know what to wear. Simple, sexy, smart and effective. As usual I wasn't wearing any bra, only a black thong. I did my make-up very simply: tinted moisturiser, black eyeliner and my fake eyelashes. I was also wearing a very sweet perfume, "Thank You Next" by Ariana Grande. I wasn't a fan of expensive luxurious perfume. I still like very sweet perfume, and even though I'm nearly thirty I don't like strong smells, because I don't want to feel old ever. I think deep inside I'm having a hard time letting go of my innocent young side. I want to remain young, wild and free my whole life.

I arrived at the hotel and walked inside towards the lobby. I texted him to say I was there. He came downstairs to meet me so we could go to the hotel bar first to get a drink and talk. After two minutes, there he was. My heart was beating so fast, my legs were shaking and I was blushing, I couldn't look at him in the eye. We walked towards each other and hugged. I couldn't believe that we were finally meeting again after two weeks apart. He looked so good with his black T-shirt, black blazer, a pair of dark denims, a Rolex on his left wrist, his grey messy silver hair, grey beard and of course his sparkly blue eyes. I was in love with his eyes. We headed towards the bar and tried to find a seat, but the whole bar was so busy that day that I suggested we get a drink upstairs in the room. To be honest, I preferred that. The whole "Let's get a drink at the bar first" was just an excuse to pretend not be a total slut who wanted to get fucked the very first hour. We walked towards the lift to head to the room; while we were waiting for the lift to come, I couldn't even stand next to him. I was so shy and goofy. We just started to laugh as I was acting like a teenager. Once the lift arrived and opened, he pushed me inside, grabbed me by the waist and kissed me deeply. I thought I was going to pass out. We arrived on our floor and walked to our room. He didn't leave an inch between us. Once we entered the room, we sat on the bed and cuddled straight away. I had missed him so much, it felt so good to be near him, even though I still felt slightly nervous and uncomfortable. He stood up and went to get something from the closet. He came back with a Chanel carrier bag and said, "This is for you, Princess." I started to laugh nervously, the first time ever that someone had handed me a carrier bag from Chanel. I opened it and found the biggest bottle of perfume you can get. "Gabrielle" was the name of the perfume. He then said, "I got it for you as I think you deserve more than wearing high street perfume." I liked my high street perfume much more than expensive perfume, but he didn't know that, and the thought behind it was just adorable. "Gabrielle" was clearly not the perfume for me, it was very strong, not matching with my personality at all, but I still thanked him and gave him a kiss. He then handed me a wallet which I also didn't like and I think he could see it in my eyes.

"I'm terrible at picking the right thing, I'm sorry. We don't know each other well yet, so forgive me." He was so cute. I usually get annoyed or disappointed when a guy buys me something I don't like, but with him I was simply grateful for everything, as I knew he would surprise me with something else at some point and just treat me like a princess every day.

I put the wallet on the side, but he told me to look inside. I opened the wallet to check it out, and there was a bundle of cash, a really big one. I looked at him, confused: "What the fuck, Connor? What is that?"

"I just thought you'd need cash for Miami, just in case things don't go as planned. I don't want you to stress about money or work and take money from your account, so I thought $1,000 would help you out, and there is also £1,000 for your return."

Was he serious? Just like that! Was I dreaming, was he actually serious? I started laughing really loud, like someone that just won the lottery.

"I hope that makes you happy, baby." For someone like him, that amount of money was probably nothing, but for me it was crazy, I couldn't believe it. I jumped on him and started to remove my clothes. I wanted him so bad, all the frustration from the past two weeks of talking non-stop and just now being so spoiled. I wanted to reward him and show him how much I appreciated him.

"I love your small perky tits hanging down," he said as I was naked, doggy style on top of him removing his trousers. Once his trousers were open, I grabbed his hard-on and started licking the tip of his penis very slowly. I knew that was driving him crazy. I was looking right at him at the same time, like I was daring him to look at me too. He found it so sexy that I wasn't shy and showing I was enjoying it as much as him. I then moved fast up and down to take it really deep. As soon as I did that, he grabbed my head to make me stay longer and deeper. There we were, starting our little game.

"Do you like when Daddy is making you go real deep?" All I could do was moan, as his penis was so far down I could not speak. The adrenaline I was getting when he was dominant and dirty was inexplicable. He then let me go, but that made me want to suck him even more.

"You are a slut, aren't you?" Those words turned me on so much. "You are Daddy's little slut, tell me that you're my slut."

"Yes, Daddy, I am, I'm a slut, a fucking slut, who just wants to please Daddy."

I loved to be degraded during sex, I loved the fact that I could let go and not be in control. Everything in my life was so organised and calculated, always looking good, acting like a lady, managing every single aspect. In bed I just wanted to be treated badly, be degraded. Me being his little slut and pleasing him was my way of showing him my appreciation. I could act that way with him and let it go fully because I knew the respect he had for me. He then grabbed me and made me lie on my stomach, grabbed the ribbon of the Chanel carrier bag and tied me up with it. My face was down on the bed, he opened my legs apart, ordered me not to move, grabbed some lubricant and started to finger me. I moaned so loudly, I couldn't handle it, all I wanted was his penis inside me. I wanted him so bad, I felt him near me, merged with him. He then went down on me, proper eating me out like a cake, licking me from front to all the way back, fingering me at the same time and playing with my anus. I thought I was going to pass out, I could not stop screaming. He then just concentrated on fingering me: he had two fingers inside me, deep and going fast. I told him not to stop as I could feel I was coming. Two minutes later, the bed was completely wet, I just came, it felt so good, I felt high as fuck, all my energy was gone.

But he was not finished with me. He then turned me around, lay me on my side and took one of my legs up and put his penis inside me, that felt amazing. I was so moist from squirting that it felt really nice inside. I had asked him to do a sexual health check before we met, so we could have sex without a condom. He rode me, grabbing my face, squeezing it and slapping me in time. Getting slapped in the face felt like getting an electrical discharge. He finally came: I loved it when he was cumming, his face was bright red but finally relaxed. He'd lost his evil face, he was back to being the sweet Connor I'd met. He took me straight away in his arms and we cuddled up. The whole afternoon was just about being with each other, learning about each other, talking about our lives, our dreams, goals, desires. I felt so safe with him and so drowned into him. We couldn't stop talking; the only time we stopped was to have sex again. We probably talked for forty-five minutes, then starting to fuck or play with each other, then talk again for another forty-five minutes.

While I was with him, I received my edited showreels. I was so excited to see them, a bit nervous, but excited to see what I looked like on camera, rather than in the videos from school. Of course, he asked me to see them, but I was too shy to show him. Weird that I wasn't shy to be completely naked and talk like a porn star, but I was shy showing him my talent. He begged me to watch them, so I let him. His face lit up the whole time and his smile was up to his ears.

"So, what are you thinking?" I said.

"You are amazing, you look so good on camera and your singing is divine. You are so natural, you definitely should pursue this. Never stop, you are really talented."

"Are you saying this because you like me, and you just want to be nice?"

"No! Not! You would see it on my face if I didn't like it. You are born to be a star, Lola, really."

My heart was going to explode, I was so proud of myself

and all the work I'd put into singing. I knew what I was meant to do and finally I had the confidence to do it! That was the best compliment someone could give me! That I was natural! I straight away sent it to Julien and Yoan the music producer, to get more than one feedback. It's not that I didn't trust Connor, but obviously he liked me a lot so anything I was doing was fabulous for him. They all responded straight away, congratulating me, blown away by my performance and how much I'd learned in such a short amount of time. Of course, Yoan pointed to a few things that I could improve on, as he was in the business and knew more than my friends or Connor, but he was still proud of me.

Time flew by. When we looked at the clock it was already 7 p.m. Connor had to go to Cambridge for his business dinner. I did not want him to leave. I wanted him to stay with me. It was only the second time we'd met, but I felt that I'd known him for years. I was so comfortable around him, we had so much to talk about, so much love and affection to give to each other, that I did not want to let it go. Connor let me stay in the room for the night, as my flight was early the next day and it was easier to depart from Kings Cross. Francesca would join me later in the evening. Connor showered and put his clothes back on, ready to leave. We stood up in front of each other, looked into each other's eyes and stopped for a minute. I could not believe that I was not going to see him for three weeks, it was going to be so hard and so long without him, I was getting addicted. He made me promise to be always a good girl out there and safe. Connor was very jealous, and he had a hard time letting me go to another country with my partner in crime, but he knew he couldn't stop me either. If he wanted to be with me, he had to accept me, the whole of me, the good side and bad side.

We kissed goodbye, and I got turned on straight away. I

never had enough of him, but we couldn't, he had to catch his train. We then hugged for at least five minutes and he then left. I was so sad, so lost: three weeks without him, how would I cope? But what I didn't know was that our time apart would be much longer than expected…

TWENTY-TWO

The World Is Collapsing

Never forget yesterday but always live for today, because you never know what tomorrow can bring or what it can take away.

Anonymous

On 4 March 2020, Francesca and I were on our way to Miami. We were both excited, but also scared, as we didn't know what to expect, what was going to happen, who we would be meeting. Were we going to work in the same club, and hustle together as we do in the UK? Would they stop us at the airport? Would customs get suspicious if we brought a lot of dollars back? We were both asking ourselves so many questions, and once again something deep inside me told me that this trip wasn't going to be as successful as we'd thought. I had a really bad sensation inside. I wasn't feeling it. Maybe I simply didn't want to go any more, as I just wanted to be with Connor. I wasn't sure, but something was telling me this trip wasn't going to be great. I was also already feeling homesick. I'm always like that when I meet someone that I truly like. If I then go away on holiday, I never really enjoy myself fully as I just want to be with that person.

A few days before our trip to the States, the world started to go crazy due to this new virus, Covid-19. Why were people freaking out? I mean, if people kept clean and washed their hands, why were they worrying? I couldn't believe that governments were making advertisements to tell people to wash their hands. I mean, to me it's just common sense. Anyway, things were only pretty bad in China at this stage, we were still fine. But once we arrived at the airport, we could see people wearing masks and hear a background voice reminding people to wash their hands. Was this virus more serious than we thought? People were starting to get mad and paranoid. We thought the media were overexaggerating everything, just to scare us. I was sure that if people kept clean, it would be fine. Security was also asking everyone if they had travelled from or to China, as if it was a crime. Seriously, this paranoia needed to stop. We could feel a small panic around us, it was ridiculous.

We finally got on our plane, and took sleeping tablets as Francesca and I are petrified of flying, so sleeping deeply would help us get through the entire journey without being too anxious.

On 5 March 2020 at 2 p.m. we landed in Miami. How nice it was to see the sun! We'd left England at the perfect time.

It was our turn to go through security. They scanned our passports and the policeman was far too serious to be pleasant. I have been to the States twice before, and I know that they're very strict about who they'll allow to enter their country. They always ask a million questions, but this time it was different, as if he knew already we were coming to work. He started his interrogation in a very harsh tone, almost aggressively. I was so confused. Why did police in the States need to be so mean all the time? Didn't they know how to speak firmly but nicely?

"How long are you planning to stay?"

"3 weeks."

"That's a very long time. What are you planning to do?"

"Visiting, just enjoying Miami."

"What does visiting mean? What do you have planned, exactly?"

My heart stopped. What the fuck did he want? Could he read my mind, or what? I was so scared, I really didn't want to end up in jail in the States.

I smiled and said, "You know, enjoying the sun, the beaches, partying obviously, maybe a day trip to the Bahamas."

He looked at me, not convinced at all. He then asked me a question I thought he would never ask. I didn't think they were allowed to ask this question:

"What job do you do?"

That question made me lose what little confidence I had. I felt distraught, my mind blanked, I didn't know what to say. I couldn't even say dancer, it would sound too suspicious, so I said:

"Self-employed."

Then he really started to get aggressive and rude. I felt like a child who'd done something wrong. I mean technically yes, we were doing something illegal, but there was no need to get aggressive. We were being polite, so why was he shouting?

"What does that mean, self-employed?! It doesn't mean anything! What do you do for work? Can you answer that, or can't you!?"

Fuck, this guy wasn't going to let it go, seriously.

"A beauty therapist, we're doing lashes."

I guess that response worked, and he finally let us go. I felt that everyone was looking at us. We were just about to go outside to take a cab when another policeman stopped us. Luckily he was much nicer, but still suspicious of us. How much was I able to take without crumbling?

"Ladies, can you stop, please. How long are you planning to stay in the States?"

"3 weeks, sir."

"And is that all the luggage you have for three weeks in Miami? That doesn't look a lot."

Now they were questioning the size of our suitcases. We'd decided to take a small suitcase each, only because it was free of charge and we didn't want to bother with too many clothes as we were here to work. What were they thinking? That we were drug dealers?

"We're renting a studio so we're planning to wash our clothes. We couldn't be bothered to carry big suitcases."

" All right, ladies, enjoy Miami."

Finally we were out, and on our way to our studio, which was in Wynwood art district. When our Uber stopped to say we'd arrived, we thought it was a joke. We were in the middle of nowhere. Next to us was a bar and a motorbike shop, and across the road an empty parking space. I was already not feeling this trip. I had a bad gut feeling about it, and where we were was not helping at all. We entered our studio and all I could smell was a strong cigarette smell. Eww! What the fuck, I couldn't breathe, it was disgusting. We dropped our bags and went outside, trying to find a supermarket or somewhere to buy groceries. We eventually found a supermarket about five minutes away from the studio. I felt I was in a bad movie. The last time I'd been to Miami was for my last TV show: we'd stayed at Miami beach, we didn't see anything else, we experienced only the good side of Miami. Now I was seeing the poor side of Miami, and it wasn't pretty. We could tell people were poor and not well, so many drugged people and junkies. We didn't feel safe at all, so we bought what we needed, like water, biscuits, cereal, milk, toiletries and left.

London also has some rough areas where I lived for a few years, such as Woolwich, Peckham, Lewisham. I even lived on a council estate, but it was nothing compared to the States, where people seemed to be either very rich or very poor. I felt that the poor unfortunate people were probably not getting any help from the government. It was really disturbing and heart-breaking to experience. I felt very lucky to be living in the country I'm in, and always in a good situation. This is also why I never started drugs: I was too scared to end up on the street because of it. I saw too many times the damage it caused people, and I really didn't want to end up like that.

We went back to our studio, showered and went to bed, just to relax a bit. It was only 6 p.m. but we were exhausted from the long journey and all the emotions at the airport.

We woke on 6 March at 6 a.m. We'd been asleep for twelve hours, how come? Jet lag? Sleeping pills? I felt so drowsy and out of energy. I opened my eyes and yes, we were still in this studio. It still smelt of cigarettes and Connor was still not with me. Francesca felt the same, not in the best mood. We decided to sleep for a few more hours and rest before starting to look for a club to work for.

We woke again around 11 a.m., finally feeling rested, time to kick our butt and make a move. What were we going to do today? Luckily Valente messaged me and told me one of his friends was from Miami and he'd asked him to look after us. He was so nice and caring, I truly adored him. He texted his friend to come and pick us up to show us Miami. He said I was a true princess and should be treated as such. How cute.

Valente's friend turned up around noon in his Lamborghini. Maybe our trip wasn't going to be all bad, after all? Connor wasn't at all happy that I was in another's man car. He kept saying he was just worried, but I knew he was jealous. Connor was very protective. I told him that the area we were staying wasn't great, and he kept telling me to come home and of course he would pay for my ticket. But I couldn't do that to Francesca. I'd promised to do this adventure with her, so I had to stick to it. I was so glad that someone was worried about me. Connor had watched my plane journey the entire time on an online map. Some people would think that was creepy, but I found it sweet. Connor was also watching me, or shall I say stalking me, from somewhere else, but I didn't know about that.

As I was scrolling down my Instagram stories to see who had been watching it, an unfamiliar account caught my attention: "Cp2605". I looked at the profile: it had no pictures, only five followers and few people were followed. I knew it was Connor, that was his initials and date of birth, but how the hell did he find my Instagram and not even tell me about it? I mean, I would have given it to him without a doubt if he'd asked me, but why was he watching me, as if he was checking I wasn't doing something wrong? I texted him straight away to ask him what was going on? He simply said that he thought I knew, that he wasn't sneaking around… I wasn't really convinced. He kept saying that he wanted to make sure I was fine. I started to think that Connor was maybe a bit of a control freak. I really hoped it wasn't going to turn into some weird obsession, but for now I was just liking him way too much to even think of being mad at him. For the first time in forever, I couldn't even try to look for an excuse to argue, he was perfect, I was simply enjoying my new relationship and it felt so good not to be a miserable bitch, I was finally the princess I always wanted to be.

Valente's friend offered to drive us to his apartment. His building had a pool and a gym if we wanted to work out and swim. That sounded cool, why not? He then said we would all go for lunch after his meeting, but for now he had to leave us by ourselves. Why not? We arrived at his building and I have never seen anything so beautiful: the lobby was probably bigger than the entire first floor of the council flat I lived in for years. It was well decorated, all white and marble, the walls decorated with arts and sculpture, an entire concierge area with approximately five ladies here to help you with anything. Was I in a hotel or a building where people live? Valente's friends showed us the pool, the gym and left. He seemed like he didn't want to stay with us, he was a bit weird. We asked the ladies if we could get changed somewhere? They told us to head downstairs to the changing room. As we walked downstairs we lost our breath. The changing room was so luxurious. The entire floor was marble, the walls were copper, the showers were individual but bigger than my entire bathroom. We had a sauna, spa and jacuzzi at our disposition if needed, a relaxing heated marble bed. I wanted to live there. I had to, one day, be able to live somewhere like that. The whole scenery was very different from where we were renting in Wynwood.

After we'd got changed, we headed to the gym area for a quick work out and then chilled by the pool. I think people could tell we were not from the building. Most rich people have this vibe about them, they look expensive. Even if most of the time they wear the worst outfits, it's like they have all those beautiful pieces but don't know how to put them together. They all seemed cold and stuck up, as if they didn't have any souls any more. I really wished that if one day I became rich, I would stay humble, happy and funny. All the girls were just ordering salads, typical.

After an hour or two by the pool, we started to get bored. Even though we were in a beautiful place, we were not feeling happy. I was missing Connor way too much.You know what they say? It's not the place that counts, but the people you're with. Well, I couldn't agree more. We tried to contact Valente's friend for lunch, as he'd been gone for a while. He then responded that it wasn't possible any more and he was too busy. He was so weird, but never mind, we took a cab and went around Miami. Once we were done doing not much, we decided to go back to our smelly studio. Back there, we were so tired from the heat, walking around and probably jet lag that we decided to take a quick nap. Yet again we woke up two hours later. We wanted to try some clubs and auditions, but the motivation wasn't there, so we decided one more time to sleep.

The next day, 7 March 2020, we had to go for auditions. We needed to start working that evening and make money, but before then we really wanted to spend the day at the pool of a luxury hotel. We decided to head to the Fontainebleau. Once we arrived, someone at security informed us that access was for hotel guests only. Really? What the fuck was going on with this trip? Why was nothing going as planned? We asked him if we could rent out chairs, but he said no, only the big bed was for rent. I knew how much a bed was, and it was out of the question to pay more than $200 to lie on a bed. The weather wasn't even that nice. Never mind, I told him that we were interested in the beds, so he let us in and told us to speak to one of the staff members. As if I was going to, now we were in. No one would know if we were hotel guests or not, we just looked around and picked two long chairs and lay down. I was always full of tricks not to queue at clubs, not pay and get access to exclusive places, even when I was not meant to. I always had my lucky star that allowed me to be privileged even when I was not meant to.

Francesca and I chilled the entire afternoon and searched for potential clubs to work for. Luckily we had two clubs not too far from where we were staying. I was also texting and calling Connor the entire afternoon. I told him we were going to audition tonight, which he wasn't happy about. He knew that men were allowed to touch the dancers in the US. He kept telling me that if I didn't feel like working I could use the money he'd given me. I seriously wanted this guy to marry me and give me a family. I was in love, so yes, of course I loved the fact that he could spoil me so easily, but I loved even more the fact that he was there for me, scared and worried, listening to me, laughing at my stupid jokes. I was finally feeling that I had a partner with me, a life partner.

The only thing I wasn't sure of was whether he had a wife or not. When I asked him, he kept saying that it was complicated: yes, he was married, but there was no love there, no sex and that they were just co-loving together for the kids; they were separated, but yes he was still married. He could give me whatever excuses, but he was still tied up to someone else. I really didn't want to be the second choice, even though in his heart I was number one; but officially I was the other one, the one in the shadows. Did I really want to be the second choice? He kept repeating that I wasn't, and it was like he was single; they did not have sex any more; he had his life, she had hers, and all he wanted was to sort this out so we could be together. Those words were really reassuring to me. Maybe I was naive for believing him, but I didn't want to get out of my happy bubble, so I acted as if he wasn't married. I knew many people who were still married just for financial reasons but were fine for their respective husband, wife to have their own life on the side. Maybe that's what they were? Connor asked me to stop worrying and just enjoy our special bond, so I did. I didn't want another man running away from me because yet again I'd got too suspicious. I had to trust him, let myself go, stop overthinking and worrying that one day out of nowhere he would disappear. No, Connor was different, he wouldn't do that, I loved him, he loved me. I felt that he was my soulmate and nothing could stop us. Seriously, I am such a hopeless romantic.

After a few hours at the pool we decided to go back to our studio, chill for a bit and get ready for our big night. Francesca and I did everything to be over the top: it was the United States, everything is a show over there, and we knew the clubs were much bigger and better than in the United Kingdom. Once we were ready, we headed to the first club. We told the bouncer we were here for the audition, so he showed us to the back door where the girls had to enter to sign in. Once we entered, someone asked us for our ID to be scanned. I was a bit scared and sceptical, but we had no choice. He then told us to go down the corridor where the changing room was; the house mom would be waiting for us. Once we entered the changing room, we felt like we were in a movie. The space was huge, mirrors everywhere, costumes, thongs, lingerie, glitter, body spray, everything a stripper needed was on sale. The changing room was on another level compared to our small one back home. The girls were all tiny, toned and mostly from Latin America. I am far from fat, but next to them I felt huge. Everyone back home kept repeating that I was too skinny for Miami, but I realised it wasn't true.

Those girls were real pole dancers, real athletes, they didn't have a tiny bit of fat.

The house mum told us to stand by ready, as it was out turn soon. We were four girls auditioning at the same time, and I was petrified. The house mom walked us to a small area, which didn't look like a club, more like a bar, a cheap bar. I felt I was in a Wetherspoons with a stage in the middle. It didn't look glamorous at all, the clientele looked cheap too, it was very different from our club back home. We got on stage and removed our bra straight away. My legs were so shaky, I couldn't dance. After less than a minute, someone told us to get off the stage. Once we were down, the house mom told us we were not successful and that we could re-audition in two weeks' time. What? How come? It was the first time someone had said No to me. I am always successful with my job applications, it was a weird feeling.

Never mind, we were not going to let this failure defeat us, so we decided to head to another club that wasn't far away. Within ten minutes, we arrived there: these clubs were so big, whereas our clubs back home are so small and intimate. Once again we had to give our ID and wait for the house mom to tell us when to go on stage. We waited so long, we were not sure why. As we were waiting, we could see the other dancers coming in and out of the changing room, some of them completely naked. This was unusual for us: back home we were not allowed even to walk around in our underwear, and over here they were completely naked. America is always on another level. We could also see them coming back with huge baskets full of dollars. We were so impressed, we hoped to make that sort of money too.

It was finally our turn. Please, universe, make me and Francesca both successful. We went onto the floor. It was a Saturday night, so the club was packed and my eyes couldn't believe what they were seeing. The space was huge, probably four times the size of our club: two massive stages, the pole was really high and the music extremely loud. The girls on stage were proper dancing, twerking, climbing the pole, changing position all the time on the pole, doing the splits and all of that completely naked, pussy out on the customers' faces, and dollars flying everywhere. The girls that were not on stage were also dancing for clients on the floor naked, being touched, grabbed, spanked. It was a new dimension for us. Francesca was loving it, I did too, I was loving the proper club, the party atmosphere which we don't have back home, but I wasn't sure I was comfortable to go on that stage and compete with those girls. I clearly couldn't compete. Me and my few lessons of pole dancing could go home and hide. I don't think I was comfortable either with the clients being able to touch me that much as well.

I looked at the price list and they were exactly the same as back home, which I thought was therefore a bit low for letting a man touch you. The only good thing was that we were able to keep all the money we made. The only time we had to give a percentage to the club was if we were using the VIP rooms, which I didn't think I'd feel comfortable going into. Everything was solid walls, no curtain to be able to see what was going on. I'd be too scared to be alone with a man in a real room, where they could do anything they wanted to. Anyway, I wasn't there yet, I still had to be successful at the audition and Francesca too. We promised each other to stay together no matter what, even if one or the other wasn't successful; we'd carry on looking for a club until we were both taken.

We headed to the upper stage, where two dancers were already on stage, grinding the floor completely naked and dollars all over them. As soon as they left the stage, the house mom told us to go on stage. We were four girls for one pole. I was lost, I didn't know what to do. Francesca was having a ball: she was already busy with a client who was sitting right in front of her. Everyone was busy apart from me. What the fuck, what was going on, why was I acting as if I didn't know my job? And then, when I thought it was going to be over for me, a couple sat right in front of me and I thought that it was about time I moved my ass, literally. I went down on my knees, removed my bra and started dancing for them. At first I was I facing them, feet on the ground, hands also on the ground and moving my hips as if I was having sex. Then I turned around, positioned myself in doggy style, elbows on the floor, back bend to the maximum and started twerking my ass completely facing them. They were both screaming and loving it. They started to throw dollars at me and tucked some in my panties. After that the house mom told us to leave the stage. Francesca was high on adrenaline, she loved it. I enjoyed it, but I don't think as much as her. My knees were already hurting; I'd danced for only two minutes, how did those girls manage it every day? They are real warriors.

Once we got back to the changing room, the house mum told the other two girls with us that they were not successful. Then she turned round and informed Francesca and me we were taken. Finally some good news! We were both so excited, we could finally start to make some real money. We could have started to work that same night, but we were feeling a bit lazy so we decided to go home and sleep.

On Sunday 8 March 2020, we woke up feeling really pleased about our performances and glad we'd both got taken at the same club. As we got up and looked out the window, we could see that the weather wasn't nice at all, so we decided to chill in our studio. As we were both on our phones, we could see everywhere on social media articles about Coronavirus. Things in Europe and China had started to get really bad. We really started to freak out: countries like Italy were flooded with cases, people were dying one after the other. What the fuck was that virus about? The world seemed in a panic, and although we seemed fine in Miami, we could feel something bad was happening. At first we'd been laughing about it, but now it did seem pretty serious, if only we knew.

On Monday 9 March 2020, the day we'd finally decided to work, we were a bit anxious about working when this virus was going around killing people. No drugs or vaccine could help, and apparently the virus was transmitted so fast from one person to another just by touching a surface or breathing. There is nowhere worse than a stripclub to transmit germs: touching dollars, which looked like the dirtiest money ever, the notes really smelly and old. Clients were allowed to touch us, and we were all touching the same pole, sitting on couches, talking to many people in one night. We really started to wonder how this trip was going to end.

I called Connor that afternoon. We'd obviously spoken about Coronavirus and how it sounded really scary. I'd also told him that I wasn't feeling comfortable working any more, knowing this virus was around; that I missed him and I just wanted to come home. He begged me to do so, but it didn't feel right to let down Francesca. I had a boyfriend who was looking after me, but she didn't. Connor knew I had the goal of coming back home with enough money not to need to work for a while, so I could finally concentrate on all my projects and move somewhere new with Francesca, where we would finally be home. If I wasn't working my ass off to earn this money, I wouldn't be able to do all this. He then stopped for a minute and offered me a proposition. He couldn't stand seeing me feeling down and worried, all he wanted to do was see me happy and stress-free.

So he offered me to send me £7,000, or the equivalent of

the $10,000 I was planning to come back home with. I couldn't believe it: I told him he was mad and that I couldn't accept his offer. I liked him way too much to take that much money off him. I would feel really bad. He then said that all he wanted was to know I was home safe and able to pursue my dreams; that he believed in me, that he wanted us to be reunited and if I needed money he would look after me. I couldn't believe that I'd met Connor just twice in my life and he'd done more for me than all my past boyfriends combined. Was I dreaming? When would I wake up? It sounded too good to be true. I'd only met him twice! Lola, this is crazy! He'd told me he loved me, that no one in his life had made him feel so alive, so appreciated, no one had ever cared for him the way I was, and after struggling for years I deserved to be treated the way I was meant to be. I wanted to cry from happiness, but also because all the pressure from all those years, all the weight on my shoulders, was finally off. For the first time I could rely on someone; I didn't need to be this warrior, always fighting, always dealing with every problem by myself. I had my other half to look after me physically, mentally, emotionally, financially. It was the best feeling in the world. He then said that he would send me the first half straight away; but the independent woman that I am refused for now, I still wanted to try to make it on my own, so I told him that I would try to work tonight, see how it was, see if I was feeling safe and comfortable. If I didn't, then I would let him send me half the money he'd offered me. He agreed. We had a deal.

One more time the universe had delivered my order. I just didn't expect to receive it like that. I'd put my intention out to the universe, to go to the States to work, to make a lot of money and come back home, find a new apartment and have the time to work on my goals without worrying about working. Well, I was going to receive the money I'd asked for, of course with the help of Connor, but I didn't know I was going to have so much time to work towards my goals, and not because I'd decided to stop working… .

Francesca and I turned up at work around 11 p.m. I had no motivation whatsoever. As we entered the club, the security who were checking us in asked us to register, as it was our first night. His first question was what stage names we wanted to use. I obviously said "Satine". After typing for a few seconds on his laptop, he told me this name was already taken. No! I couldn't be anything other than Satine! Then I asked if Lola was available. Nope, Lola was also taken. Jesus Christ, what name could I have? Then after thinking for a few minutes I asked if I could take Paris; not that I liked this name, but nothing else was coming through, so there I was, named Paris. When I told Connor about my new stage name he laughed; he said that it didn't suit me at all. Once we'd finished our registration, we got changed and went onto the floor.

The club was empty! All the girls seemed worried. We thought it was because maybe Mondays were quiet, the same as in Europe, but no, the other girls explained this was unusual and that everyone was probably scared of catching Coronavirus. Seriously, could this trip go any worse? I knew from the start that I wasn't feeling it, but I never expected it to be that bad. Francesca and I tried everything to get some money. We then realised that all those dollars being thrown on stage were only $1 notes, so at the end of three songs on stage, yes, you ended up covered in dollars, but after counting you didn't end up with a lot. Those girls were working their ass off for not much, I have to say. Francesca and I were trying to get clients to the big VIP room, but every single client was asking us what we would do in there. We were confused, and then one client told us that if a guy takes you to a private area and pays $400 an hour, it was not to chat, see some tits and talk; obviously more than dancing was happening in there. We were shocked: all our hopes of making $10,000 by dancing were ruined, so we decided to take a break and went to the changing room.

As we were chilling, I went to see the house mom and asked her about it: she would probably be more honest than a client. I told her that in Europe we hear stories about girls in America making a minimum of $10k a month by stripping, and that is why we'd come over. She stopped me straight away and said it was all bullshit, that yes some girls were making that, but only because they were doing more than dancing. That was truth: it was the exact same as back home, the same type of money, nothing was different apart from the fact that, for the same amount of money, men were allowed to touch us; and I wasn't happy with that. I texted Connor straight away and explained everything. I knew that he wasn't going to let me work, for sure. He told me to not worry. I then received a notification from my bank saying that a payment of £3,500 had been made to my account. Fuck, he really didn't bullshit me! What had I done to deserve someone so good to me? I couldn't wait to be home to show him my gratitude. All I wanted was to be in his arms, make love and be his little slut. After that I told Francesca I wasn't going to work any more, but that I would still come along with her and just wait until she was done. That night after paying the DJ, the house mom and security, she came home with $50. Clearly this job wasn't worth it.

On Wednesday 11 March 2020, Francesca still wanted to try her luck at work, so as promised I went along with her. All day long we heard more and more stories about Coronavirus, how thousands of people were dying around the world, countries shutting their borders. We couldn't believe it, what the fuck was this chaos about? We felt as if we were in a movie. I really started to be scared of getting stuck in the States, or the United Kingdom not letting us re-enter the country. We didn't know what to do any more, but for now Trump and Boris didn't seem worried about it. So we carried on our lives thinking we should be fine.

As we reached work, we could see girls panicking, washing their hands all the time, as were we. The house mom disinfected all the surfaces. You could feel fear, tension and panic. The floor was empty, no clients were in. After a few hours of hustling, Francesca was devastated for not making any money and told me to go home.

On Thursday 12 March 2020, Trump decided to shut the borders, and whoever was visiting the United States had to find a way to return to their countries. We couldn't believe it. What dimension were we in? How long would this last? We were petrified. Connor asked me to change my flight as soon as possible and come home.

On Friday 14 March 2020, after a long day of trying to find a flight to London, we finally managed to get on a plane. Francesca and I had no words: we had spent $3,000 on accommodation in Miami, probably $100 on Ubers for the entire week, money on food, restaurants and we hadn't earned any money. Lucky me, Connor was looking after me, but I couldn't imagine how Francesca was feeling. We also received a message from our club back home saying it was closing until further notice. What were we going to do? How were we going to earn money? How long would this last? The whole world was in panic, more and more people were wearing masks, gloves, avoiding other human beings. I just couldn't believe we were living this nightmare. It felt like a bad joke. I couldn't believe I'd been laughing about the situation a few days ago. We would have never imagined how the world would turn around…

On 15 March 2020, we finally landed in London. A taxi was waiting to take us home. Connor had arranged everything for me, what a sweetheart. How had I lived without him for so long? I decided to put myself in quarantine, even though England was still acting as though nothing was happening, and were just advising people to "wash their hands"; how ridiculous!

On 23 March 2020, ten days after we'd arrived back from Miami, the United Kingdom was finally put into lockdown. The whole world was in lockdown: all the borders were shut, clubs, restaurants, bars, non-essential shops, transport, the world stopped running and we were all struggling to get toilet paper. Who'd have guessed that toilet paper would turn into a luxury item? It was such a weird feeling. As the French president, Emmanuel Macron, put it, we were at war, at war with an unknown and invisible enemy. Everything seemed so surreal, I could never have imagined living through this. You always think this sort of thing could only happen in another era. We would never have thought our lives could be put on hold. I really understood the idea of not taking life for granted any more: all those nights of eating out in fancy restaurants, going out clubbing, walking down the streets of London shopping, or simply seeing friends. I'd always been grateful and happy for it, but I don't think I truly was.

Now I was spending my days inside, sharing my room with my roommate, going to bed at crazy times, waking up in the middle of the afternoon. I had no motivation at all for anything, either writing or working out. My productivity was at it lowest point. I had the time to be productive, to be honest. I'd received what I'd asked for one more time: I'd wanted to be off work, and here I was off work. I must always remind myself to be more precise when I ask for something from the universe.

Thankfully I had Connor to talk to everyday, but I was really worried where this would go. We didn't know when we could see each other next. I was worried it would end, even if he promised me he wasn't going anywhere. I needed to see him and talk to him constantly, but him being at home 24/7 with his wife and kids was really hard. The only time we could talk was when he was going to sleep in his bedroom, as he and his wife were not sharing a bed any more. I mean, that is what I thought. Connor and I started to Skype once a week, when he went to his office. We spent hours talking to each other and having "cam sex". Even via a screen, I could feel this crazy sexual tension between us, I was still madly drawn to him. Connor was also giving me hopes: he kept repeating that being away from me made him realise that his life was a complete lie, and at forty-five years old it was time for him to be truly happy. He and his wife had separate lives, and he'd had enough of sharing a house with a stranger. I wanted to believe those words so badly, but once again my gut instinct kept telling me to not fall for it. Even though until now everything Connor had said to me did happen: as promised, once I was in London, I did get the rest of the £7,000 he'd promised me.

But still, getting a divorce and starting everything from scratch was another level of commitment that not many men are capable of doing. He had four kids, a huge house in Ireland, businesses with his wife, a horse ranch, friends, family. Was he really going to let everything down to start something new with me? I knew he wanted to, but was it more of a fantasy that kept him alive, or was he actually serious about it? He promised me that once all the lockdown rules were over, he would contact a lawyer to make things official with his wife. He also kept mentioning how much he was fantasising of me being a virgin. He was obsessed with being the only man in my life, the first man to be inside me and cum inside me to impregnate me. I think the psychology behind this fantasy is linked to possession. Connor was obsessed with marking his territory, he kept repeating how I was his and no one else's, that I would get punished for letting so many men see me naked and touching me for all those years. I know it can sound a bit freaky, but I was loving it; I loved the fact he loved me so much that he wanted me for him only.

By 23 April 2020, it was now one month that we'd been officially in lockdown and I was mentally exhausted. Even though we weren't doing anything, I was constantly feeling tired. I wasn't happy at all, I was feeling lonely, unproductive, unmotivated. I felt like a lion in a cage. I needed to go out, socialise, move. I was getting really anxious about my future. We would see the number of deaths rising higher and higher every day. I was getting paranoid every time I went outside to buy food. I would clean everything I bought. I was living in psychosis.

Connor and I also started to argue a lot. I was getting frustrated at only talking to him at night time. I couldn't understand why he had to hide from his wife if they were technically not together any more? I also didn't understand why out of the blue he was sleeping in the same bed as his wife if they were not meant to be together any more? I could feel he was hiding something, but even though we argued, we always managed to get back together and we were more drawn to each other.

One day after two weeks of non-Skyping, I was finally going to see him. For the occasion, I decided to wear the sexiest glittery dress that he loved without any underwear. I did nice make-up and my hair was in a high ponytail, exactly the way he liked it. Connor and I hadn't argued for a few days, everything was calm and lovely. He had even bought me a pair of shoes the night before to show me he wasn't taking me for granted and he still wanted to show me he could be romantic. I was seriously a lucky girl.

At 1 p.m., I logged into Skype, waiting for Connor. I was so excited to show him how sexy I looked, just for him.

At 1h05, my phone rang. Connor was calling me, probably to tell me he was going to be late or something. I picked up, so happy to hear his voice and get talking.

"Hey baby, I'm already on Skype, just waiting for you."

"Hey… Lola… How are you?" His voice was shaking and sounded cold. He never called me Lola, he always called me princess or baby. Why was he calling me by my name?

"Listen, I don't know how to do this, but I can't do this any more."

My heart stopped. What did he mean by he couldn't do this any more? I was very confused so I told him we could change our Skype day if he was too busy, naively thinking he was talking about Skype. He then said:

"No, I can't do this, I can't be with you any more. I mean, it's not like we're together anyway, we've only seen each other twice, and we don't know when the next time might be. My wife is driving me crazy for being on the phone constantly, and I've been on the phone to my accountants this morning, and I'm fucked. I have no money left. I have to concentrate on making things right for my kids."

I didn't know what to say. I knew that at some point he would wake up and do this, but I didn't expect it now. Once again I was being dumped, right before my birthday. How could he abandon me when he'd promised me he wouldn't go anywhere? Was it all fake? All a lie? My heart was crushed into pieces, my body was flooded by sadness, but weirdly I had no tears coming. I think I was too shocked by what I'd heard, or simply I'd cried enough in my life that my body couldn't produce tears any more. After feeling lost and confused, I started to feel angry at him for being such a coward. I told him that I didn't care about his money; that even if he was broke, I wanted to be by his side and support him. He kept saying that he had always been honest, and what he was feeling for me was real and he was gutted, as he would probably never meet anyone like me in his life ever again. But his family was his priority, and he couldn't go back to being poor as he'd been when he was a child. I asked him if I'd done something wrong, but he promised me not. I didn't know what to say any more. I had no words so I hung up on him.

As if a pandemic wasn't bad enough, I had to be dumped and heartbroken on top of that, with no distractions to make me forget about him. Once again, I imagined finishing my days with a man who'd promised me the world and ended up abandoning me like all the others. For the first time, I hadn't been a miserable bitch, I'd been chilled, understanding, forgiving, attentive, funny, everything he wanted me to be. What was the problem? Even when I was the best version of myself, I ended up being dumped.

When we hung up, I started to cry, I was heartbroken. I felt that one more time I'd lost my best friend, my other half, and I had to start everything all over again as usual. When was the universe going to give me a break and let me live the life I'm meant to? But I knew that in order to receive something better, the universe had to remove people or situations from my life. This is simply how it works: in order to receive something, something else has to be removed.

TWENTY-THREE

The Higher Power

> *To have faith is to trust yourself to the water. When you swim you don't grab hold of the water, because if you do you will sink and down. Instead you relax, and float.*
>
> Alan Watts

By 29 May 2020, it had been more than a month since Connor and I broke up. And even though it was really hard at first, I decided once more to fight as usual. Just like the previous year, I read *The Magic* again, followed every advice and practised all the daily exercises. Once again I felt much better and things started to look brighter. I now had the motivation to write my book and it was almost finished. I was practising yoga every single day, which helped me big time to feel calm mentally. I was working out, money was coming to me from unexpected places: either it was a refund for plane tickets, or regulars from the club sending me money, or benefits from the government. I found an apartment in the perfect location, a safe upper-class neighbourhood in London for a very good price, with a very easy landlord who was not asking for too much paperwork.

Really my life was getting better and better each day. I realised that what I'd asked for a few months ago had manifested itself: a large amount of money, time off work and a beautiful apartment in a privileged area. I realised that once I let go of everything, that I wasn't holding on so tight to whatever was happening to me and understood that it was happening for me and not against me, that even bad times are a blessing in disguise, it made me feel very light and content. I was feeling truly blessed and peaceful. I had no artificial things to make me happy, no extra people, I was on my own and I was fine. I was living in the moment and not worrying about the past or the future. Embracing each day as it comes was the best thing I have ever done. I know it can be hard, trust me! I have always worried about the future, and always victimised myself, even with what was happening in the world. I was so frustrated at first with what was happening, but then I understood that I had to accept it even if it was hard at first, because complaining about Coronavirus, lockdown and my break-up wouldn't get me anywhere.

I had two choices: either to accept it and work around it, or to moan about it and be miserable. Even though it was hard at first, once I accepted it all and was at peace with it, life changed around me and it was the best feeling. Life is a long, weird journey and the best thing you can do is to work with what you have and not going against it. That will create only more blockages and pain. The universe, God, however you want to call it, has a plan for each one of us. Sometimes the process is painful and hard, sometimes it doesn't go as planned, but somehow something out there is protecting you and has a better plan for you. Just trust the divine time, and in the meantime be grateful because, as the Evangelist Matthew says in the Bible: "For whoever has, to him shall be given and he shall have more abundance; but whosoever has not, from him shall be taken away, even what he has." Trust me, I am not religious and for some it might sound a bit too spiritual and "woohoo", but somehow it does make sense, trust me. Every time I complained about my life or took things or people for granted, somehow something was taken away. But if I was grateful, even during hard times, miracles happened. You don't have to believe in it, but I do believe that it doesn't cost anything to be positive, kind and grateful. It is much better than being a moody cow, believe me!

But one weird coincidence was the best of all, or shall I say something that the universe sent me. After my break-up with Connor, I decided to go on Tinder, only to keep my mind busy. I wasn't even planning to meet anyone in real life, I just needed to talk. One day I matched with this guy, Andrew: he seemed like the only decent guy on the app. He is a lawyer, and at least he was polite enough to say something simple like "Good afternoon, how are you?" compared to all the others who said "Hey sexy", "What's up", "Oi oi", the sort of words that made me cringe. We started talking online before I moved to my new place, and then when I told him that I'd moved house we realised that we were living in the same area. How crazy was that! But the craziest was that out of nowhere I asked him some legal question about my book, which I was hoping to publish one day. He got really interested in it, and said that if it was helpful, he knew a publisher who lived in the same area as us. I asked him if he knew which road she was on, and when he sent me the name of her road I couldn't believe it, she was living right behind my building. What were the odds of meeting someone on Tinder who knew a publisher living right behind my new place! Once more, I felt that the universe was on my side and that all the manifestations and meditations I was doing were working. But I never expected them to be so powerful and surreal. I was so excited and happy. It didn't mean that my book was going to be published, but I still felt it was a big step forward.

Andrew contacted her straight away and asked if we could be in contact and potentially meet to discuss how my book could get published. A week later, I finally met this mysterious editor who was living right behind my house. We met on the square that was situated between our streets; that was the only place where we were allowed to meet, as restaurants, bars, cafes were still closed. How funny that I was meeting her when I hadn't met Andrew yet! We sat on a bench and talked for two hours, about my book of course but also about life in general. She found my story interesting and told me she was willing to help. I was over the moon. I still couldn't believe someone was willing to help me. I'd asked many of my clients if they knew a publisher, but none of them believed in my project apart from Connor. But I couldn't contact him, could I? I felt relieved that I had a positive opinion from a professional. All I had to do now was finish the book and send it to her so we could start working on it. I thanked her for her time and help, and left full of hopes and dreams.

Life couldn't be better: lockdown was eased, the number of deaths and infections from the virus was getting lower. I was living in a nice area, in a brand new apartment, with restaurants, bars and cafes probably re-opening in July. My singing lessons re-started soon, we even heard that the club could potentially re-open mid July, everything seemed great. I was walking back home, looking around me, hearing the birds singing, feeling the sun warming my skin, listening to my music. Life was much simpler than a few months ago when I was out every night, and I was feeling genuinely happy, learning to appreciate the simple pleasures even more. Nothing could disturb this feeling of joy, I thought, but the universe decided to give me just one more life lesson.

On 16 June 2020, I was having a fantastic day: non-essential shops had re-opened, so I could finally meet with some friends to do shopping in Central London round Oxford Circus. The weather was amazing, I was just feeling great in general; it was so good to finally see the streets of London being a bit busy and buzzing with life.

Out of nowhere Zach, my ex-boyfriend from years ago, called me to ask me if I wanted to go to a barbecue in Chelsea. I thought, why not? It would be good to socialise a little. I went to the house Zach and his friends had rented for the occasion. After an hour I realised it wasn't my scene at all: drugs, weed, alcohol, so I decided it was time to leave. It was nice to socialise, but It was better for me to go. As I walked down the street in Chelsea, a car that was parked caught my attention: a beautiful black Ferrari. I love sports cars that make a loud noise when driving fast. I had learned during lockdown how to live a more simple life and appreciate it, but still deep at heart I appreciated luxury; it would be a lie to say I didn't any more. I realised the driver kept staring at me, which made me smile. I hadn't had a man's attention for a while, so it felt good somehow. Suddenly I saw him getting out of his car. Oh my God, please don't come and talk to me, I'm not ready for a chat with a man! Even though I'd learned not to let the break-up get to me, to be thankful for my time with Connor and try my best not to feel anger towards him, I couldn't stop thinking about him and missing him. I couldn't forget this sort of connection, so it just made me feel weird. Even weirder, when I was on my way to Chelsea, the bus stopped and I couldn't believe what I saw on the wall above: "Connor Street". In ten years living in London, I'd never seen a street with that name, and that street had to be near where I lived. Once again, it was odd. As soon as I saw the street sign, I felt in my gut that I would hear from Connor; which a few hours later did happen, but I would have never expected it to be in this way…

As I arrived home, content with my day, my phone rang. At first I thought it would be the guy I gave my number to in Chelsea. I'd managed to hold a painful two-minute conversation and given him my number, but no, when I saw the number my phone was indicating, it was from Ireland. I screamed! It was Connor! I had deleted his number, so as not to be tempted to harass him and try my best to move on, even though I could see him every day still looking at my Instagram stories. I never understood why guys break up with you but still want to have a look at your life. I was sure it was Connor calling me. Who else would be calling me from Ireland? I tried to calm down and act as reasonably as possible.

"Hello?" I stuttered.

"Hello… is this Lola?" It wasn't Connor, it was a woman's voice, and as soon as I heard it I knew exactly who it was.

"My name is Laura, I am Connor's wife."

For fuck's sake, why was she calling me? I didn't know what to do, what to say, so I stayed quiet.

"How do you know my husband? Where did you meet? Are you still seeing him?"

I responded vaguely that I barely knew him. It wasn't my call to tell her the truth. It was his responsibility. On top of that, I didn't know what she'd found out, what he'd told her, if she even knew anything about it. A part of me wanted to be honest with her, as if this happened to me, I would appreciate the truth from the other woman. But Connor had told me his version of the story, that they were technically not together any more, so what was I supposed to do? It was their marriage, not mine. For once he had to face his issues like a grown up, so I just said that I vaguely knew him, that we'd met once over lunch via friends, and that I wasn't in contact with him.

She then started to get angry and said: "We have four young children, so stay away from him. Next time you meet someone married, back off." Her words pissed me off so much. Of course I understood and why she was angry at me, I would have too, but she didn't know what her husband had told me and made me believe. Yes, I should have stayed away, but I didn't ask for any of this. Connor did everything in his power to make me feel that what we had was real; he did everything to see me, have me on the phone, it wasn't like I chased him and begged him to be mine. Why was she blaming me? Blame your husband! He was the one with a situation, not me. So I told her that I wasn't in contact with her husband, and if her husband was unfaithful, she should blame him and discuss it with him, not with the other woman, and I hung up.

Women love to blame the other woman. They don't want to face the fact that their marriage failed because of their husband or them. It is much easier to blame someone else in order to feel less guilty, and not feel that they were living a lie. I do not consent to having affairs and cheating, but she should ask herself why her husband needed to be with other women. In some cases, men have no excuse; but in Connor's case, according to what he had told me, he always felt that she wasn't listening to him or didn't care, she was constantly moaning and arguing about everything, how he was never home and she always had to be alone with the kids. She wasn't even working, she had nannies to help her, cleaners and chefs to cook for the family, so what was she complaining about? She would use his credit card to buy whatever she wanted and never be grateful for it. That's why Connor loved to spoil me, because he could see that it was making me happy and I was appreciative of it. Connor could also talk about personal stuff with me, such as the death of his brother and his mum; he could tell me his darkest secret and desires without feeling judged. And of course, even if it happened only twice, he was free in the bedroom with me, which of course he wasn't with his wife.

After I hung up with her, I immediately contacted Connor via Instagram and asked him to call me to say what was going on. When he rang, I could hear his tone of voice being so different from the one I was used to hearing. He had no soul left, he sounded as if he was about to die. He told me she'd kicked him out of the house, he was staying in a hotel and she wasn't allowing him to see the kids. She had found a receipt for flowers he'd sent me when we met. She'd found my name, address, phone number and what it said on the card: "I can't wait to see you on Tuesday, Princess xx." He still wasn't sure how she could have found out: he'd deleted everything, so he thought she'd probably hired someone, as this receipt was dated from March, we were now in June. He then said she was obsessed with me, she'd found my Facebook, my showreels on Youtube, that I was pole dancing and she told everything to the kids. She kept saying to the kids that their dad didn't love them; if he did, he wouldn't have done that; that he preferred to be with his "princess" than them, and that maybe they should have a pole at home as a reminder of me. She was out of control. Why tell the kids? It wasn't their problem, she was not behaving like an adult. I understand that she was angry, but be angry with your husband; be smart and leave the kids alone. If she was always acting like this, I understood why Connor was looking elsewhere; but he was still wrong for not getting real and filing for divorce in the first place, knowing she wasn't the one for him.

We then spoke for a bit and decided to video call. It was so weird to see him: he looked aged, he had more white hair now, his eyes looked tired, they were not as bright and happy, I didn't recognise my Connor. As usual, even though Connor had hurt me, I couldn't help but feel sorry for him. Once again here I was listening to him and helping him somehow. It was good to catch up with him. We stayed on the phone for two hours; he kept repeating how he was thinking about me every single day, that he was missing me so much, he was sorry for what happened, but for once he wanted to make things right for his family. After a while we naturally started to get turned on; even though he was looking a bit rough, I was still attracted to him and we started to have cam sex. He was surprised that he was even able to get hard, as for the past days nothing was sexually stimulating him. After that, we hung up. I texted him goodnight. He then asked for a yoga video of mine as he loved to watch me doing yoga, where I executed myself like an idiot. I told you that sometimes it takes me a while to learn my lesson. I then asked him to text me if he enjoyed the video or not. I woke up the next day to no text from Connor. I was a bit upset, but never mind.

At 9 p.m. the same day, I received a text from him finally, but I didn't like what I read at all:

"Hey, I'm going home tonight. The kids are bawling. So don't text me."

I couldn't believe how cold his text was. I felt used. Once again he'd needed a shoulder to cry on. I'd been there for him, he wanted to perv on me, release his tension. And then ignore me and just send me this impersonal, formal text. I then realised he had blocked me. What a fucking bastard. I had so much esteem for Connor, even after the break-up, but now my view of him had changed completely. I was hurt, angry, disappointed, sad. I could only see a coward in Connor, and not the man that I'd loved for the past four months. But I wasn't going to let it get to me. I promised myself that I was better than that. I sat down again, thought a lot, thought about my life, all the men that I'd met in the past, all the bad situations, the good ones, work, money, health, opportunities, my future career, my dreams. I breathed deeply, closed my eyes and there I was, calm and happy.

Conclusion

I can say that I am happy and proud of myself. No, I'm not a millionaire, I'm not a famous singer yet, even though Yoan, the music producer, has finally decided to look after me and produce me; we are working on my first album. I am not some rich man's wife, I am still single; I don't know when I will finally meet the real love of my life. I haven't worked in a long time; I don't know when the club will re-open, or if it ever will.

But as I wrote my story, I realised how far I had come. I have achieved so much as a person in my career. I have elevated myself, I am mentally stronger than ever, not letting anything bring me down. I accept my failures, I accept my challenges. I enjoy the present and try to not worry about the future. I turn every negative situation into a positive. I know now that, no matter what, being with someone who is married in any sort of way is toxic and bad; even though we don't choose who we fall for, I know that I don't want to be the second choice. I know my worth. I can now say I love myself physically and mentally. I don't take anything for granted any more. I am happy with nothing artificial around me; and maybe all of that, all the growth, all the life lessons and challenges make me rich in my own way. I am rich in knowledge, life, intuition, perseverance, and no matter what I am going through, I will carry on fighting for my dreams in the healthiest way possible, and stay kind, humble and positive.

I have accomplished many things that were on my life's list of goals, but as I grow up the list is always extending. I wish one day that my story can inspire people to feel better and live a life true to themselves and not for others or because of society. I wish for women to be more equal and stop being judged on their jobs, clothes or whatever they decide to do. I wish for mental health to be a subject in schools, to avoid kids growing up negative and angry, but believing in themselves. I wish many people could feel happy in the way I am at this exact moment as I type the last words of my diary. I am at peace with myself, my thoughts, my body and accepting who I am; this is the best accomplishment I've ever achieved, and I am grateful for my life experience, and especially the club I was working in, for giving me this confidence that I never had before and opening my eyes to the world. I don't know when I will see the club again, but sometimes I close my eyes and imagine myself with Jasmine, Francesca, Amber and the other girls, partying with Valente and all his friends, all of us dancing in the dark with those red lights, the loud music, everyone laughing, enjoying life and appreciating the moment, as it could be the last time.

My Summary and Best Tips

- Be true to yourself; do things that are aligned with you and you only, not what society thinks or says.
- Don't surround yourself with people who don't make you feel good; they don't have to be the same as you, but as long as you feel happy when you're with them, that's all that matters!
- Don't get stuck in a job you hate; I'm not saying just leave it from one day to another, like I do most of the time! I know some people have kids and responsibilities, but try to find a way out, even by taking small steps and actions.
- Ask yourself what makes you happy. Don't think about what society wants you to do or have. The best way is to think what were you doing as a child. (When we were kids we were innocent, with no imprint of society yet.) The best way to raise your vibration is to have fun, so what were you doing as a child? Was it dancing? Drawing?

Colouring? Acting silly? Cars? Football? Reading? Your options are limitless.

- Take actions everyday, even if they are small. Trust me, I'm lazy, so I have to deal with procrastination every day! Sometimes you just have to kick your butt a little.
- It going to sound cheesy, but be healthy. I know you've heard it many times, but unfortunately it's true! I'm not talking about diet (diets are the worst); just try to eat reasonably, not excessively, and work out. You will see the difference it makes to your day to breathe some fresh air, move your ass and eat well.
- Have time alone; meditate even for five minutes; it will help you breathe properly, and breathing exercises are the best thing when you get anxious!
- Don't put yourself down! The words you say to yourself are extremely important! Tell yourself good things, love yourself, appreciate who you are.
- Identify your goals, write them down, record yourself, talk out loud or in your mind, whatever you prefer, but make sure you put an intention out there.
- Don't judge others: it will only affect you. If you don't agree with someone's lifestyle or haircut, for all I care, just keep it to yourself. We are all different; we cannot agree with everyone, but let it be! If you have nothing nice to say, keep quiet!
- Don't pretend to be perfect; accept negativity and bad times. Trust me, I still moan and act miserably sometimes, but hey, we're only humans. The key is to not let negativity take over our entire life, or even a single day!

- Be fucking grateful!!!!!! If you can walk, breathe, taste, have a roof and clothes, you are more than blessed. Trust me, some people have none of that.
- (Try to not fall in love with someone who is already taken.)
- Don't judge a woman for what she is wearing, saying or the work she does (a stripper, for example 😊)!
- You have no idea of people's past or what happened to them, so stay kind no matter what, and do not judge a book by its cover.
- We have one life on earth, so make the most of it! Laugh, have sex, travel, read, learn, eat different cuisine, be kind, tell your loved ones you love them, expend yourself, go after your dreams. Life is weird and harsh sometimes, but it can be beautiful and worth it, trust me.
- Favourite books: *The Secret*, *The Magic* and *Miracle Morning*.

Printed in Great Britain
by Amazon

17282973R00203